A LIFE IN A WOODEN O

NEW HAVEN & LONDON, YALE UNIVERSITY PRESS, 1977

A Life in a Wooden O

MEMOIRS OF THE THEATRE   BEN IDEN PAYNE

Published with assistance from
The Kingsley Trust Association Publication Fund
established by the Scroll and Key Society of Yale College.

Designed by Sally Sullivan
and set in Baskerville type.
Printed in the United States of America by
The Alpine Press, South Braintree, Mass.

Published in Great Britain, Europe, Africa, and
Asia by Yale University Press, Ltd., London.
Distributed in Latin America by Kaiman & Polon,
Inc., New York City; in Australia and New
Zealand by Book & Film Services, Artarmon,
N.S.W., Australia; and in Japan by Harper & Row,
Publishers, Tokyo Office.

Library of Congress Cataloging in Publication Data

Payne, Ben Iden, 1881–1976.
　A life in a wooden O.

　Bibliography: p.
　Includes index.
　1.　Payne, Ben Iden, 1881–1976.　2.　Theatrical
producers and directors—United States—Biography.
3.　Shakespeare, William, 1564–1616—Dramatic
production.　I.　Title.
PN2287.P29A35　1977　　　792'.092'4m　　　76-48988
ISBN 0-300-02064-3

Can this cockpit hold
The vasty fields of France? Or may we cram
Within this wooden O the very casques
That did affright the air at Agincourt?

Henry V, Prologue

CONTENTS

ILLUSTRATIONS

PUBLISHER'S PREFACE

Genuine modesty is a rare virtue that is perhaps nowhere more rare than in the theatre. Yet Ben Iden Payne, who spent seventy years of his life as an actor and director, was a truly modest man. It is not that he was self-effacing or lacked conviction or was unwilling to exert authority—far from it. But his thoughts were always on the job to be done and not on himself. Moreover, they were totally engaged by the present, never the past. Payne's students and colleagues importuned him repeatedly to record both his experiences in the professional theatre and the approach to the production of Shakespeare's plays that he called "modified Elizabethan staging." For fifty years he resisted these pleas, saying rather impatiently, "This is something to be done, not written about." Only when he retired from active production —at the age of eighty-eight—did he at last find the time to review the events of his own life. He finished this book in his ninety-first year.

It is a most unusual theatrical memoir. There is almost nothing in it of Payne's triumphs or the honors and praise he received. If he records successes they are essentially successes of ideas—repertory theatre, a new kind of drama, a method of staging—not of B. Iden Payne the man. If he mentions great names—Yeats, Shaw, Frank Benson, William Poel, Miss Horniman, the Barrymores, Helen Hayes—it is because he believes that his readers will want to hear about *them*, not the fact that B. Iden Payne knew them and worked with them. When King Edward VII attends one of his performances it is his accent that interests Payne, not his presence.

If this modesty was one of Payne's most endearing traits, it has also posed a problem for his publisher. For every well-known name that Payne recorded he left out several. One would never know, to cite one example, that among his actors at the Gaiety were Sybil Thorndike, Clarence Derwent, and Rebecca West. Nor does one learn that actors, directors, and designers trained by Payne or by his students are to be found today in prominent roles in the theatre, radio, television, and the drama departments of universities. We intrude upon Payne's memories with this preface and a few footnotes solely for the purpose of filling in blanks and placing his achievement in a wider perspective.

Ben Iden Payne was born at Newcastle upon Tyne, England, on September 5, 1881. After his first appearance, with Frank Benson's company in 1898, he toured the provinces with a variety of companies. In 1907 he was briefly the director of the Abbey Theatre in Dublin, before the Abbey's chief financial backer, Miss A. E. F. Horniman, placed him, at twenty-six, in full charge of a new venture, at the Gaiety Theatre in Manchester. There, over a period of four years, this young actor-director molded the first true repertory theatre in England, performing almost untried works by Shaw, Galsworthy, and playwrights whose talents he fostered. It met with failures as well as successes, but its influence was great and carried across the sea to America. Payne went with it. His first wife, the actress Mona Limerick, remained in England with their children, and their marriage was eventually dissolved. One of their daughters also became an actress, as Rosalind Iden, and later married the Shakespearean actor-director Sir Donald Wolfit. Lady Wolfit and Sarah Payne live in England today; Payne's son, Padgett, lives in America.

For several years, working for the Shuberts, Charles Frohman's successor Alf Hayman, Ziegfeld, and the Theatre Guild, Payne was one of the busiest directors on Broadway. But he was unhappy with the star system, typecasting, and other evils of the professional theatre of the day. Early on he enjoyed an experience of working with students in the theatre department of the Carnegie Institute of Technology, in Pittsburgh, the nation's first professional school for theatre arts in a university. This led him gradually into the career of teaching and directing in universities, which would occupy most of the rest of his life.

During Payne's tenure of sixteen years at "Tech," now the Carnegie-Mellon University, he developed what he considered his chief contribution to the theatre: the method of producing Shakespeare's plays on an approximation of an Elizabethan stage. It was inspired by his brief association with that eccentric genius William Poel, founder of the Elizabethan Stage Society. In 1934 Payne left Carnegie Tech (though he returned briefly later) to direct and act at the Goodman Theatre in Chicago with his old Tech colleague Thomas Wood Stevens.

Payne was invited in 1935 to become general director of the Shakespeare Memorial Theatre at Stratford-upon-Avon. His eight years in that post were among the most frustrating of his career. The management of the Stratford theatre had little sympathy for Payne's unconventional approach to Shakespearean staging, and the huge proscenium stage at Stratford was in any case poorly adapted to his purpose. Payne was unhappy and so, for the most part, were the critics. Characteristically, Payne criticizes no one in his account of this period; he merely has little to say about it.

Payne returned to the United States in 1943. Thereafter, except for directing a couple of Broadway productions, he devoted the rest of his life to the educational theatre. Although he taught and directed at many universities, he made the University of Texas his home base for the last twenty-three years of his teaching career. Finding many congenial and appreciative colleagues and students there, he continued teaching and directing until 1969. In 1950 he married Mrs. Barbara Rankin Chiaroni, a former ballet dancer who had assisted him with his productions. During the last weeks of his life Payne learned that his memoir was to be published and that a new theatre at The University of Texas was to be named in his honor. And an emissary from Queen Elizabeth II presented him with the Order of the British Empire. A few weeks later, on April 6, 1976, Ben Iden Payne died, in his ninety-fifth year.

Payne says much in his memoir about his physical staging of Shakespeare's plays but little about his directorial methods. Fortunately, Rex Pogson, in his *Miss Horniman and the Gaiety Theatre, Manchester*, describes them in some detail.

It has already been suggested that Payne's approach to production was imaginative rather than realistic (in the usual sense of that word) and consequently plays calling for poetic and imaginative treatment, in particular plays calling for spiritual insight, appealed to him most strongly. Almost as strongly developed, however, was his sense of fun, a Puck-like quality which popped out happily and unexpectedly, a sense of fun dependent less on verbal dexterity than on the external humours derived from the contrast and clash of character, the oddities and eccentricities of individual personality, the absurdities of human snobbery and pretentiousness. . . . It was this clear understanding of the basic humours of human behaviour, no less than his deep sense of character, which gave Payne's productions, at their best, that fine sense of balance and of contrast, of sincerity and spontaneity, for which the Gaiety company became widely famed. Payne never became wedded to a theory of producing; he approached each play on its merits as an individual work of art, to be interpreted as the dramatist had conceived it, not to be fitted into some already formulated mould.

In relation to his actors Payne was constructive and quietly authoritative. His complete grasp of a play and his ability to relate every speech to the whole character or the whole play inspired confidence. There was no attempt to dragoon his actors. If he were asked how a certain speech should be spoken, he would not speak it for the actor; he would tell him why it was spoken, precisely what significance it had for the character or the play and then he would leave the actor to attempt to give that significance in his own way. It was the same in little bits of stage business. If a window had to be opened or a door shut, he would not attempt to show how it should be done, since every actor, even in so small a matter, would behave in an individual way. So long as what was done did not falsify the author's intention and did not upset the overall balance and conception of the play, the actor was allowed freely to express his own personality. This method had its dangers and did not always succeed, but it was a method which expressed perfectly the temperament of Payne and was ideally suited to a permanent company fully conversant with the personalities and abilities of their fellow actors. It maintained interest, prevented staleness, and induced study. Like Stanislavsky, Payne had the peculiar faculty of creating the atmosphere in which actors, so to speak, found themselves, and in which they developed, rather than in creating a pattern into which they had to fit themselves.

In later years, no doubt through long experience with student actors, Payne became somewhat more authoritarian in his approach. Nevertheless, he managed to inspire in his students both respect and devotion. Franklin Heller, one of his students at Carnegie Tech, writes of him,

Mr. Payne's effect on his students is legendary. He was a most charismatic teacher, yet, personally, he was shy and retiring. His appearance was dramatic and striking. Even in his old age he was alert and active. With his white hair, his pink English schoolboy complexion, and his beautiful speech, combined with that prodigious memory, he made a unique contribution to the culture of any community into which he came. Although short in stature, he could assume terrifying authority, which sometimes frightened students, but he was adored by them all for everything that was characteristic of a great teacher who wanted to share his vast knowledge, his love of language, his tremendous enthusiasm for creativity, his professional skill, and his abundant love of the theatre.

As an actor Payne was limited in the range of his roles (though he played hundreds) by his very slight figure. He excelled, however, in certain comic parts. His Puff, in Sheridan's *The Critic*, won recognition on both sides of the Atlantic, and both Pogson and Derwent attest to the excellence of his Lickcheese in Shaw's *Widowers' Houses*. Shaw himself deplored Payne's portrayal—but Shaw was often dissatisfied with performances of his own plays, and Payne made a substantial success of a play that Shaw had dismissed as a failure. The two men's association continued for many years.

Today, although the name of B. Iden Payne is remembered with something close to reverence by hundreds of former students, it is hardly known to the general public. This is due in part to his total lack of interest in self-advertisement, but more to his long immersion in the educational theatre. Payne's influence, however, can be found in many places. Most obviously it can be traced in the English and American repertory theatre movement. Pogson has written, "During the four years of Payne's connection with it the Gaiety more closely approximated to the ideal repertory theatre than any other venture in England has done." That ideal was taken up with growing enthusiasm in the United States. Today professional regional theatres across the country are evidence of its vitality.

Payne's other chief interest, the rediscovery of Elizabethan principles in the staging of Shakespeare's plays, did not originate with him, and he gives full credit to Poel. But the fact is that Poel's idiosyncrasies, his antiquarianism, and his insistence on using amateur actors stood in the way of its success. Payne, for all his eventual dedication to his method, was above all a practical man of the theatre. He used his modified Elizabethan technique not because it approached historical accuracy but because it worked on a stage. Hundreds of Payne's students left their universities convinced by their own experience that he was right. A few applied his principles in theatres built on Payne's model, such as those in San Diego and Ashland, Oregon. Others adapted them to new situations on thrust stages or in theatres-in-the-round. Thousands of playgoers have discovered the effectiveness of Shakespeare on a quasi-Elizabethan stage.

In view of the resistance to Payne's ideas that he met with at Stratford he would have been gratified to know that for the 1976 season a smaller stage, designed to suggest that of an Elizabethan theatre and to bring actors closer to the audience, was built inside the large stage. In the same year an Elizabethan theatre designed by C. Walter Hodges was constructed in the remodeled St. Georges Church in London.

It is evident that the ideas and practices that Payne has bequeathed to the theatre will have a long life. Only a few decades ago the answer of most theatregoers to the Chorus's query in *Henry V*

> . . . May we cram
> Within this wooden O the very casques
> That did affright the air at Agincourt?

would have been an amused no. Today, thanks to Poel and especially to Payne, it is for a great many audiences a resounding yes. It is our hope that this memoir will make Ben Iden Payne himself more widely known.

The manuscript from which this book is mainly derived comprised, in effect, two parts: Payne's recollections of his professional career and detailed accounts of many of his modified Elizabethan productions. The present volume includes all of the first part and enough of the second to give the reader a clear idea of what his method was like. To these elements have been added excerpts from a remarkable series of talks that Payne delivered over WFAA, the radio station of The University of Texas, in 1956. Payne's memory at the age of ninety was remarkable; it is not to be expected that it should have been infallible. A few minor lapses have been either pointed out in footnotes or silently corrected by the editors.

A bibliography of Payne's writings, prepared by his colleagues at The University of Texas at Austin, will be found at the end of this book. However, readers may be interested in more information on some of the people with whom Payne was associated. The following books are useful sources.

Bowmer, Angus L. *As I Remember, Adam: An Autobiography of a Festival.* Ashland, Oregon: The Oregon Shakespearean Festival Association, 1975.

Flannery, James W. *Miss Annie F. Horniman and the Abbey Theatre.* Irish Theatre Series. Dublin: The Dolmen Press, 1970.

―――. *W. B. Yeats and the Idea of a Theatre: The Early Abbey Theatre in Theory and Practice.* New Haven: Yale University Press, 1976.

Pogson, Rex. *Miss Horniman and the Gaiety Theatre, Manchester.* London: Rockliff, 1952.

Speaight, Robert. *William Poel and the Elizabethan Revival*. Cambridge, Massachusetts: Harvard University Press, 1954.

Trewin, J. C. *Benson and the Bensonians*. London: Barrie and Rockliff, 1960.

Many former students and colleagues of Payne have provided helpful information. We are particularly grateful also to Dame Rebecca West, Anthony Quayle, and James W. Flannery. The original manuscript of Payne's memoir was prepared by Barbara Payne. Mrs. Payne joins the publisher in acknowledging the generous assistance and encouragement of many persons, only a few of whom can be mentioned here. They are:

The late John Rosenfield, of the Dallas Morning News; Dr. F. Loren Winship, retired chairman of the Department of Drama at The University of Texas at Austin and friend and colleague of Payne; Dr. David Nancarrow, also of the Department of Drama; Dr. W. H. Crain of the Hoblitzelle Theatre Arts Library, The Humanities Research Center, The University of Texas; Elizabeth Kimberly, Director of Drama Alumni Relations at the Carnegie-Mellon University; Robert Schenkkan, President and General Manager of the Communications Center, The University of Texas; John F. Sollers; and Neville MacDonald.

Martha Mahard of the Harvard University Theatre Collection; Ted Fetter, Director of the Theatre Collection of the Museum of the City of New York; Paul Myers, Curator of the Theatre Collection of the New York Public Library of Performing Arts; Louis Rackow, Curator of the Walter Hampden–Edwin Booth Theatre Collection and Library of the Players Club; Elizabeth Leach, Arts Librarian at the Central Library, Manchester, England; Raymond Mander of the Raymond Mander and Joe Mitchenson Theatre Collection, London; and John Bustin of the *Austin Citizen News*.

Craig Noel, Producing Director, The Old Globe Theatre, San Diego; Angus Bowmer, founder, and Jerry Turner, Director, Oregon Shakespearean Festival, Ashland, Oregon; the Royal Shakespeare Theatre, Stratford-upon-Avon; and Ron Christopher, Goodman Theatre Center, Chicago.

CHAPTER 1

*M*any well-known actors point with pride to having inherited theatrical traditions from several generations of their forebears. If there was actor's blood in my family, it was a well-kept secret. In a weak moment my grandmother had long ago admitted to having some collateral relationship with the Siddons family. My mother said that her father used to pester his wife to tell him what the connection was. He thought she should be proud of being related to the great Sarah. My grandmother was shocked that he would even mention it. "He thinks he'll get it out of me," she would tell my mother, "but he never will. No, he never, never will."

In spite of my grandmother's embarrassment, it seems to me that an atmosphere of theatrical activity floated in the air of my home. My father, a Unitarian minister, encouraged the putting on of plays at entertainments held in the Sunday school of his church in Manchester, in the British Midlands. In these performances my sister Nellie, fifteen years older than myself, and my brother Alfred, ten years older, were always eager participants. When there were young enough parts available even my sister May, five years my elder, took part. There was much sewing of costumes, and my brother had a makeup box well stocked with greasepaints and crepe hair, with which he made elaborate disguises. He was also the makeup man for local amateur theatrical clubs. And then there was Colonel Thomas, a retired army officer who visited us. He had been connected with the professional theatre, and nothing was talked of when he came to see us but actors and acting.

It was through Colonel Thomas that I made my first appearance on any stage. He organized a semiprofessional entertainment in the shape of what would now be called a revue. Something went amiss backstage, and Colonel Thomas came out front to my parents and whispered a request that they permit me to take part in the performance. I was to represent a poor lost child, leaning against a lamppost while a song was sung. My parents readily agreed, and soon I found myself dressed in ragged clothes and placed in the appropriate position. Although I had been given no instructions, when the song began I could tell by the singer's words and gestures that I was supposed to be a starving waif. I responded by acting the part with passionate fervor. The climax to my emotional performance came when I happened to look down at the front row of spectators and saw my father wiping his eyes. This was more than I could bear and I burst into tears myself.

My parents were regular and eager playgoers, and it cannot have been many years later that I saw my first Shakespeare play. I was taken to a performance of *Twelfth Night*. I could not follow the details of the dialogue, but I had been briefed about the story and a child's imagination is swift and vivid. I was entranced by the whole performance and fell in love with the actress who played Viola. She seemed to me to be particularly fetching when disguised as Cesario in a short, white evzone skirt, embroidered gaiters, a scarlet bolero over a white blouse, and a saucy red porkpie cap. I think it must have been then and there that I began to revolt against a more or less tacit understanding that I was to "follow in my father's footsteps" as a Unitarian minister. At any rate, on my father's untimely death at fifty-two, when I was eleven years old, I began to take it for granted—though still keeping it a secret—that my life's work would be that of a professional actor.

Within a year or two I began memorizing Shakespearean soliloquies. I declaimed "To be or not to be" and "Now is the winter of our discontent" in my bedroom when, as often happened, I was alone in the house. Alone, that is, except for our trusted housemaid, who was my ally.

My mother's only source of income was a slender annuity. For her to assure my continuance at a private preparatory school must have been a financial problem, until I was fortunate enough to win a foundation scholarship at the Manchester Grammar School. During my second year there, it was announced that a performance of *The Merchant of Venice* would be held. I wasted no time in applying for a part and was cast as Bassanio. It was a wonderful experience, setting the seal upon my resolution.

Soon after this—I think it was the same year—the great actor Henry Irving was on tour and paid a visit to the Manchester Theatre Royal. Of course I had to see him. As I could afford to attend only one performance out of his repertoire, I naturally chose *The Merchant of Venice*. My attitude toward the production was slightly condescending. I admired Irving's Shylock for its dignity, but I thought he played too quietly. My friend who played Shylock in our school production seemed quite his superior when it came to the impassioned passages. As for Bassanio, I thought the actor very handsome. Above all, however, I envied him for being allowed to make love to Ellen Terry. Her charm and grace of movement no one who saw her ever forgot. I enlisted in the vast army of her devoted slaves, and after nearly three-quarters of a century I remain one still.

My brother, meanwhile, had become an enthusiastic actor. He was capable, too, and always in demand. If he had had his way he would have been a professional—and indeed he became one for a few years, long afterward, under my management. His ambition in that direction prompted him to subscribe to *The Stage*, the more popular, and the less expensive, of two weekly trade papers of the theatrical profession. Each week there were columns of advertisements for actors and actresses, sometimes for whole companies. Many specified "lines of business," and frequently they warned that applicants must "dress well on and off the stage." These advertisements were inserted by managers of companies touring the smaller theatres; the managements of higher standing did not need to advertise for actors.

One day, when I was about fifteen, my eyes lighted on an advertisement inserted in *The Stage* by a manager whose company was playing at one of the three or four Manchester suburban theatres. He needed a juvenile lead for the melodrama in which he himself was starring. I decided that I would apply for the part. Accordingly, I walked self-consciously into a small shop and bought a straight-up collar, which was then the customary grown-up neckwear. I could hardly present myself in my schoolboy's turned-down Eton collar. The problem was how to change the collars. Near the Regent Theatre, whither I was bound, I found a field where there were some bushes to hide behind. There I made the transformation, concealing the Eton collar in my pocket. Soon I was walking nervously back and forth in front of the theatre, trying to summon up courage to storm the stage door. But it was in vain. My courage failed to respond, and in deep humiliation I returned to the field to resume the schoolboy collar. Such was my first attempt to enter the profession.

Every year several touring repertory companies, a few of them mainly Shakespearean, came to Manchester. They played not at suburban theatres such as the Regent but at one or another of the centrally located theatres, of which there were fewer than five. Among them, the Theatre Royal was the most prominent. It was primarily used by the leading London actor-managers on their annual provincial tours. Not far behind the Theatre Royal came the Princes' Theatre. It was generally occupied by the best touring musical comedy or opera companies. The Comedy Theatre, later known as the Gaiety, had a slightly lower but still respectable status. It was host to a mixed group of companies of good but secondary repute.

At Christmas each of these theatres staged a pantomime—that peculiarly English form of entertainment composed of song, dance, low-comedy interludes, and spectacular "transformation scenes," the whole being superimposed upon a lightly sketched fairy tale. It used to end with a brief "harlequinade" especially for the children's delight. Only the harlequinade was true pantomime, played without words by Harlequin and Columbine, Pantaloon, a clown, and a policeman. Pantomimes were amazingly popular and ran for several weeks, even months, drawing audiences not only from Manchester itself but from all the encircling cotton-spinning towns.

Fourth in rank was the Queen's Theatre, which performed a special function. It was known as the blood-tub, for it was dedicated almost wholly to melodrama. It gave no pantomime, but its manager, a notable figure named Richard Flanagan, furnished a special form of Christmas entertainment that I shall have occasion to describe later. The fifth and last theatre in the city was the St. James, which subsisted on a mixture of lesser attractions.

Of the Shakespearean companies that visited Manchester, quite the most important, and the only one ever booked at the Theatre Royal, was Mr. and Mrs. F. R. Benson's Shakespearean and Old English Comedy Company—to give it the full title it enjoyed on the billboards. In the fall of 1898 I wrote to Mr. Benson, asking for an interview when he came to Manchester for his annual visit. By keeping careful watch I managed to intercept the postman every day so as to receive the mail before the rest of the family. To my great delight, a reply came in a brief note from his secretary, informing me that Mr. Benson would see me shortly before the Saturday matinee, the last day of his Manchester engagement. At the prescribed hour—nay, at the very moment—I presented myself to the stage-door keeper, proud that I had the right to do so. He invited me to wait inside the door, that antechamber to the temple of art.

It is difficult to convey the aura of glamor that in those days glowed about the mystical words "behind the scenes." This was not so only in

4

the romantic imagination of a stagestruck youth; the feeling was shared by all theatregoers. No one with good manners dreamed of asking to go backstage unless he had business there or was acquainted with an actor. The actors carefully fostered this feeling that the theatre was a world apart, all details of which should be kept secret from the profane eyes of the uninitiated. The footlights were the moat surrounding a fairy castle, and the drawbridge was seldom let down.

You may imagine my excitement, then, when a short, chubby man appeared, asked my name, and ushered me farther within the sacred precincts. This gentleman, who wore the most luxuriant handlebar moustache I have ever seen, was Joe Richmond, Mr. Benson's valet. He led me through the greenroom, the lounge where actors while away their moments offstage. (The Theatre Royal was one of the few theatres that still retained this amenity.) Then we came to the star dressing room. There I was greeted by Mr. Benson, an actor whom I regarded with nothing short of reverence. As he proceeded with his makeup he asked me, as if it were a matter of course, to recite something from Shakespeare. Very wisely, I now realize, I did not attempt something beyond my capacity—not to speak of my comprehension—such as the Hamlet soliloquies. Instead I chose to repeat Hotspur's first speech, his defence for having withheld his prisoners after his victory over the earl of Douglas at Holmedon. This speech was a required one in the competition for a special elocutionary prize that I had twice won at the Grammar School.

Mr. Benson stopped making up and watched me closely. When I had finished he called for Richmond and told him to ask Mrs. Benson to come to his room. Mrs. Benson's arrival was a moment to be remembered, for she was the lady who had so impressed my fancy as Viola when I first saw *Twelfth Night*, years before. Mr. Benson asked me to repeat Hotspur's speech for her. Although I saw no particular significance in this, I recited the speech for Mrs. Benson with added gusto. Mr. Benson ended the interview by making inquiries about my situation at home and at school. He then told me he would like to talk to my mother. He handed me two passes written on visiting cards, one for myself to *The Taming of the Shrew* that afternoon, the other for two orchestra stalls for the evening performance. I was to take my mother and bring her around to meet him afterward.

Since my family were such ardent playgoers, I was not surprised, on reaching home after the matinee, to find that my mother and eldest sister had already left to attend the evening performance at the Theatre Royal. The reason for their early departure was that the ground floor of English provincial theatres was divided into two parts. In the front were

5

Frank Benson as Richard III

Mrs. Benson as Juliet

five or six rows of "orchestra stalls," with separate seats comfortably upholstered. At the back of the stalls was a low barrier, behind which was the "pit," where the rest of the audience sat crowded together on benches. The pit was not booked beforehand, so for a popular attraction people assembled hours before the ticket offices were opened. Promptness was rewarded—but at a price. There were three pit doors: the "extra-early doors," which opened fully an hour before the play began; the "early doors," where people were admitted half an hour later; and finally the "ordinary doors," which opened to fill the remaining seats during the last fifteen minutes before curtain time. The price of admission at the Theatre Royal descended from three shillings and sixpence for the extra-early to a shilling for the ordinary doors.

My mother and sister were always among the "extra-early" entrants. For them it was part of the evening's entertainment to sit in the front row of the pit behind the low wooden barrier separating them from the stalls. There they were able to watch and comment upon the spectators as they assembled in the more expensive seats. Consequently, as I said, it was not much of a surprise for me when I hurried home to find no one but the younger of my sisters. For her it seemed to be the chance of a lifetime to be able to go with me—and under these extraordinary circumstances. Excitedly she put on her best dress and, after a hasty meal, we made our way to the theatre. We arrived so early that we were the first to enter the stalls. Imagine, then, the astonished faces of my mother and eldest sister as they saw us emerging from the side door to occupy the exclusive seats!

I hastened over to explain the situation to my mother. She was almost as excited as I had been at the prospect of meeting Mr. Benson, but hesitated because she was not wearing her best clothes. My sisters and I persuaded her that a word of explanation to Mr. Benson would suffice, and so, after the play, she and I went backstage together. Mr. Benson said that, in his opinion, I had acting talent and should be encouraged to go onto the stage, and the sooner the better. At first my mother demurred, but she finally gave her approval when Mr. Benson suggested that I should continue at school for the final year. My own disappointment at this delay to my career was alleviated by the promise that, when Mr. Benson came to Manchester for his autumn season the next year, I should join the company as a "walker-on." He called this a trial engagement, which made it seem thrillingly important.

I don't know how I managed to get through that year at school. Concentration upon my studies was impossible, so it was not surprising that I failed to graduate. But the waiting time, dragging its slow length along, finally came to an end. The next autumn, when Benson had an unusually long season at the Theatre Royal, I became a member of his company. Though I had no speaking parts, I was technically a full-fledged member—a "walking gentleman," as the position was defined in the stock companies. This must not be confused with a mere supernumerary. I had my assigned place in a dressing room with the regular members. The characters I represented were diverse and sometimes not without significance. For instance, in court scenes I was one of the silent lords; in other scenes I was a peasant, a townsman, a beggar, or a servant who handed out tankards of ale. Once—the proudest moment of all—I made an entrance to present a scroll.

At that time, the Benson company was at the height of its provincial popularity. In later years, after the First World War and a series of financial difficulties, a company bearing the Benson name continued to tour with scenery dilapidated by long and continuous touring. Benson himself had gone to seed and was supported by inferior actors. The troupe was no longer even fully under his own management. The decline of this once outstanding company was a sad story. A younger generation naturally passed judgment upon it as it then was, not as it had been. The best that Tyrone Guthrie could later say about seeing Benson's troupe while a student at Oxford was that "they threw open windows which would otherwise have remained shut. They may have been rather dusty, grubby old casements which creaked open, but they gave onto the foam of perilous seas in faery lands forlorn."

I am thankful that I never saw the company in its decay. By that time the acting doubtless deserved the strictures laid upon it. But when I joined in 1899 it was of a very high quality. Benson himself had certain peculiarities in the delivery of verse that were not universally admired. But for him and all his subordinates, sincerity and simplicity were the keynotes of acting. Above all, the actors were inspired by Benson's enthusiasm, and they conveyed to their audiences a sense of joy in the performances. As J. C. Trewin has written in *Benson and the Bensonians*, they thought of Shakespeare "not as dead beneath a chancel slab, but as a living man whose work must live through the actors."

In the theatrical profession Benson's company was universally regarded as a great nursery of talent. It is amazing how many leading actors and actresses on the London stage, including such stars as Oscar Asche, Matheson Lang, and Henry Ainley, were "old Bensonians." Several, too, came to hold important positions in the American theatre.

The distinguished author Arthur Machen, who for a time was an actor with the Benson company, wrote in *Theatre Arts Monthly* for September 1931: "Here was acting, a curious and beautiful art, with its inward part and its outward part, with every detail, every gesture full of significance; and everything open to discussion, to a reasoned enquiry into the right or the wrong, the more graceful and the less graceful way of doing it. It has always seemed to me that the Benson way is the way to make actors who think, who delight in nice enquiry into every detail, who have an intelligent joy and interest in the art they follow."

A younger generation remained aware of the Benson influence. Anthony Quayle, speaking at the unveiling of the Benson panel in the Memorial Theatre in Stratford-upon-Avon in 1950, said that as he looked around the picture gallery he "saw all over the room actors and managers from whom we younger ones have learnt everything. They in their turn were taught by Frank Benson, so that the younger ones who are learning today are also being taught by Frank Benson."

My own family was doubtless typical of many who looked upon the annual visit of the Benson company almost as the return of old friends, for many of the principal actors remained with Benson year after year. But spectators were mere observers. What an exalting experience it was for me during those four weeks of humble but full participation to pass, before each performance, the long queue waiting for the pit doors to open—a queue extending all down the side and along the back of the theatre and broken only by a gap for the stage door—and to stride proudly through that gap into the inner sanctum. I imagined that I was watched enviously by the bystanders, who would be able to take only a passive part in the coming celebration.

On days when there were matinees the assistant stage manager met me alone to give me instructions about what I was to do in that day's performance. Every other day there were long rehearsals, not only of that night's play but of plays that were to be revived after being neglected for several weeks.

Benson's indefatigability was notorious. At these rehearsals I had my first experience of the Bensonian "bun-fund." This was a unique device for keeping actors content without any break for lunch. After about a couple of hours rehearsal, Richmond would appear with huge sacks in each arm containing freshly baked and most delectable buns. He walked quietly around the back of the stage, well behind the action being rehearsed, and stopped by each of us to let us dip into the bags. He would then place the packages on a table where the actors who were rehearsing at the moment could help themselves as they made their exits. Benson, celebrated for his abstemiousness, never took the least notice, much less a bun for himself. This distribution was called a fund because it was theoretically paid for by a system of fines inflicted for such misdemeanors as being late for an entrance or a rehearsal. As the occasion for these fines rarely arrived, however, the actors knew that the cost of the buns was really defrayed out of Benson's private purse.

Though the actors showed no signs of regarding Mr. Benson with the reverence that I felt for him, it was obvious that their attitude toward him combined affection and respect. When he was not present, in the dressing room, for instance, he was always spoken of as "Pa," but I doubt that even the most outspoken called him this to his face.

Rehearsals began promptly at eleven and lasted until about two-thirty, or more often later. I soon noticed that they were occasionally cut short when Randle Ayrton, the stage manager, reminded Mr. Benson that they were booked for a hockey match that day. Later on I learned that Benson and his company were notorious throughout the profession for their enthusiasm for outdoor sports, not only hockey but also cricket and water polo. It was even rumored (though falsely) that it was impossible for a male actor to procure an engagement with Benson unless he was proficient in one of these games. A farfetched story had it that once when Benson sent a telegram to an actor asking if he could play Rugby (Dr. Caius's servant in *The Merry Wives of Windsor*), the actor wired back his regret that he played only soccer.

Henry Herbert, whom I later knew more intimately in America as a successful character actor, at that time superintended the wardrobe. Every day he fitted me with costumes, including all necessary accessories, even wigs. Had I been under contract as a full member of the company, not on a trial engagement, I should have had to supply three pairs of tights—black, brown, and "fleshings"—and two pairs of shoes, black velvet and russet leather, as well as a pair of eighteenth-century buckled shoes, if the repertoire required them. All these things, and wigs, if needed, constituted the established requirement in all stock or repertory contracts. Herbert had assistants, including an "armorer." The Benson company was so well supplied with arms—swords, halberds, and pikes, not to speak of full suits of armor—that it was necessary to have someone especially employed to keep them polished and in proper condition.

Except at rehearsal I saw very little of the principal actors, but those with whom I did come into contact, especially in the dressing room, accepted me as one of themselves. They treated me with neither indifference nor condescension, as they might so easily have done.

The four weeks of my trial engagement passed all too swiftly. At its close I had an experience that I had somehow not expected. The very polite acting manager handed me an envelope containing a check for four guineas. It was exciting enough to hold in my hand the first remuneration of any kind I had ever received for anything whatsoever. But how inconceivably wonderful to be paid for what had been the most delightful experience of my life! The form of the payment, too— a check inscribed for payment to Ben Iden Payne—seemed to give it so much added importance. The excitement did not end there either. Before I had fully recovered my balance, Richmond came to summon me to Mr. Benson's dressing room. I went there buoyed up with the hope that I was to join the company as a regular member then and there. In this I was overconfident, for the interview turned out to be something of an anticlimax. I was not offered an immediate engagement. I was promised, however, that, if I spent a year working with some smaller troupe, I could rely upon an engagement as a full member of the Benson company when the autumn tour started in the following year. Mr. Benson explained that I needed experience and that the best way for a beginner to procure it was to find work in a repertory company. There were, he assured me, several available.

CHAPTER 2

Young actors today will marvel that Mr. Benson could speak so confidently about my finding work in the theatre. The explanation is in fact a simple one. Motion pictures, radio, and television were yet to be invented. There were variety theatres, as our vaudeville houses were called, but no lady could attend them, and many gentlemen did not care to be seen in them. They offered, to be sure, certain conveniences. For example, there was always a handy little shelf on which a customer could rest his mug of ale while the master of ceremonies, who sat on the stage, announced the turns between sips of the same refreshment. There were also minstrel shows, respectable enough, but only very occasional. So among those who preferred more serious entertainment, the theatre reigned supreme, feeble though it often was. Even small towns had their theatres, which either housed resident stock companies or played host to a succession of touring stock companies.

With all this activity, it is not surprising that the supply of actors could not equal the demand—or at least the supply of male actors, who were needed in larger number and (in very relative terms) commanded larger salaries. The companies touring in the smaller provinces had perennial difficulties in filling their casts. Consequently these smaller, poorer managements were willing, even eager, to take on a beginner, at the tiny salary he was glad to accept. Mr. Benson gave me the names of two or three to which I might apply. About one of them, he said, he had heard only vaguely, but it was under the management of a French woman with some such name as "Great-Tiny." It had been running, he believed, for some time, with a repertoire about which he was ignorant. But repertoire it was, and repertoire, he said, was the way to gain experience.

Searching the long list of companies on tour printed weekly in *The Stage*, I learned that a Mlle Gratienne—obviously French so probably the Great-Tiny one—was booked the next week at Chorley, a small town conveniently situated only about thirty miles from Manchester. This proximity was a stroke of luck. I wrote to Mlle Gratienne, timing my letter to reach her on her arrival at the theatre named. By return of post there came a letter in large, scrawling handwriting asking me to see her as soon as possible. I should find her, it said, at the theatre rehearsing every day.

There was an old, established publishing house that issued, under the title of *Dick's Penny Plays*, an enormous list of dramas old enough to be free of royalty. They ranged from the classics to one-act farces. Since they were indeed sold for two cents apiece, it is not surprising that they were little more than thin paper pamphlets, printed in minute type with double columns to the page. *Dick's Penny Plays* were invaluable to the still existing companies playing in wooden, transportable theatres known as "the booths," as well as to the companies in the few remaining "tent theatres" at fairs.

I had purchased some of these plays by mail and, with them, a special item from the catalogue entitled, in large type, *The Actors' Handbook*. Below, in smaller type, was promisingly added *With a Guide to the Passions*. This publication was larger and fatter than the plays and cost no less than fourpence, "or sixpence if sent by post." It informed one, in a chapter devoted to the etiquette of the theatrical profession, that when an actor joined a company, certain conventions were to be observed. The actor was first to give his name to the doorkeeper, the doorkeeper would take him to the stage manager, the stage manager would introduce him to the manager, and the manager would then present him to the members of the company. Although I was not yet a member of Mlle Gratienne's company, and was doubtful that I ever would be, I anticipated that at least the first part of this procedure outlined in *The Actors' Handbook* would be followed.

I was disappointed that my reception, when I arrived at the theatre, lacked this formality. I could find no doorkeeper, for none existed; I had to work my way alone through a dark passage to a dim and unoccupied stage. There I waited disconsolately, half inclined to beat a quiet retreat. After a time three or four men and women, obviously members of the company, drifted in. They took no notice of me and I pretended not to notice them. Soon after this, however, a short, middle-aged woman erupted—one can call it nothing less—onto the stage and bore down upon me like a charging bull. She asked me, with a marked French accent, whether I was the young man who had written to her for an engagement. When I admitted it, she told me abruptly that I looked all right, that she would pay me a guinea a week, and that I was to join the company on Sunday morning at Crewe Station at eleven-thirty. The company would be there on their way to Gloucester, where they were booked at the Theatre Royal for the following week.

I returned home elated, and on Sunday morning an early train took me to Crewe Station in plenty of time to meet the company. Crewe, though a small town, is a busy junction on the London and Northwestern Railway. At that time touring was in its heyday. All day long on every Sunday there were frequent arrivals and departures of "theatrical specials," trains made up exclusively of touring companies, each of which was provided with its separate coach and a baggage van attached thereto. On arrival at Crewe the trains were split up. There was much shunting of coaches into new arrangements in preparation for departures in different directions. Consequently, actors could depend upon a long wait in Crewe, and the platforms were centers of excitement as the specials pulled into the station. Actresses rushed frantically from one platform to another to find out what companies were on the newly arrived trains. This was followed by a search for acquaintances and screams of joy when they were found. There were eager inquiries about how much time there would be for chatter and gossip. The men took it more calmly. They generally retired with their friends to the refreshment room to discuss matters over a glass of beer, for as bona fide travelers they could purchase alcoholic beverages during legally restricted hours.

Since it was customary for theatrical companies to paste print-sheets of paper on the windows of their coaches proclaiming their names in large type, I had no difficulty in locating the Gratienne company. Mademoiselle greeted me and told me to take any seat I wished. There were no corridors in the trains; each coach was divided into separate, isolated compartments. I had only one companion in the compartment I happened to choose. His sardonic countenance made him seem to me quite old—indeed he may have been as much as forty years of age, which was antiquity in my young eyes. He spent the time grumbling about the financial condition of the company and making contemptuous gibes against all his fellow actors. His conversation was depressing and I was happy to escape from him on our arrival at the station in Gloucester, where he angrily seized his bag from the rack and hurried away alone.

For a few moments I felt like a lost sheep as I stood aimlessly on the platform, but my plight was noticed by two young men, members of the company, who asked me if I would like to share rooms with them. So all was well, and I made my first acquaintance with theatrical rooms and theatrical landladies, those now vanished conveniences of touring days.

The rooms, or "digs," as they were generally called, were invariably stuffy and overfurnished, though usually spic and span, for a good landlady prided herself on her cleanliness. The mantelpieces were so crowded with bric-a-brac—often cheap china ornaments labeled "A present from Brighton" or some other seaside resort—that it was difficult to avoid knocking them off. Most landladies were friendly, genial souls who loved to be on good terms with their tenants. If you addressed one as Mrs. So-and-so, she was likely to look hurt and say, "Just call me Ma." They often liked to chat about their early experiences, especially when they had worked in the theatre themselves. Once, after serving my breakfast, my landlady returned and shyly leaned a photograph against the teapot, where it was bound to catch my eye. She stood there, elderly, stout, and grey haired. The figure in the photograph was a young woman with crisply curled hair, tight waist but broad hips, and laced boots reaching almost to the knees. She was instantly recognizable as a vaudeville dancer of a type that had flourished a generation earlier. I am glad to say that I had the presence of mind to ask, "Is that a picture of you?" She beamed with pleasure as she told me proudly that she had been "the champion buck-and-wing dancer of Australia."

At another time, in the south of Wales, a landlady quietly pushed open my door but did not appear herself. A few seconds later I heard the twanging but pleasant tones of a musical instrument with which I was unfamiliar. Of course I had to investigate. I found my landlady sitting on a stool just by the door playing on a Jew's harp. I stood listening. When she finished I praised her skill and asked her about the tune. She explained that it was an old Welsh ballad about a farmer's widow who was forced to sell her most precious possession, a dearly loved pig, in order to pay the rent for her cottage to her grasping landlord. She assured me that it was a very sad song, as indeed I had guessed from the tune.

For most actors London, or rather that central part of it known as the West End, was a far-off Mecca it was most unlikely they would ever reach. They anticipated only an indefinitely continuing life on tour. Consequently, one of their most closely guarded possessions was a notebook containing an alphabetically arranged list of provincial towns with the names and addresses of landladies to be found there. Sometimes there was an added note about the price paid and the quality of the accommodations. It was a proof of affection for an actor to let another actor see and copy from his book.

Older actors generally wrote ahead for rooms already entered in their books. However, during each week letters addressed "to the members of the company" were to be found on a rack in the theatre. They were sent by landladies from the next town to be visited. The writers had found out from the manager of their local theatre the name and current address of the company to play there the following week. They gave information, sometimes in not very legible handwriting, about what they had available in the way of sitting rooms and bedrooms or of "combined rooms," which were single rooms furnished as both a bed and sitting room. They were remarkably inexpensive. The standard rate for the week was about twelve to fourteen shillings for bedroom and sitting room and eight to ten shillings for a combined room. The price was not only for the accommodation but for meals cooked and served by the landlady. If she was instructed by mail to buy food she did so and inserted the cost of her purchases in the bill at the end of the week. But the inexperienced actor was warned that it was extravagant to let the landlady do the buying for she would boost the prices she had paid. Accordingly, actors usually brought their own food in a basket and handed it to the landlady with instructions as to how it was to be prepared. Then, before going on to the next town, all the remaining transportable food was packed into the basket and carried to the train.

Landladies kept "testimonial books," placed always in a prominent position in the room, in which one was expected to write a few words of commendation at the time of departure. You looked through them in search of names of acquaintances, not without curiosity as to what they had written. Most compliments were short, dull, and repetitious, but every now and then one came across some special expression of approval such as "Don't miss Ma's apple pies; her pastry is tip-top," or "Ma's beefsteak puddings are extra special." Sometimes an illiterate or careless landlady would permit a derogatory remark to remain in her testimonial book. One of these comments read, "I recommend careful addition and scrutiny of the items in your bill." Presumably the landlady had laboriously spelled the message only to the second word!

Among the companies that could be relied upon to appear at the

Theatre Royal in Manchester once every year was Mr. and Mrs. Edward Compton's Old English Comedy Company. (The Comptons were the parents of Sir Compton Mackenzie, the popular novelist.) Like the Benson company it was an important provincial institution. We never failed to see one or another of its offerings nor to join in the applause that greeted the first entrance of each principal in the play of the evening. These actors held a lofty place in our theatrical pantheon. It was therefore a shock when I came upon their names in one of the testimonial books. I had supposed that such exalted personages would never lodge in humble theatrical digs. But this feeling quickly gave place to gratification, as if the aura of their presence still clung to the rooms they had inhabited.

Such experiences would come later, however. My first night in the digs was uneventful enough. The next morning at rehearsal I became acquainted with my fellow actors. Mlle Gratienne's company was a small one—about ten of us, or possibly a dozen at the most. Besides Mademoiselle, I can remember only two ladies. The male members of the company were mostly young and comparatively inexperienced, though not quite such greenhorns as I. There were two older men in the company when I joined it, but the discontented one who had been my companion in the railway compartment did not remain long with us. His departure was unlamented, for everyone had disliked him. Unfortunately, however, there was nothing unusual about such sudden departures. The personnel was continually in a state of flux. Every few weeks Mademoiselle had to advertise in *The Stage* for a "responsible gentleman." Consequently there were daily rehearsals, even when we were not adding another play to our curiously mixed repertoire. The plays were of various ages, but none was new, for, since Mademoiselle could not afford to pay royalties, they had to be in the public domain.

On the first day in Gloucester we rehearsed *She Stoops to Conquer*, the play announced for the following night. I was delighted to learn that I was cast for the low comedy role of Diggory. I had seen the play and knew how good a part it was. As for the play to be given on the first night, I was told that I needed no rehearsal because I had only one line to speak. I was to dress myself in my darkest clothes and appear once in the second act as a manservant. All I had to do was to enter carrying a salver with a note upon it, take it to the man in the middle of the stage, and say, "A letter for you, sir." I prepared myself accordingly. When the act was in progress the stage manager took me to the door at the right side of the set and stood beside me. I waited, keyed up with nervous tension. Suddenly, in a low whisper, the stage manager gave me the word "go," and opened the door for me. From the dimness behind the flats I emerged into what seemed to be a blaze of light. My advance, thanks to my nervousness, was made with slow and ponderous steps. On reaching my goal—the man in the center of the stage—I declaimed my one line in the deepest, fullest, richest tones I was able to command. Even to this day I can see the surprised look on the face of the recipient of the note as he took it from the salver. I turned away with stately dignity and, with the same solemnity with which I had advanced, stalked off the stage. As I approached the door, my ears were assailed with loud laughter from the audience, laughter that was followed by ironical applause as I disappeared from sight. Possibly I may have the distinction of being the only actor who has left the stage to a round of applause on his first speaking appearance in a professional company!

Happily the next night was a different story. I had been thoroughly rehearsed and it was the right kind of laughter that I evoked. Diggory became one of my favorite parts. Mademoiselle was pleased and said so. More important, she gave me several substantial parts then being played by an actor who had given notice. Since our company was composed mostly of either inexperienced actors or broken-down has-beens, the quality of our performances must have been appalling. In this appraisal I include my own efforts, of course. But at least I knew my lines, which could not always be said about the others. Sometimes I not only spoke my own lines but had to fill in for others who dried up.

I also had to be prepared to meet emergencies of one sort or another. One of these occurred on the first night that I played my first long part, that of the Reverend Mr. Chadband in *Poor Jo*, a dramatization of *Bleak House*. One might imagine that no misfortune could exceed Mademoiselle's insistence on casting herself in the title role, the pathetic little cockney crossing-sweeper, Poor Jo. Apart from looking her age—she was well into her fifties—she spoke with a strong French accent, which she never attempted to disguise. But that was a continuing disaster, not the emergency I am speaking of. As I walked offstage with the other actors from a front scene we were met by Mademoiselle. Taking me by the arm, she turned me forcibly around and whispered fiercely, "The scene is not yet set; go on and gag!" Thereupon she pushed me back onto the stage. Fortunately I knew Dickens well, and Chadband was one of my favorite characters. I was strangely calm when I again faced the audience. Coining phrases vaguely reminiscent of Chadband's in the book, I launched into a hypocritical sermon in the sanctimonious Chadband manner. I was pleased and surprised to find that my impromptu effort was greeted by responsive laughter. I could have continued indefinitely and was actually disappointed when Mademoiselle signaled from the wing that the setting had been completed.

Meeting emergencies quickly developed a variety of technical skills. In this respect Mlle Gratienne's company proved an unusually valuable training ground. Among her other eccentricities, Mademoiselle had a curious idea about makeup, especially in a straight part such as that of a pretty army nurse in *The New Magdalen,* another dramatized work of fiction.* When playing young parts she contended that she looked best in a strange face of her own devising. Ghastly pale, entirely without rouge or mascara, she painted out her eyebrows and drew on narrow, brown half-moons above them. In the first act of *The New Magdalen* the heroine was taking shelter in a hut while a battle raged without. I, as an army officer, had to make a hurried entrance, see the nurse, and exclaim, "My God, what a beautiful woman!" The first time I played the scene, my articulation was loud and clear and the audience responded with a hearty laugh. However, I quickly learned to trick the line with a quick turn of the head and a slight muffling of the dangerous adjective.

Mademoiselle was a glutton for acting. There were occasions when the leading part did not satisfy her insatiable appetite. If an actress failed to please her in a small part in a scene in which the feminine lead did not appear, she would announce at rehearsal that on that night she would double the part to show how it ought to be done. The fact that her French accent would make her instantly recognizable did not trouble her at all; double the part she would and did, if for that night only.

That was bad enough. But when one morning Mademoiselle said that she would double as a midshipman in the navy, the company was moved to protest. No one ventured to stress the element of unsuitability, but there was also a problem of time to be considered. All that happened on the stage between Mademoiselle's exit as the leading lady and the entrance of the midshipman was a soliloquy, which it was my lot to speak as another naval officer. At the normal pace, this soliloquy did not take more than three-quarters of a minute at the most. Argument was unavailing. "I will underdress the part," she said, "and I will wear a moustache so that they will not know me." Our contention that a midshipman would not be allowed to wear a moustache was dismissed

*This play was presumably A. Newton Field's adaptation of a story by Wilkie Collins, first produced in 1882.

with a shrug of the shoulders. All appeal was uselsss. She quashed it with an irritable, "I am the manager, am I not?"

On the fatal evening, Mademoiselle made her first appearance as the heroine, looking even thicker in the waist than usual. The increase in bulk was due, of course, to the midshipman's trousers under her dress. The audience accepted this strange appearance, perhaps because Mademoiselle Gratienne projected her own sublime indifference to her appearance. But in time the action brought us to Mademoiselle's exit, which was made downstage on the left. The set for this—an open space at a seaport—had open wings, so there was especial need for quietness offstage. But almost before Mademoiselle was out of sight she was loudly calling, "Maman, where are you? What are you doing? Unbutton my dress." ("Maman," known to the rest of us as Madame, was Mademoiselle's mother, eighty if she was a day, who served as her dresser and also as wardrobe mistress for the company.) We—myself and the audience—could trace her route as she went, first upstage and then across behind the backdrop audibly directing Madame, until she finished her change of costume and arrived at her entrance upstage on the right, where she was to come down a ramp as the midshipman. As this noisy journey proceeded, I spoke louder and louder in a vain effort to drown her offstage exclamations, and slower and slower to give her more time for the costume change. I could judge her progress by her orders. "Give me my jaquette. Where is my wig?" The audience could have marked her passage visually as well as audibly, for I could hear her banging the backdrop as she and her mother traversed the narrow space between it and the back wall.

The inevitable moment came. I turned upstage to meet the midshipman, and Mademoiselle came tripping down the ramp. The laughter of the audience drowned our words. Her plentiful hair had been only partially thrust into a man's wig, making her head look enormous. On top of it the middy's cap was precariously balanced. Her tunic was not fully buttoned, and I noticed that she had not had time to affix the promised moustache.

When at long last the laughter subsided we proceeded with the lines. A little later, while I engaged in a brief dialogue with another actor, the midshipman had to go upstage. Presently there came an even louder burst of laughter from the audience. My back was turned toward the midshipman, but I managed to steal a glance over my shoulder. Mademoiselle was standing ·with her head and torso offstage hidden behind one of the wings, so that only her posterior and legs were visible.

What on earth could she be doing? The mystery was solved with her cue to speak. As she stood erect and turned toward us, we saw that she had used her silent interval to complete her concept of the character by affixing the missing moustache!

It was customary in prosperous companies for the acting manager to come around to the dressing rooms on Friday nights to distribute the weekly salaries in envelopes. This process was referred to somewhat irreverently by its beneficiaries. An actor coming off the stage in one of the earlier acts would inquire on his arrival in the dressing room, "Has the ghost walked yet?" But Mademoiselle could not afford the luxury of an acting manager. An actor in each night's cast who did not make an entrance until late in the first act, or perhaps did not play in that night's bill at all, was delegated to manage the front of the house. This task entailed walking about the theatre while the audience was assembling, looking important, and watching (or appearing to watch) the ticket takers at the various entrances to see that customers handed in the tickets they had bought at their respective entrances. The takers then placed the tickets in locked boxes from which they were subsequently taken and counted.

In the same way, late in the performance, an actor free at that moment was called upon to join the local theatre manager in unlocking the boxes and counting the tickets. He then signed the night's "return" in duplicate and took the company's copy to Mademoiselle. This count could not take place until the "half-timers" had been admitted. Ticket offices were kept open until an hour and a quarter after the curtain rang up. At that precise moment spectators were admitted for half the regular price. I need hardly say that it was disconcerting for the actors in a quiet or emotional scene to be suddenly interrupted by a loud clatter of hobnail boots as the late patrons scampered into the pit or down the wooden steps of the gallery, the favorite place for half-timers. Nevertheless, this was a good way of adding to a sparse night's take.

Occasionally it was my task to join the local manager in his office and assist him in making the count—that is, seeing that we got our just due. The boxes were unlocked. The tickets, as well as the passes, if any, were tossed onto his desk. We counted them together, comparing our count with the numbers handed in from the ticket office. The manager then made out the night's return. I disliked the job at best, and I have not forgotten one particularly unpleasant checking experience. The manager was too drunk to undertake the counting. In fact, soon after I arrived in his office he passed out completely. The keys were on the table, so I was able to unlock the boxes and do the checking myself. Then I shook him out of this stupor, forced a pen into his hand, and compelled him to sign the return as I had made it out.

It will perhaps not come as a surprise that with Mademoiselle's company the checking was often an all too simple task. With a capable and popular company, Monday night was the poorest house of the week and business regularly improved from night to night. With us, I am afraid, Monday was generally the best night and the takings decreased as the week went on. In retrospect, it surprises me that there were not more nights—I can think of only two or three—when there were so few in the house that the money was returned and we disconsolately went home. I say disconsolately because "No play, no pay" was the recognized principle.

I found that it was common talk among the actors that Mademoiselle's finances were in bad shape. At the end of my first week I had the opportunity to determine the truth of this rumor myself. Had the Gratienne company possessed a ghost, it would not have walked that Friday. Instead we were told to go to Mademoiselle's dressing room after the performance on Saturday night. I knocked at her dressing-room door, heard an imperative "Entrez," and found that Mademoiselle had removed her stage costume and anything else she may have been wearing beneath it but had not yet had time to put on her civilian gear. I gasped, but mánaged to take no notice of her appearance and riveted my attention upon the few pounds in gold and silver coins that were scattered on the dressing table. "How little can you get out of the town with?" Mademoiselle inquired.

Although I responded modestly that first time, it did not take me many weeks to learn that it paid to name more than was necessary and come down shilling by shilling in one's demand. Twice I was unable to squeeze out enough to pay the bill at my lodgings. The first time I left my traveling rug with my landlady. (I missed its comfort on those cold journeys in train compartments unheated except by flat metal containers of hot water for our feet. Sometimes even these were unprocurable.) On the second occasion my watch served as a pledge with my landlady. After a few weeks I was able each time to send the money due, so both rug and watch came back.

It was not unusual for us to travel "on the baggage," as the practice was called. The railway would carry us to the next town even though there was no money to pay for our transportation there. But our baggage van was retained in a siding until the fares were paid. On Monday the manager of the theatre would advance the money to free the baggage so that we could open. He then subtracted it from the company's share of the takings at the end of the week.

On Sunday evenings a few of us were sometimes invited to forgather at Mademoiselle's lodgings to discuss the possibility of introducing devices to improve the performances. None but male members of the company were ever present. Let me describe one such meeting. Mademoiselle is seated at a large table drawn up to the fireplace, which is at her back. Pen, ink, and paper are spread before her and freely used. The dining table has been converted into what she sees, I am sure, as a kind of parliamentary table, before which we sit as her cabinet council. Madame is sitting by Mademoiselle on a low stool, gazing into the fire with a look of ostentatious resignation. The talk, mainly sustained by Mademoiselle, wanders on and on without being interrupted by inspiration. Eventually poor old Madame's store of patience becomes exhausted. After a series of sighs of mounting intensity, she looks up and loudly but half apologetically says, "Allez-vous-en!" Mademoiselle turns upon her and shouts, "Maman, tais-toi!" At last, after several repetitions of the same protest, the old lady sums up the situation as she sees it. "My daughter is mad," she exclaims, "exactly mad." Then with a shrug of the shoulders and another dismal sigh, "Ah, my daughter is very mad!"

One generally futile suggestion at these meetings was the addition of a song in one of the plays or a dance in another. The idea may have been sound; the futility resulted from its being always incompetently and carelessly carried out. Once, and once only, however, the incompetence was nearly converted into an asset. To everyone's astonishment Mademoiselle blandly allocated a song to me. My assurance, eagerly confirmed by the others, that I could not tell one note from another meant nothing to Mademoiselle. As usual, she overrode all opposition. The band parts were prepared and the orchestra rehearsed. When the music struck up the introduction I was—after a moment of sheer terror—suddenly and unexpectedly inspired. I found an escape from the imminent catastrophe by accompanying the song with gestures and facial quirks that lent it a kind of burlesque interpretation. Fortunately, I was playing a comedy part. Instead of giving vent to the catcalls I expected, the audience, though puzzled, refrained from laughter and ironical applause. Much to my relief, however, Mademoiselle did not persist with the experiment.

One may wonder how it was possible for such a company as Mademoiselle Gratienne's to exist at all, much less to limp along for years, as it managed to do. The answer is that, in spite of the multitude of companies on tour, theatres in the small towns were often hard put to keep open. Even up to Thursday, when *The Stage* was issued, a small-town theatre was sometimes compelled to insert a desperate advertisement offering to book a company for the following Monday! Similarly, the Gratienne company might have reached that day still unbooked. Then there was a hasty exchange of telegrams. When we were accepted there was rejoicing in our company and the necessary posters were sent posthaste for urgent delivery. Such late bookings were inevitable in the smallest towns that could boast a theatre. The theatres, like the companies playing in them, were fighting a losing battle for survival. The coup de grace, both to the companies and to the theatres that housed them, was administered a few years later with the advent of the newly invented moving pictures.

Some of the theatres we played in were structures as decrepit as the companies they were able to engage. This was particularly noticeable backstage. In a few theatres the wash basins did not function and in the dressing rooms buckets of cold water were the only provision. There were but meager supplies of coal for the fireplaces that were the only means of providing a modicum of warmth. Then there were the rats. The proverbial poverty of church mice was at least as endemic in theatre rats. They would doubtless have starved if careless actors had not unintentionally provided them with nocturnal feasts of greasepaint and powder puffs by leaving their makeup materials loose on dressing tables when they went home at night. The theatre managements deserved more to be pitied than censured for the discomforts we endured. Grumbling actors blamed it on the penny-wise, pound-foolish policy of the managers. More likely their excessive economy resulted from grim necessity.

Since one could always depend on local stock scenery, it was possible to start a company on tour in the smaller theatres simply by inserting an advertisement in *The Stage* reading (as it often did) "Whole company required. Must dress well on stage and off. Apply at ———." Nevertheless, companies so recruited, with no financial backing except for the required printing, were generally short lived.

But how did this French lady, with little or no professional experience and no reputation as an actress, come to enter this precarious field? I learned after a time that Madame, her mother, had once been comparatively wealthy, the owner by inheritance of vineyards in Burgundy that had been devastated in the Franco-Prussian war. She also owned a little real estate in Paris and still retained it at the time she emigrated to England. In London her daughter, who had theatrical ambitions, found that Sunday night performances were sometimes given in workmen's clubs in various suburban districts. Payment, if any, for these performances was so tiny that the clubs had difficulty in finding bookings. Mademoiselle could afford, by engaging a few out-of-work actors, to put on such shows. Her performances were so enthusiastically received at the workmen's clubs that her head was turned. Not surprisingly, she overestimated her acting ability and decided that it deserved a wider scope. Mlle Gratienne's Repertory Company was thereupon launched into the troubled waters of a touring system that, though few realized it, was already beginning to decay.

Madame's property in Paris meant a lot to her actors because the rentals came to hand at quarterly intervals. When Mademoiselle announced, "My rent money has arrived," the jubilation of the company was touching. We knew that we should receive what was owing us; moreover, salaries would be paid in full for that week at least, and possibly for a week or two more, if the takings were not at the lowest ebb.

Though I cannot applaud Mademoiselle's capacity as an actress, in one respect she was something of a pioneer. She never let the acting be careless or haphazard. In dealing with the company at rehearsals Mademoiselle was always direct and incisive. Because she knew exactly what she wanted, no one dreamed of contradicting her. Moreover, she differed from the touring managers of most repertory companies in her insistence that everything in the acting relate to the play as a whole. In short, Mlle Gratienne was a forerunner of the modern stage director.

She was also a tyrant in her demands upon the local stage carpenters. She always demanded—in spite of grumblings and mumbled curses, which she calmly ignored—that they unroll every back-cloth in the theatre before she made her selection for the play being given that night. She considered the possible use of each one before making her decisions. Some of the theatres were very old and had formerly been the home of stock companies who had their own scenic artists. Sometimes the scenery was as old as the theatres, so it is quite possible that we acted in front of drops painted as early as the eighteenth century. Some of them, even though faded, were quite beautiful, with feeling for a realistic style that is now lost. Moreover, they were the product of considerable technical skill. In 1944 Stewart Chaney, the designer of the scenery for *Embezzled Heaven* (a play I directed for the Theatre Guild with Ethel Barrymore as the star), agreed with me that a realistic depiction of an exterior background would be right for one scene. But when he looked for a scene painter capable of producing the charming picture he designed he might as well have been asking for the moon.

Mademoiselle, as one might expect, was in debt far beyond the limits of her credit. One day I was called for at my lodgings in the late afternoon and told to hurry down to the theatre. When I arrived the other male actors were also assembling. We were told that the bailiffs were in. Most of the company's wardrobe, its only valuable asset, was carried in a few large trunks. Mademoiselle requested in a whisper that each of us please lay claim to one of the trunks as his personal property. We rose to the occasion and everyone pointed out one or another of the trunks as his own. Mademoiselle's admitted belongings dwindled down to one small basket containing stage properties that had very little value and were easily dispensed with!

Apart from uniforms, mainly military and police, the company's wardrobe was, of course, entirely for "period" plays. Theatrical contracts stipulated that present-day clothes had to be supplied by the actor. In an ill-paid company such as Mademoiselle's, plays not too antiquated to pass as contemporary were costumed, for the most part, with a strange hodgepodge of cheap misfits. I picked up at a pawnbroker's shop swallow-tailed evening dress that, I later realized, must have belonged to an impoverished waiter. My brother had recently bought a new top hat, and so was able to give me the one he had discarded. It became the top hat of the whole company! On one occasion, as I walked off stage in a garden scene I gave my hat to another actor, who rushed round behind the backdrop to make an almost immediate entrance on the other side. But then a new problem had to be met. My hat was so large for him that it tended to rest on top of his ears. But necessity in the Gratienne company had mothered an inventiveness equal to any challenge. As the actor made his entrance he let the audience see him taking off the hat. After nonchalantly wiping his brow with his handkerchief, he carried the hat for the remainder of the scene.

I stuck it out with the company as it limped along until the closing for the summer of all provincial theatres except those in holiday resorts. These were comparatively few and Mademoiselle's company was too obscure to compete for their occupancy. She gave up for the time being but assured those of her actors who had "stood by her" that she would resume operations in the autumn. Characteristically, she was quite certain that everything would brighten up for her then and she would be on the way to success. What's more, she did reopen. For years afterward curiosity made me occasionally consult *The Stage* to see whether her company was playing that week. It generally was, and I wondered if it was still traveling on the baggage.

CHAPTER 3

*B*efore I finished the tour with Mademoiselle I received what I had anxiously and eagerly awaited: notification that I was called for rehearsal for the autumn tour of the Benson company. I could hardly believe that this time I was to be a fully accepted Bensonian—a fledgling, to be sure, but with an official place in the nest.

As was to be expected, only small parts came my way. Oddly enough, my first opportunities for real acting were elderly roles. My great chance (as I saw it) came when I was cast for Egeus in *A Midsummer Night's Dream*. The Benson company gave it as a special production, running for four weeks at the Theatre Royal, Birmingham, in place of their usual Christmas pantomime.

As was customary at that time, the settings and costumes were Greek and the music Mendelssohn's. To my mind, the high spot came in the last act. An altar was set in the center of the stage with a low flame burning on it. As the grand tones of the wedding march burst forth, the principal characters (and Egeus was numbered among them) advanced from the side, one by one or two by two, walking solemnly to the rhythm of the music to the center of the stage. Then they turned to the altar, raised their arms in obeisance, and moved on to their allotted positions for the tableau when the dialogue began. For me it was a thrill indeed to play an individual role in this exalted procession!

Among the smaller parts that I particularly enjoyed was that of the Priest in *Twelfth Night*. He leads Olivia and Sebastian to their marriage in the penultimate scene, and in the last scene he is called upon to confirm the marriage in a center-stage speech of eight lines of verse. I did not start the tour with that part; it was given to me later when it chanced to become free. Although I was rehearsed for the part only by the stage manager, I noticed as I spoke the lines at the performance that Mr. Benson, who generally arrived on the stage just before his entrance as Malvolio, was standing in the wings. Later I learned from the stage manager that Mr. Benson had spoken to him favorably about my speaking of the part. Such was my awe of the great man that this was for me the high point of the season.

During my first year with Benson the tour included the principal towns in Ireland. I was amazed at the enthusiasm of the audiences. I soon discovered that Mr. and Mrs. Benson were great favorites in Ireland. Early one Sunday evening in the city of Cork, we found, besides the usual jaunting cars and cabs, an open carriage waiting for Mr. and Mrs. Benson. There was nothing unusual in that, except that standing around it was a small group of young men, from the local college, we were told. No sooner had Mr. and Mrs. Benson taken their seats than the students, who had cheered their appearance on emerging from the station, unharnessed the horse, took positions at the shafts of the carriage, and trotted off with it. Mr. and Mrs. Benson, they explained, should be taken to their hotel in style.

I went to Cork several times in my touring days and always lodged at the same address. On the first visit I found rooms in a house owned by a widow with three children, ranging from about twelve years down. On this visit, a rather startling incident occurred. One morning I was seated at the table in my sitting room with books and papers spread before me, the paraphernalia of a correspondence course in English literature that I was taking from the newly instituted Ruskin College in Oxford. The door opened with startling suddenness. A very white-faced man of about thirty-five darted in and swiftly shut the door behind him. Snatching up a chair, he sat down opposite me. Then, assuming a businesslike manner he took a sheet of paper and a pen from my table and stared across at me, pen poised as if waiting for dictation. I confess to having been a little disconcerted, but I sat still and waited to see what my visitor would do next. Suddenly he asked in a very strained voice, "Has the meeting been going on for long?" I assured him that it had not. He paused a moment, then barked out, "In that case I suppose I may be excused." Leaping to his feet, he hurried out of the room.

A few moments later I heard a loud crash and a scream. I jumped up and opened the double doors that led to the kitchen. There the table had been overturned and smashed crockery covered the floor. My landlady, wary but unafraid, stood watching the man who had interrupted my studies. His eyes were fixed on the upturned edge of the table, from which he was frantically trying to wipe something away.

My landlady hurried over to me and whispered, "The poor fellow has the d.t.'s, God help him." He was, it seemed, wiping away imaginary serpents that troubled his vision.

Presently the twelve-year-old daughter hurried in with a medicine bottle filled with a colorless liquid. This turned out to be holy water from a nearby church. My landlady sprinkled some of it wherever the snakes appeared to the victim. This seemed to calm him for a time, but suddenly he dashed out of the kitchen, seized his bowler from the hat stand, and again ran into my sitting room. As I watched from the doorway, he knelt at the armchair by the fire and, employing the hat as a telephone, rang up Heaven. Having made the connection, he held the hat over his eyes and prayed into it for release from his suffering. My landlady, meanwhile, had summoned attendants from a mental hospital. The man rose quietly and, pitifully tremulous, allowed them to take him away. This incident created a friendly bond between my landlady and me. On subsequent visits I never failed to seek the same lodgings.

On my first tour with the Benson company I was so absorbed in my work at the theatres that I took little notice of the towns we played in. Newcastle upon Tyne was an exception. My curiosity was aroused beforehand because it happened to be the town where I was born, though my parents had left it before my first birthday, and I had no recollection of the place. But the reason Newcastle was to stand out strongly in my memory afterward was an unexpected occurrence.

I had no lodgings when we arrived, but a member of the company recommended some. When I asked the landlady what the terms were, she looked at me severely and said, "It doesn't matter." My natural retort was that to me it mattered very much and I must really be told. "Don't you know?" she demanded, with the same severe manner. "The world will come to an end next Thursday." When I confessed that I had not heard of this event, she assured me that many people in Newcastle were aware of it. She admitted, however, that my ignorance was shared by a considerable majority, and in deference to it, she consented to mention a figure. It was satisfactory, so I took the rooms.

My landlady's dire prediction proved wrong, but only in degree. On Thursday night that week we played *Macbeth*, a play theatrical superstition regards as unlucky. After the performance I went home, ate my frugal supper as usual by the sitting-room fire, and went to bed. I had hardly settled down when a bright glow attracted me to the window. The sky was illuminated by a great conflagration that seemed far away. It was a fine spectacle. I watched it for a long time with interest. Not until the next morning did I learn that it was the Theatre Royal that was ablaze.

The theatre was reduced to a shell. Everything had been destroyed. Like most actors I kept practically all my clothes in my theatre basket so as to have only a portmanteau to carry to and from the railway station. But my personal loss was nothing compared to the overwhelming financial blow to Mr. Benson—a blow from which he never fully recovered. All the very costly and historically accurate costumes for *Henry V*, with which he intended to open his great venture, a London season at the Lyceum Theatre the following spring, had arrived in Newcastle that very week. Neither these, nor any of his cast's regular wardrobe, nor the large stock of scenery was insured. Everything was lost.

Mr. Benson showed no outward perturbation about the catastrophe. He hurried off to London to rent costumes. A special train brought them, including those required for *The Merchant of Venice*, which we were to put on at a hurriedly arranged matinee in a suburban-Newcastle theatre the following day. The owner of the theatre and the manager of the touring company then playing there had generously offered to cancel their regular matinee in order that we might appear instead.

Mr. Benson brought in everything for the *Merchant* with one slight exception; shoes for the actors had been overlooked and we had to wear our everyday boots. (These articles, known in America as high shoes, were laced well above the ankle and called boots in England.) But that was a trivial matter. What is memorable is a public response that revealed the respect in which Benson was held and also the importance of the theatre in the lives of the English at the time. In spite of the short notice that could be given for the performance, the theatre was packed. When Mr. Benson made his entrance as Shylock, the applause was wildly enthusiastic. It lasted longer than I have ever heard in any other theatre at any time under any circumstances.*

Despite the fire and its disastrous results, Benson was able to proceed with his projected occupancy of the great Lyceum Theatre. There I suffered a bitter disappointment, very poignant at the time but, as I realized later, inevitable. The few parts of any worth to an actor that

*Apparently not everyone in Manchester shared this admiration for the Benson company. In *Benson and the Bensonians* J. C. Trewin tells this anecdote: "At about two o'clock the roof crashed in with a final gust of smoke and flame. By three the fire was controlled, but most of the watchers stayed until dawn. An old man, by Constance Benson, said to her after watching silently, 'Are all the company in the theatre?' 'None, thank God,' she replied. At which, exclaiming, 'Good Lord, I've been waiting here three hours!' he hurried off in anger."

had come my way in the touring repertoire were given to more experienced actors, added to the company for the London season. My own share in the productions was reduced almost to the "walking on" that had characterized my trial engagement. I also performed the useful but unrewarding function of understudying, the value of which the beginner fails to realize. At the moment, the blow was severe. I felt that the stigma of failure was laid on me. For a time I seriously wondered whether I should not give up all hope of being an actor. When I went home at the end of the season I even discussed that possibility with my mother. She wasted no time in opening a correspondence with influential friends of my father in the Unitarian church. But before her diligence could bear fruit, her hopes and my depression were cut short at a single blow. Out of the blue came a reply-paid telegram, signed Carlyon and Charlton, asking if I was available to play the juvenile lead in a melodrama called *In the Shadow of Night.* As my mother sorrowfully remarked, the receipt of the telegram was like the smell of gunpowder to a war-horse. She recognized that it was useless to offer resistance, and I wired my acceptance.

CHAPTER 4

*I*he name of the firm of Carlyon and Charlton was not altogether unfamiliar to me. Its important sound had impressed me when I was regularly consulting *The Stage* before joining Mlle Gratienne. But although the name had stood out, I had dismissed it from my mind. I was looking for a repertory company and the advertisement was for a "full fit-up company" for a single play. I wanted a wider range of experience. Besides, I did not know what "fit-up" meant. Now I was going to find out what it meant. I soon discovered that the "fit-up" of the name consisted of a portable proscenium and drop curtain, a frame from which to suspend drops, limelights, gas footlights, and battens, as well as all the scenery for the play. In short, it was a complete proscenium and stage made to be "fitted up" in halls that were rented for various purposes besides stage shows. Fit-up companies even traveled with a small piano and pianist to supply the music.

I hoped that my mother did not realize how low in the theatrical scale were the fit-ups. It was a consolation to remind myself that even lower were the "booths." These traveling shows not only fitted up the stage but carried the theatre with them as well. This was wooden structures which could be carted from town to town and erected in nearby fields rented for the occasion. These companies had very extensive repertoires of plays and would often act in one town for several weeks, changing the bill each night. ("Day-bill," the old term for a theatre poster, testifies to the daily changes of program in stock companies, but these were limited to modest repertoires at best.) I once asked a man who had played in the booths how the actors managed to learn their parts. His answer was that they did not attempt to do so. Each morning they met, the plot was explained, and the actors worked over the scenes in their own words. That was the rehearsal. The actor assured me that most of the company developed a good deal of skill in improvising dialogue. Moreover they learned never to show any hesitation, though they would often have to pull up when they found that two of them were speaking at the same time. "I beg your pardon, you were saying?" was the usual escape. Unusual aplomb was called for, however, when two actors asked the question at the same time!

An actor forced to appear with the booths could console himself with the knowledge that there was one form of dramatic entertainment even lower on the scale of quality. That distinction was held by those performances that were given in tents at fairs. By the end of the 1800s, these shows were very seldom encountered. I must confess that, although I occasionally saw the outsides of tent theatres at fairs, I never witnessed a performance in one. I have since regretted that I did not snatch at that opportunity while it still existed. Those who did told me that the tent performances were almost unbelievably crude. Moreover, the tents themselves were small and rickety, very different from those used by "tent shows" in America, which, to judge by the one I saw in Iowa City, were palatial in comparison.

When I joined Messrs. Carlyon and Charlton, I learned that the company toured annually, always with a melodrama and generally over the same very extensive route, which covered most of England and Wales. I arrived as the company assembled on their usual date early in the fall. Rehearsals were held in a disused and fine old tithe barn in a charming little market town in the south of England called Ringwood. Mr. Charlton, a bachelor in his middle forties, played an important character part in the play and Mr. Carlyon, whose wife traveled with us, was in command of the business side of the undertaking. The management was a model of efficiency. Nor did it suffer from the impecunious condition that harassed Mlle Gratienne. Year after year, it seemed, Messrs. Carlyon and Charlton earned a substantial income from their fit-up tours.

Usually we played in town halls or corn exchanges. We visited, as did all fit-up companies, small towns only, so that the bookings were always for one night, except on occasions when in somewhat larger towns we played both Friday and Saturday. With Sunday free in any case, we then had a very welcome break. This was all the pleasanter because the managers chose attractive towns, often seaside resorts, for the three comparatively restful days.

Throughout the tour daily life flowed along calmly and pleasantly, not unlike a long holiday, except for one all too frequent annoyance, the difficulty of finding lodgings. Because visits from theatrical companies were infrequent in these towns, there were no regular theatrical rooms. The train had hardly stopped at a station before there was a rush to the hall where we were to play, in the hope that the hall keeper would have information as to where rooms were available. Generally he could say no more than that we "might try" this or that address. We left our bags at the hall and off we dashed. More often than not the hall keeper's suggestions led to our being told that a landlady used to let rooms or had done so sometimes but would not now. Generally, however, she suggested other addresses we should try.

It became customary for me to join two other men in setting out on the search. If, as often happened, we came upon a landlady who could offer only one bedroom, I insisted upon my companions having it. They offered to toss a coin, but I refused because it was distasteful to me to share a bed. Then I was on my own, and my solitary quest would go on sometimes for hour after weary hour. Occasionally I almost reached the point of desperation. What a relief it was when the landlord of an inn, as happened two or three times, took pity on my plight and persuaded his wife to let me have their spare bedroom. Once two actors who had the luck to find a room gave it up to a couple of despairing actresses who could find nothing. The gallant actors spent the night, as our stagehands generally did, sleeping in the hall on the company's big baskets, which were used for transporting the properties and lighting equipment. Curtains were their coverings.

Brought up, as I had been, in a household with a tolerant and liberal outlook, puritanical disapproval of the theatre always astonished me. Sometimes in the pursuit of rooms a door was opened, or only cautiously half-opened, by a woman of sour and forbidding demeanor. When that happened I knew what to expect. Fixing me with a suspicious eye, the landlady was sure to ask whether I was "one of them actors coming to the hall." When I confessed that I was, she would say, "I don't have nothing to do with them folks," and bang the door in my face.

Earlier, when I was still with Mlle Gratienne, I had had a different kind of encounter with the puritanical spirit, in a mining town in southern Wales. Going home from the theatre one night I saw dimly in the poorly lighted street a figure approaching with uncertain steps. I would have avoided him, but he ambled across and stood right in my path. He held up a crumpled cigarette and asked me to give him a light. I struck a match and held out the flame. As he puffed at it I noticed that he was looking at me with an odd sort of grin. Presently he asked me in his lilting Welsh tones, "Maybe now, you are one of the play actors at the theayter?" When I confessed it he brought his face close to mine and exclaimed, "Devils! Devils!" Then he laughed, slapped me on the shoulder, and lurched away down the street, cackling maliciously.

It may seem extraordinary that such an attitude had persisted in some quarters since the late Middle Ages, when small strolling bands of "common players" were classed in legal statutes with "rogues, vagabonds, and sturdy beggars." There were reasons then and even later for such an attitude. In Tudor England, "masterless men" constituted a serious social and political problem. With the breaking up of the great feudal houses in the War of the Roses and the dissolution of the monasteries under Henry VIII, the country was flooded with destitute men who had formerly been dependent, in one way or another, on those vanished institutions.

Under Elizabeth I, who was sympathetic to the theatre, companies of actors achieved legal status by attaching themselves to noblemen as, at least in theory, their servants. Shakespeare's company, for example, was known as the Lord Chamberlain's Men, and later—a signal honor— the servants of His Majesty King James I. But the battle for respectability was not won. Many Puritans, who were achieving ever increasing power in government, opposed the theatre for reasons that somehow mixed religious scruples with social disapproval. Stephen Gosson, one of the most violent critics of the theatre and of actors, admitted that "it is well known that some of them are sober, discreet, properly learned, and citizens well thought of among their neighbors at home." Several members of Shakespeare's company were church wardens. Yet such was the stigma still clinging to the actor that Shakespeare, in his Sonnet 111, upbraided Fortune

> That did not better for my life provide
> Than public means which public manners breeds.
> Thence comes it that my name receives a brand;
> And almost thence my nature is subdu'd
> To what it works in, like the dyer's hand.

In 1642 the Puritan enemies of the profession gained the upper hand with the beginning of the Civil War. They promptly closed the theatres, and they were not reopened until King Charles II came to power in 1660.

During the Restoration the theatres enjoyed a new freedom. For the first time feminine roles were played by women instead of boys and men. Yet the average actor remained low on the social scale for a long time thereafter. An anecdote about James Quin—the highest-paid actor of the mid-1700s and a formidable rival to David Garrick—illustrates the prevailing attitude. Quin was invited to the table of a nobleman and delighted the other guests with his noted wit. The appreciative peer, recovering from his laughter, said, "What a pity it is, Mr. Quin, that you are an actor!" (Quin's retort was, "And what would you have me be—a lord?") A century and a half later such prejudices, especially where they were supported by religious beliefs, had by no means disappeared.

Railway journeys were short for the Carlyon and Charlton troupe. Moreover, they were generally full of interest. My fellow actors were always on good terms with each other. It would be an exaggeration to say that we became close friends, but a kind of congenial companionship sprang up among us. We swam in the ocean, sometimes rented a boat and went for a sail. Or, in the inland towns, we hired a trap and drove a sober old horse along pretty country lanes, sometimes to some locally recommended beauty spot such as a waterfall or a fine view. (I wonder what disapproving puritans would have said if they had known how innocent were our amusements.)

Apart from the problem of finding nightly accommodation, that long tour of *In the Shadow of Night* from autumn to early summer stands out in my memory as an unbroken series of halcyon days. The play, as I was aware even then, had no merit. Still, it was not ill constructed along the conventional lines of the school of domestic melodrama, appealing to unsophisticated spectators who loved to have their emotions stirred. Our audiences enjoyed the play, and we enjoyed rousing their enthusiasm. It was no mean satisfaction for me, as the hero, to work up a round of applause for a moral or heroic sentiment.

I do not know just what I had expected a fit-up company to be, but I was pleased and surprised to find that both the managers were men of culture and refinement. There was nothing crude about the actors either. The naive simplicity of the plot of *In the Shadow of Night* was a constant joke among us. This, I feel sure, was the attitude of most of the actors in all the popular melodramas of the day. But they must have realized, as we did, that the plays were the source of our livelihood.

We realized too, though, that spectators who paid for admission deserved to be met on their own level. It followed that, however preposterous the plays might be, it was incumbent upon the actors to perform them as seriously as if they were literary masterpieces. The place of the old melodramas has now been taken by certain kinds of moving pictures and by television soap operas. Actors today must surely have to act them with similar integrity. Perhaps this is the reason, then, that there is something distasteful to me in the present-day fashion of ridiculing Victorian melodrama by exaggerated burlesque.

As the juvenile lead, I was the son of the "old squire." Under the cloak of pretended friendship, my cousin, an unmitigated villian, sought to rob me of my inheritance by causing me to be arrested on trumped-up evidence for a crime that he had himself perpetrated. Among other dramatic adventures, I had to save the villain's accomplice from drowning in the Serpentine River in Hyde Park. Moved by my heroism and my magnanimity, the accomplice subsequently repented, to the cheers and applause of the audience. As I jumped into the lake, the property man, hiding behind the ground-row representing a low wall, threw up handfuls of rice to simulate the splashing water. In addition to saving a miscreant, I had also to rescue the heroine from a burning building, in which she had been locked by the villain. I smashed the door and dashed through high-mounting lycopodium flames for this exploit. But the most thrilling adventure came when I had to flee from the grasp of the police into a windmill and climb rapidly to the top of the building. Even as the door was battered down and the police were dashing into the mill, I appeared on the roof and descended by holding on to one of the revolving sails. There were loud cheers as I ran off and the thwarted police looked helplessly out of a window.

Fit-ups were considered to be lower in the theatrical scale than companies touring in theatres; yet a comparison between Carlyon and Charlton's company and Mlle Gratienne's company is all in favor of the former. There is a further paradox in the fact that, because Mademoiselle was starring in her own company, she could claim to belong to that elite group the actor-managers. These remarkable people were able to organize, own, and manage their own companies, as well as act the leading parts in them. Although there was discussion as to the advantages and disadvantages of the system at the turn of the century, few people—least of all the actor-managers themselves—realized that the end of their era was already beginning. It was still taken for granted that any enterprising actor who had sufficient public support would naturally branch out into managing his own company. He would, to use the picturesque phrase then current in the profession, "don the purple."

Though there were later actors of no mean stature who donned the purple—Arnold Daly and Richard Mansfield in America and Fred Terry and Beerbohm Tree in England, to name only four of the best known—the last of the really great actor-managers in America was Edwin Booth and the last in England was Henry Irving. *Sir* Henry Irving, he ultimately became; he was the first actor ever to be honored with knighthood. When the possibility of knighthood was broached to him he pooh-poohed it. In his estimation the actor was above the necessity of any extraneous tribute. Later, when Irving realized that knighthoods were being awarded to distinguished painters and musicians, he decided that he should accept the title to show that acting was on a par with any of the sister arts.

Even at that time much was said about the weakness of the actor-managerial system. Few actor-managers were obsessed with thoughts of the box office, as was sometimes claimed; most genuinely loved their art. But another charge was leveled against them with some justice. Many were tempted to make their own roles greater than the whole and to choose plays less for their intrinsic merit than because they offered vehicles for individual display. Yet this tendency to subjugate artistic values to the exploitation of personality was not forced upon an unwilling public. It was possible only because of a complicity between actor and audience. If the leading actor's name appeared in large type on the day-bills, it was because it was he (or she) whom the public had come to see.

Max Beerbohm was a dramatic critic in the heyday of the actor-managers, and his brother, Herbert Beerbohm Tree, was one of the last outstanding members of the breed. In a radio broadcast Beerbohm later recalled that "people had come not so much to see a mere play as to see a play with their idol in it. They hoped the play would be a success for *his* sake. If it seemed to them a failure the pit and gallery booed the author for having betrayed their idol. They were in no mood to stand any nonsense from an author." Beerbohm spoke of a play in which Lewis Waller portrayed an important Anglo-Indian soldier in command of a province. In the second act a subordinate who had been refused a petition drew a pistol and fired at him. "I was in the back row of the stalls," said Beerbohm, "and was almost deafened by a young lady in the front row of the pit who screamed, 'How *dare* he?'"

Waller was a fine masculine actor with classical features and a lovely voice full of rich cadences. Not only in London but in all the big cities in Great Britain—for of course these princes of the theatre toured at intervals through their minor dukedoms—you would occasionally meet young ladies (and some not so young either) who wore buttons bearing the capital letters K O W. Such a button proved that the wearer was a member of the almost mystical society of the "Keen Order of Wallerites."

Lewis Waller had no London theatre of his own, nor was he always his own manager, but within his realm he was an uncrowned king.

Then there was George Alexander, the darling of the ladies, who reigned at the St. James's Theatre. This was at a time when women's fashions were very elegant, and to set off an afternoon costume a "picture hat" was an absolute necessity. This was a perfectly enormous structure surmounting an elaborate coiffure. Fortunately picture hats were not worn at night; they belonged to the afternoon toilette. But imagine the problem they created in the theatre at matinees! It was impossible to see the stage from behind them, but objections from outraged theatre-goers were futile until George Alexander had the temerity to ban the things from his theatre. This bold action was celebrated in a parody of the old song, "The British Grenadiers." The first verse went something like this:

> I sing of Alexander, the hero of today,
> A very handsome man, sir, as all the ladies say,
> But courage too and bravery he surely did display
> Because he sat on the terrible hat of the British matinee.

No greater proof can be cited of the esteem in which the actor-managers were held than the fact that ladies still flocked to see George Alexander even after he denied them the opportunity to show off their picture hats.

Beerbohm truly said that the actor-managers "inspired something deeper than interest. It was with excitement, with wonder and reverence, with something akin even to hysteria, that they were gazed upon. There he was in his own theatre and giving to that theatre a definite in-dividuality of its own. It was not merely a building, it was a kind of temple with its own special brand of worshipers."

With such emotional rewards awaiting the successful actor-manager, it is not surprising that the temptation to don the purple was very strong. Even stars of the second magnitude might succeed in building up suf-ficient provincial reputation to tour as actor-managers without ever trying their fortune in the metropolis. But disaster quickly followed a too-rash aspirant. One such was William Mollison. My friend Whitford Kane was with him on his first tour under his own management. They visited a Scottish town where the usual admission to the upper gallery, known colloquially as "the gods," was fourpence. But prices varied according to the attractions. Mollison, having become his own manager, raised it to sixpence. One night Kane, who was playing the First Grave-digger in *Hamlet* and so finished early, was standing outside the theatre as it began to empty. He noticed three or four young men waiting at the gallery exit. They recognized a friend descending into the street and pounced upon him with the question, "Was it worth the money, Jock?" The shrewd Scotsman pondered a moment and then pronounced judgment. "Weel," he said, "he's better than a fourpenny Hamlet, but he's no a sixpenny Hamlet."

Perhaps this anecdote hints at the answer to a tantalizing question: Given the great and unabating popularity of the better actor-managers, even in the early years of the twentieth century, why did the system fall into decay? The answer is neither a lack of loyal audiences nor the excesses of egotistical actors. It is not even the serious dearth of good plays. No, the cause of the decline was almost wholly economic. The costs of producing plays, and of maintaining a theatre or touring with a company, were mounting catastrophically. Few actor-managers were strong enough financially to bear the growing risks. So their places in the managerial sphere were gradually taken over by entrepreneurs and syndicates.

Something was gained, no doubt, in financial stability. But something was lost, too. However great the popularity of an actor hired for a single production in someone else's theatre, the rapport that he builds with a given audience is inevitably short-lived and impersonal. The bond between the actor-manager and his audience, even on tour, was one that ripened and grew stronger year by year. There was about it a quality of glamor, an aura of romance, that has vanished forever from the theatre.

CHAPTER 5

*I*he long fit-up of the Carlyon and Charlton company ended late in the spring. For the first time in my life, and perhaps more sharply than ever again, I felt the poignancy of the dispersal of a group of actors who have worked in close partnership. When all the members of a group share the same central interest a strong camaraderie develops among them. We parted sadly.

At the beginning of 1902 I began my third stint as a Bensonian. The Benson company had for a time divided into two parts. Mr. Benson continued to tour in the "number-one" towns in the north of England and in Scotland, while a sort of splinter company, with Mrs. Benson at the head, went to Ireland and then toured for a few weeks in the south of England. I did not inquire into the reason for this temporary separation; it was enough for me that I was sent for when the second company was formed. My contract stipulated that I not only was to play "parts as cast" but was also to be the assistant stage manager. If I had realized at the time that I was about to take the first step in developing into a stage director, I might well have declined this chore. For the moment, knowing that the additional work was not burdensome, I accepted it with no particular interest.

The decision to divide the company may have been a sudden one. Our repertoire consisted only of the regular standbys, and rehearsals were very brief. I was delighted to find that the fine actor Frank Rodney was to be the leading man, though I noticed that he was evidently far from well and frequently had to speak in a strained whisper.* When at

---

*J. C. Trewin records that Rodney was suffering from cancer of the throat, which killed him only a few months later.

times his voice cleared, it was again a joy to listen to the beauty of his exquisitely natural delivery of the verse. When the tour started, however, the vocal strain increased. On our second night in Londonderry, as J. C. Trewin recounts in his *Benson and the Bensonians*, Rodney broke down completely while playing Petruchio in *The Taming of the Shrew*. His brother, Stratton, was traveling with us, and for a night or two he struggled through parts for which he was entirely unprepared. Evidence of the close relationships among those who have long played together was the degree to which we were all upset and nervous. Startling things happened to the dialogue. When the curtain went up on *The School for Scandal*, Lady Sneerwell converted Sheridan's opening line, "Have you inserted the paragraphs, Mr. Snake?" into "Have you inserted the snakes, Mr. Paragraph?" To which the bewildered Mr. Snake replied, "Yes, Your Majesty!"

We recovered our equilibrium after the arrival of William Haviland, who had been wired for. He was an accomplished, versatile actor who well deserved his high reputation. Since he had played all the leading parts, a better substitute could not have been hoped for. His sense of character was acute and he spoke verse with a rich and vibrant voice. I have never known anyone who became quite so absorbed in whatever part he was playing. One night when he was playing Shylock he forgot to remove the property coins from his wallet. When, in the trial scene, Portia asked to see the bond, he drew out the purse and some of the coins fell out. Instantly Shylock was on his knees, his eyes glinting with miserly rapacity, as he snatched up every piece of property money.

Most of my duties as assistant stage manager were simple. They included sending on in advance the stage "plots" for the local theatre's carpenter—we carried only a part of the scenery—and property plots that I wrote out on foolscap. I also made out a call for the orchestra to be posted on the board. The main Benson company always took along its own musical conductor, a position that Vaughan Williams later held. But in Mrs. Benson's company, as I came to call it, we had no musical conductor. The task devolved upon me as assistant stage manager to rehearse each local orchestra on the morning of our arrival.

These groups were usually competent enough to satisfy our simple requirements, but there were occasional exceptions, at least of a temporary nature. We opened our week in Limerick on the day after St. Patrick's Day. When I met the small orchestra on Monday morning, neither the conductor nor his instrumentalists had recovered from their celebrations of the night before. They were friendly and jolly enough but quite unable to read the band parts. Since they were not only to provide music between the acts but also to accompany the minuet in *The School for Scandal*, it seemed imperative that something be done. I went off to hunt up the owner of the theatre, who lived next door. I found him in a room lined from floor to ceiling with well-filled, dusty bookcases, on which there stood a row of classical busts. He was an elderly, stout figure with a rubicund face. The whole scene suggested an illustration by Phiz for some Dickens novel, but in my agitation I was unable to appreciate it. The theatre owner sat with a bottle of whiskey before him and kept helping himself from it as I explained the situation. When I had finished he rose, slapped me on the shoulder, and said with a genial laugh, "Naughty boys!"

That was the end of the discussion. Fortunately, Mrs. Benson had a keen sense of humor and laughed heartily at my tale. There were times in even the best-organized touring company when the only possible response to an insoluble dilemma was laughter.

CHAPTER 6

*A*fter finishing the tour with Mrs. Benson, there came a series of unremarkable engagements, but at least I was always working and always on tour. Twice the engagements were for "special weeks," as they were called in advertisements in *The Stage*. In the first case the manager was trying out a new play, which, happily, he soon abandoned. The second special week was quite different. An actor named Arthur Hare had the idea that he would experiment with the long-popular sentimental comedy *A Pair of Spectacles*, by Sydney Grundy. It was an easy play to put on, and after only one week's rehearsal in London we played it for a week at the quaint old Theatre Royal in the quaint old town of Stafford. Mr. Hare was so much encouraged by the response that he decided to take the play on tour. He engaged me to act as stage manager and to play the short part of the butler. Having the stage management annoyed me, but the tour, a lengthy one, was otherwise pleasant enough. Unfortunately, the one memorable event of the tour was what must have been as disgraceful a performance as was ever presented by a professional company.

In the Boer War, a few years earlier, Arthur Hare had served in a volunteer cavalry troop known as Padgett's Horse. Colonel Padgett, its leader, was now a country squire living near Shrewsbury, one of the towns we visited. Padgett invited Hare and the other men of the company to visit him on the Sunday preceding our opening. I was unable to go, but all the other men—there were six of us—accepted the invitation. On Monday I carried out my stage manager's duties with the local stagehands and then retired to my lodgings. Later, as I was arriving at the stage door for the performance, a four-wheeler cab drew up. Out of it tumbled—literally tumbled—Arthur Hare followed by the others.

Before my eyes, the entire male strength of our company fell in a heap on the sidewalk. Obviously Colonel Padgett's hospitality had not been stinted. The cabman and I helped the sodden actors into their dressing rooms. I doused their heads in the washbowls and sent out for a supply of soda water. In one way and another I got everyone onto the stage at his entrance cue. But the dialogue, for the first part of the play at least, must have kept the audience in a state of perpetual bewilderment. Even today I shudder at the memory of that nightmare evening.

On the next day Arthur Hare signed a pledge of total abstinence for the remainder of the tour and prevailed upon the other culprits to do the same. What is more they kept their word—but at the cost of heroic self-discipline. When two or three of us were together and Hare felt that a drink would normally be in order, he would take us into a chemist's shop and rap with his silver-topped ebony cane on the counter. The shopman arriving, he would say sharply, "A round of sal volatiles, please." The shopman never failed to show his astonishment, but would serve us all the same. When we had drunk off the ghastly medicine someone would politely invite the others to have another round. Needless to say, the offer was always refused.

We could play only at the "number-two" towns. The number-one towns were held by *John* Hare, a very distinguished actor whose name had long been associated with *A Pair of Spectacles*. It had been one of his great successes, and he sometimes took the play on tour in the big provincial cities. When Arthur Hare secured the rights to the number-two towns from the owners of the copyright, John Hare was furious that anyone but himself with the name of Hare should tour the play. He claimed that it was a catchpenny device to give the impression that the great actor himself was visiting the number-two towns! If he had been able to he would have prevented us, but, since he had no legal resource, he merely wrote an angry letter demanding that we end our tour. Arthur Hare was quite unmoved. He made no direct reply, but afterward the advance paragraphs in the local newspapers of the towns we visited contained the following statement: "Many people are under the impression that Mr. Arthur Hare is related to Mr. John Hare. This is not the case. Mr. John Hare assumed the name for professional purposes, whereas Mr. Arthur Hare is the son of Rear Admiral Hare and the heir apparent to the Earl of Listowel."

A Pair of Spectacles did well on the road. After visiting all the better number-two towns, Arthur Hare decided to make what was regarded at the time as a bold move. He determined to tour *The Importance of Being Earnest*. Since the scandal of Oscar Wilde's trial and imprisonment, no one had ventured to give performances of his plays. Hare persuaded the copyright owners to let him do so without announcing the author's name, which would still have been unthinkable. So all the billing and the programs stated that the play was "A comedy by the author of *A Woman of No Importance*." The device worked and we had a successful tour, which started at the New Theatre, Oxford.

This choice of a theatre turned out to be more right than we knew. Besides again acting as stage manager, I played Canon Chasuble. On the opening night I happened to be in the property room shortly before my first entrance. A row of black-bound books on a shelf inspired me with the notion that it might be appropriate for the canon to be seen holding what looked like an open Bible. My entrance was imminent, so as I pulled out one of the books I had time only to notice that they were annual registers of the students resident at Oxford University. As I reached the center of the stage I opened the volume and, looking down, saw the words "Oscar Fingal O'Flahertie Wills Wilde." The coincidence so startled me that I almost forgot the words of my entering speech.

The tour of *The Importance of Being Earnest* preceded my fourth experience as a Bensonian. A prominent shipping company had built a fine new ship, the *Port Kingston*, especially for traffic to Jamaica in the West Indies. Its officials conceived the notion that it might help to increase tourist interest in Jamaica and other islands in the Caribbean if a Shakespearean company could be induced to visit them. Mr. Benson was approached, but he could not afford to abandon his English dates even for a time. However, he agreed to form a special Benson company for this purpose. I had the good fortune to be invited to join it.

The West Indian company was a strong one, composed almost entirely of present and former Bensonian actors. Matheson Lang, not yet the star actor he later became, played most of the male leads, and Nigel Playfair, who will be remembered for his notable productions at the Lyric Theatre, Hammersmith, was the principal comedian. The other men, all capable, included George Fitzgerald and Halliwell Hobbes, both of whom became established actors in the American theatre. Alfred Harris, W. E. Holloway, and E. A. Warburton are also now recognized names. That lovely Shakespearean actress Dorothy Green shared the leads with Hutin Britton (Mrs. Matheson Lang).

Rehearsals for the tour were far too short, however, and although we continued rehearsing throughout the twelve-day voyage, there were some strange readings at the first performances in Jamaica. I remember that Matheson Lang, who had to cope with the longest parts in the repertoire, floundered desperately in *Richard III*. The last act gave him the most trouble. Every time he forgot a line he would pace across to the prompt corner, repeat the sharp command, "Up with my tent" and wait for the word. Charles La Trobe, our stage manager, and later for many years stage manager at the Haymarket Theatre, London, maintained that by his count the order was given more than twenty times in one evening.

We played in Kingston for two weeks on our arrival and again at the end of the tour. Also we visited Barbados, Trinidad, and Georgetown, in British Guiana. The voyages up and down the blue Caribbean were a delight in themselves, but they were ten times more gratifying because each of them brought a much needed interlude of three to five days between performances in almost intolerably hot theatres. Air conditioning, of course, had not been invented, and even electric fans, because their noise would drown the dialogue, could be used only in intermissions. The heat was sometimes almost stupefying. It is no wonder that one night, after being stabbed behind the arras as Polonius, I fell into a sound sleep. When the stentorian voice of Matheson Lang rang out with "For this same lord, I do repent," as he drew aside the curtain, Polonius was discovered, if not dead, at least dead to the world.

Back in England the company did not immediately disband but went on a tour of south-coast seaside resorts. Their location was a lucky stroke for us because the change of temperature from tropical heat was less violent than it would have been in north or even midland England. As it was, the company suffered an epidemic of influenza. More and more understudies had to go on, until there came a night when none was available for the First Murderer in *Richard III*. I was the Second Murderer, and such was our predicament that Charles La Trobe, who never acted, had to go on with me and mime the First Murderer's motions in the fairly long scene of the Duke of Clarence's assassination! I spoke all my lines in a little higher pitch than usual. Then, turning my back to the audience, I used my deepest possible bass tones for the First Murderer's speeches. I hope that La Trobe's anguished expression as he endeavored to move his mouth in a lame synchronization with my own lip movements did not look as comical to the audience as it did to me.

As the summer advanced, the tour closed. We were all sorry to separate. I should have felt it even more if I had known that never again should I work under the Bensonian banner.

This parting also meant that the first phase of my Shakespearean work was over. If someone then had asked what Shakespeare meant to me I should probably have said that he provided magnificent opportunities for acting. I should have added that, of course, he was the author of fine plays that stirred me emotionally. Finally, I would have said that his verse was a perpetual delight to speak and to listen to when it was properly spoken. But if someone had asked me how the plays should be produced, I would have been bewildered. The manner of production meant nothing to me. Production was dominated by use and custom— what else need be considered? If anyone had told me that I would spend most of my life attempting to answer that question, I would have been incredulous.

CHAPTER 7

*J*n the two years after leaving the Benson companies for the last time, I had long engagements, again combining acting and stage management, with two repertory companies. The managers of the first, Mr. and Mrs. A. B. Tapping, seemed to be trying to establish themselves as a sort of minor Mr. and Mrs. Kendal. The Kendals were players whose names were always coupled together. Mrs. Kendal, who first appeared as Margaret Robertson, was the sister of the dramatist T. W. Robertson, whose plays were popular for many years and are now regarded in academic circles as an important step in the direction of realism. While still young she became known as an accomplished actress. After her marriage to William Kendal she always worked with her husband, though he was never regarded as her equal in skill.

In the case of the Tappings their capacities were reversed; Mr. Tapping was far more accomplished than his spouse. The discrepancy was all the more marked because Mrs. Tapping was not aided by her appearance. Indeed, it would be an exaggeration to say that she was even passably good-looking. Then, too, Mr. Tapping was a little above average height, while Mrs. Tapping was positively diminutive. The contrast did nothing to enhance the many scenes they played together— especially the love scenes.

Even in rehearsal both Mr. and Mrs. Tapping conducted themselves in a curiously aloof manner. Offstage, they were markedly uncommunicative and rarely to be seen. I could not avoid the feeling that both were unhappy. Certainly Mr. Tapping was a lonely man who enjoyed taking long solitary walks. I too took long walks in country lanes, and when I met him he passed with a hasty nod. Mrs. Tapping never appeared apart from rehearsals and performances, except at the railway stations.

Most of the plays the Tappings did required curtain raisers. It was customary in all companies that when the main play was not thought long enough to give ticket buyers full value, the bill began with a one-act play called a curtain raiser. Whether this was comic or tragic, it was always referred to by the stagehands as the farce. Later, when I was touring with the Abbey Theatre company, Synge's grim one-act tragedy *Riders to the Sea* sometimes served as a curtain raiser. The actors in it were immensely amused when I told them that as I was standing in the prompt corner looking onto the dim stage and listening to the doleful dialogue, the local stage carpenter tiptoed up and whispered, "How long does the farce last?"

But in the Tapping company the curtain raisers were Victorian farces such as *Box and Cox* and *Poor Pillicoddy*. It was Mr. Tapping's custom to take the lead in both plays on the evening bill. This unusual industry—for so it was regarded—amazed some of the older actors in the company. One night, while I was making up during the curtain raiser, Mr. Tapping's voice on stage was clearly audible in the dressing room. An actor well up in his fifties, with whom I was sharing the room, turned to me and said in a tone of sardonic amusement, "Just listen to him. He must *like acting!*"

It was not the first time that I had met with this attitude on the part of some elderly actors to whom their work was no more than a means of earning a living. I had been astonished by it years earlier during my trial engagement with Benson. He was adding *Coriolanus* to his repertoire and, of course, conducting rehearsals himself. At a slight pause in rehearsal, Benson remarked that someone not in the scene in progress was needed to try out a new piece of stage business that involved crossing the stage with a barrel on his shoulder. I noticed how an old actor who had recently been taken on for a few small parts—out of pity, it was rumored, because he was down and out—quietly glided away and hid himself behind a wing, while on this and similar occasions I and other young actors made ourselves as prominent as possible, hoping to be selected.

In some smaller towns the performances of the Tapping company were advertised by means of an interesting survival, the town crier. This dignitary wore an official uniform consisting of a long, gold-braided coat and a tricorn hat. His occupation was to walk from street to street, stopping at set places to shout out a list of current local events that he read from a sheet of paper. The announcements were prefaced by the loud clanging of a bell that he carried on his peregrination. He had been selected, doubtless, for his stentorian voice, and I used to listen with interest when he bellowed out the information. Between advertisements of such things as a soiree at a church and a special sale at a furniture shop, he announced that Mr. and Mrs. Bernard Tapping's company would appear at seven-thirty at the theatre in *Still Waters Run Deep*— or whatever the play of that evening might be.

At the end of the tour in the late spring* I was immediately engaged by a well-established touring actor-manager, Mr. Norman V. Norman, for a summer tour of seaside resorts. When I went to call on him for a preliminary interview, I thought that his somewhat grandiose name fitted him well. He was a fine figure of a man with great elegance of mien. On the tour that followed I noticed how, as he paced the promenades, his stagely passage aroused the curiosity of visitors to the resorts, who would ask each other who he could be. I am not sure that his pompous manner was not deliberately accentuated as a sort of stock-in-trade, for I discovered that he concealed a sense of humor behind the mask. I met him many years later when I was director of the Stratford-upon-Avon Festival Company and he had become a successful actor in London. All his pomposity had disappeared and his manner was gracious and friendly.

One person who was not impressed by the Norman manner was William Marshall, his terribly overworked jack-of-all-trades. The tasks Mr. Norman imposed upon him were so many and various that I wondered how he managed to fulfill them all. Few men can have performed such diverse functions at the same time, yet I never heard him complain, even when he was obviously so weary that I feared he was nearing the end of his tether. It gives me great gratification to be able to report that sometime later I was able to engage Mr. Marshall in a much easier and more agreeable job—that of assistant acting manager at the Gaiety Theatre, Manchester. He was ultimately promoted, thanks to his faithful and talented services, from assistant to manager.

The names by which Mr. Norman referred to Marshall could be catalogued. To townspeople where we were playing he was "my valet"; to theatrical friends who happened to drop in he was "my dresser" or "my property man," according to which of those functions Marshall might be fulfilling at that precise moment. He was "my secretary" when he was attending to Mr. Norman's correspondence in the afternoon and "my man" when exercising the two King Charles spaniels that appeared in *Nell Gwyn*.

*This was not the last that Payne saw of Mrs. Tapping. In 1908, while he was the director of Miss Horniman's repertory company at the Gaiety Theatre, Manchester, he engaged Mrs. Tapping. She continued to play in the company at intervals for some years thereafter.

Mrs. Tapping as Mistress Quickly

Norman V. Norman as Coriolanus

Madge McIntosh

Speaking of Marshall reminds me of another victim. A middle-aged gentleman of good family—I will call him Mr. Renshaw—having no knowledge or experience of business affairs, thought he might find it interesting to take up theatre management. He advanced a sum of money to Mr. Norman to be initiated into what was to him an unknown world. All Mr. Norman did was to make him his acting manager and instruct him in the routine of looking after the front of the house. (An acting manager, in spite of his title, has little to do with the actors and is principally concerned with the box office.) Mr. Renshaw was nervous and shy in manner, but his duties were not onerous and I am sure he fulfilled them conscientiously. With anyone weak enough to be bullied, however, Mr. Norman was always high-handed, and he expected "my manager," as he labeled Mr. Renshaw, to be always at his beck and call. There was trouble if he did not turn up quickly in answer to a summons.

One night after the show I had to go to Mr. Norman's dressing room for a consultation about the casting of a play that was to be added to the repertoire. I found that Mr. Norman was impatient because Mr. Renshaw had not yet brought him the night's return. Marshall (at that moment "my dresser") was sent to fetch him and very soon Mr. Renshaw hurried in. "Mr. Renshaw," said Mr. Norman, "you are late; you have been drinking at the bar!" Mr. Renshaw anxiously assured him that this was untrue; he had been talking to an old friend who happened to live in the town. "Don't lie to me, Mr. Renshaw," said Mr. Norman severely, "you have been drinking at the bar!" Mr. Renshaw had endured many insults and indignities but this was the last straw. He almost threw the evening's return onto the dressing table and stamped out of the room. Next day we learned that he had left town. Soon it was rumored in the company that Mr. Renshaw was accusing Mr. Norman of not fully acting up to his agreement and that he was demanding the return of at least a portion of the money he had advanced.

One morning at rehearsal a few days later Mr. Norman suggested that I join him, as I sometimes did, for a swim in the ocean during the afternoon. A time was arranged when I should call for him at his lodgings. When I was shown in at the hour appointed, Marshall was sitting at the table with pen and ink and a pile of correspondence before him. Mr. Norman was pacing the room with a letter in his hand. He greeted me and said, "Please take a seat for a few moments, Mr. Payne, while I finish dictating to my secretary." Flourishing the letter, he added, "That fellow Renshaw threatens me and I suppose he must have a reply." Mr. Norman wandered over to the window. For a short time he stood gazing thoughtfully at the view of the sea. Then he turned and said sharply, "Marshall, write." He threw the letter onto the table and continued, "Mr. Charles Renshaw. Sir: Pooh! P-O-O-H exclamation mark. Yours, etc. That is all I have for you today." He picked up his bathing suit and towel. "Now, Mr. Payne, I'm ready."

Since Mr. Norman managed a company that was on a sound financial basis, the repertoire was not confined to plays in the public domain. *Nell Gwyn* was a contemporary play, and while I was with him Mr. Norman added a dramatization of a popular novel by Stanley Weyman, belonging to a still more recent vintage. This play required special scenery that had to be carried with us. Consequently it meant more work for poor Marshall, in the role of "my carpenter." In one play we were touring I played a dumb servitor whose tongue had been torn out. The part not only gave me good acting opportunities but it opened the door for me to a much fuller understanding of the value of significant gesture, a lesson that has been of service to me as director as well as actor.

It began to look as though I might remain indefinitely with Mr. Norman, jogging along what was becoming my accustomed path of acting and stage management. Then something happened that made me feel a new and different kind of interest in the theatre. Indeed, it influenced my whole outlook on life. A fellow member of the company brought a copy of George Bernard Shaw's *Plays Pleasant* to rehearsal. When he was called to rehearse a scene he left it on the bench where we had been sitting together. Curiosity made me pick it up. I turned the pages idly at first, but my interest was quickly gripped. When he returned at the end of the scene I was absorbed in reading. He told me that this book and the succeeding volume, *Plays Unpleasant*, had been given to him as a birthday present, but he couldn't make head or tail of them. He insisted that I take them off his hands. The next day he brought me *Plays Unpleasant*. I read both volumes avidly. They were a revelation. Here were plays quite different from anything I had previously met with. Some were on subjects never before dealt with in a theatre. I found them exciting, stimulating, and provocative. Shaw quickly led me to Ibsen, whom he so greatly admired. Ibsen struck deeper still—even, as it seemed, into the inmost recesses of my being. A new world was opened to me.

I suppose that it must be very hard for anyone of the younger generation today to realise how positively cataclysmic the impact of these revolutionary authors could be to one of my generation who was ripe to receive them. I began to have a distaste for the old-fashioned plays in the repertoires I had been engulfed in. For a long while the stage had been dominated by the "well-made play." This kind of drama deserved the epithet only to the degree that a machine is well made. Mechanically it was neat and efficient in its construction, but it lacked an animating soul. The well-made play did not develop from a core of passion—a passion arising inevitably from the clash of character and circumstance. It was the artificial product of a passionless machinery. Sentimentality was as near to passion as it could reach, and sentimentality as George Meredith defined it: "Harping harmonies upon strings of sensualism."

The most successful dramatist of the period, the high priest of the cult, was the French playwright Victorien Sardou. He described his method, frankly enough, as finding an effective theatrical situation and then building actions and characters around it. (Shaw coined an apt epithet for the products of this method: Sardoodledum.) These plays should not be despised for the way they carried out their intent; technically they were highly adroit. But beyond their surface effects they had nothing to say. They were bound by conventional viewpoints; the life they expressed was one of empty propriety; and when, rarely, they dealt with serious social questions, they never challenged the accepted standards.

Thanks to my chance introduction to the plays of Shaw and Ibsen, I was eager for an opportunity to act in the New Drama, as it was called. But it was nowhere being acted, except in single performances by independent groups. The plays were generally regarded as literary freaks, and theatrical managers thought they were entirely without commercial value. But surely, I said to myself, it ought to be possible at least to shake off the dust of these moldy survivals and act in plays dealing with contemporary life.

The opportunity came—indirectly so far as plays related to contemporary life were concerned—when I met Madge McIntosh, an accomplished actress of high standing. She engaged me to act in a few "pastorals" (as open-air performances are called in England) in Hurlingham, the park surrounding the famous polo club. The play was Rostand's *Les Romanesques* in a beautiful rhymed verse translation by George Fleming called *The Fantasticks*.* Immediately afterward, I again worked with Miss McIntosh when she organized a tour of *Mollentrave*

---

*A musical adaptation by Tom Jones and Harvey Schmidt, *The Fantasticks*, opened in New York City in 1960 and achieved the longest continuous run of any musical ever produced there. It was dedicated to B. Iden Payne.

on Women, by Alfred Sutro. It had no affinity with the New Drama but was a mildly satirical comedy that had recently run in London. Nevertheless it was refreshing and had an up-to-date outlook, so I regarded my playing in it (I also stage-managed) as a step in the right direction. Moreover, the cast was a skillful one and I learned a good deal about the technique required for the acting of realistic modern plays.

CHAPTER 8

*I*t must not be thought that Ibsen and Shaw had obliterated or even decreased my love of Shakespeare. The ancient and modern streams ran parallel courses, as far as my interest was concerned. Therefore I was delighted when, toward the end of the *Mollentrave* tour, I received a letter from Mr. Ian Maclaren, at that time unknown to me even by reputation. He invited me to join a Shakespearean repertory company he was about to start. The nature of the offer aroused my enthusiasm, and I accepted with alacrity.

Ian Maclaren was an actor with fine presence and a rich and sonorous voice. A few years later he became established as an actor in America, principally in moving pictures. With his physical advantages it was perhaps inevitable that he had the notion that he ought to play Shakespearean leads, especially the great tragic roles. There was something of the soldier of fortune about Maclaren. It was this that prompted him to launch his company with very little capital beyond his unbridled self-confidence. I did not know this when he wrote to me, but if I had it would have made no difference. The bait he held out was irresistible. I was engaged to play what were known as the "seconds"—Laertes in *Hamlet*, Mercutio in *Romeo and Juliet*, Bassanio in the *Merchant of Venice*, Jaques in *As You Like It*, Macduff in *Macbeth*, and, above all, Iago in *Othello*. What an opportunity! It would have been more than enough reason for me to jump at the chance to join the company, but I was also relieved to find that there was no mention of stage management—a job I had reconciled myself to but never enjoyed. Soon I was to discover that stage management is an excellent preparatory step to a more responsible job—one that did not yet exist.

The company met at Kendal, a pleasant little town nestling in the

Westmorland Hills, where we were to begin the tour after three weeks' rehearsal. Even when I add that we were to give only four of the six plays in our repertoire during the week at Kendal, this may seem a very short rehearsal period. But it must be remembered that a manager starting a Shakespearean company took care to engage actors who had already played in Shakespeare. Even if they were given parts that were new to them, the lines were familiar, for they had often heard them spoken. This led to rapid memorization, although, of course, there is more to rehearsal than learning one's lines.

No sooner had we assembled and been introduced to one another than Maclaren drew me aside. In an easy-going, almost casual, manner he suggested that, since he did not know the plays half so well as I did, perhaps I wouldn't mind "producing" them for him. A few years later Maclaren would not have been so debonair in making his request, nor should I have been so lighthearted in accepting. At this time "producing" (or "directing," to use the American term) meant no more than arranging the movements of the actors on the stage. This was the prerogative of the leading actor, often partly in consultation with other actors in important parts, especially the leading lady. The reading of the lines was left almost entirely to the judgment of the actors themselves. Touches such as tempo and pauses were expected to develop spontaneously.

Whence came the necessity of a new functionary called a director? It is frequently attributed to the enormous increase in the expense of putting on a play. According to this theory, the financial backers of so costly an enterprise felt the need of an intermediary between themselves and the actors. Someone had to attend to the more and more complicated trappings of production—settings, costumes, and the newly invented lighting instruments. (Later on more separate functionaries developed, such as the lighting expert.) There is probably a modicum of truth in this contention, but I doubt that it is the basic answer. Something else was happening at about the same time that suggests a more tenable explanation.

The necessity for a director arose with the advent of Ibsen and Shaw. Their influence on the theatre was not direct, of course, for their plays were rarely performed. But they had a profound influence upon playwrights, who began to write plays with much more psychological import than the popular theatre had theretofore produced. Motives for action were less obvious than they had been; they were frequently veiled and so required explanation and guidance for the actors. Then too there were more plays in which "atmosphere" was of the utmost importance. A guiding hand became indispensable to its achievement.

There are many who believe that today directors often overstep the rightful limits of their function with destructive instead of helpful effects upon the artistry of the theatre. If so, that is at the opposite end of a scale from what Ian Maclaren thought he was requesting of me. I was to make the conventional cuts in the scripts and tell the actors where they came on and went off or where they crossed the stage and perhaps give them a few essential bits of traditional stage business. For my own part, I had much the same idea about what my duties should be. In this I soon found out that I was making a mistake.

Rehearsal had hardly passed beyond a first reading when I began to realize that the actors needed all sorts of advice if they were to do justice to their parts and to themselves. This was not because they lacked talent. The general level of competence was fairly good. The company included Frank Cellier, who was afterward for many years one of the leading actors on the London stage. He played the King in *Hamlet* and other important parts. Florence Glossop-Harris (the daughter of Sir Augustus Harris of the Drury Lane Theatre), who later managed her own repertory company, played the feminine leads. Also in the cast was Aubrey Mather, a useful actor who for many years was never out of work in America either on Broadway or in the moving pictures. None of the actors was entirely without experience. All of them took their work seriously. Mona Limerick, who was shortly to become my wife, was then a beginner in classical drama and so was engaged for small parts, but her forceful, even electrifying, personality, the keynote of her power, manifested itself whenever she appeared.

Only one of the actors presented a problem, and for this I was to blame. Through him, at the very beginning of rehearsals, I learned my first lesson as a director. The first morning was devoted to *Hamlet*. I roughed out the action up to the play-within-the-play scene. Shakespeare gave only one speech to the Second Player: "Thoughts black, hands apt, drugs fit and time agreeing . . ." I thought at that time that he had meant it to be overacted. What was my amazement when the actor cast for the part—a sallow-faced, lantern-jawed fellow called Midgeley, almost a comic drawing of an old-fashioned strolling player —delivered the lines with a deep and throaty voice, extravagant gestures, and rolling eyes. I took this to be a clever burlesque of the kind of overacting Hamlet condemned. When we broke off for lunch I congratulated Midgeley upon his exciting performance. I told him that it was nothing less than brilliant. I thought he looked surprised and soon discovered why. That same afternoon we rehearsed *Much Ado about Nothing*, in which Midgeley was cast as a simple and kindly old gentleman. He read his lines in exactly the same manner and with the same intensity and gestures that he had displayed as the Second Player! I found that it was useless to point out the difference in the

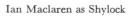
Ian Maclaren as Shylock

Cyril Keightley as Young Marlow

Mona Limerick

character. This was Midgeley's idea of acting, no matter what the part might be.

As you may imagine, in the other plays I used him only in the very smallest parts. I fear that Midgeley was disappointed in me. He was laconic by nature and never complained about his tiny roles, but I had to become accustomed to sour looks whenever we met out of the theatre. Still I have to thank him for teaching me never to judge an actor's work from a first reading, and sometimes not from several readings of a part.

Throughout the tour that followed I was aware that I was taking a new and different interest in Shakespeare. I found that I wanted to help the actors in their interpretations, and in doing so I began to realize that it was necessary to know far more about the plays themselves than the acting opportunities they afforded. It struck me that each play revealed itself as a world of its own. To enter into that world it was necessary to know the play as a whole, not merely as a series of separate but related scenes. I became conscious of my ignorance of Shakespeare's drama, except as an acting medium, and I began to read the commentators. They opened a gate into new and unexpected regions. A. C. Bradley's *Shakespearean Tragedy* delighted me particularly. The author's broad outlook, combined with meticulous analysis, widened my horizon. It was pleasant to agree with him and pleasant to disagree with him. In either case, I found that sharing his thought stimulated the imagination.

I was able to share this new interest with a few of my fellow actors. With them I enjoyed discussions about the plays. But I made the discovery, confirmed so often since that I have come to take it for granted, that many actors are interested only in their own parts and prefer to leave their realization to instinct without thought. They are deaf to suggestions. It seemed a serious drawback that my manager, Ian Maclaren, belonged to the latter category. This does not mean that he lacked the equipment of an actor. On the contrary, as I have already mentioned, he possessed qualities that made him much admired, his presence and his voice. He had a fine, upstanding appearance, but his head was rather small for his more than six-foot height and, though his voice was rich and resonant, his delivery of verse tended toward the declamatory. Unfortunately this was especially true at moments that call for overwhelming bursts of emotion. He did not exactly overdo his acting by tearing the passions to tatters, but his emotion was forced and lacked spontaneity. However, audiences, if measured by the index of applause, were ignorant of this limitation.

Spectators at an efficient but mechanical performance of a great Shakespearean tragic role are unaware that their emotional response would be much deeper, almost different in kind, if they were watching an actor borne along on waves of natural instead of forced emotions. All really fine acting, though differing in externals according to the social manners of the age, must have been natural in essence. Once during my tour in the Ian Maclaren company I saw the most striking proof of this in my experience. When we were booked at a Lancashire town called Burnley, Mr. Maclaren told us that the owner of the theatre, Jonathan Dewhurst, was an old actor who had long since retired. Yet, though he was over eighty, whenever a Shakespearean company came to his theatre he made a practice of appearing with them at the Friday performance in one of his great parts as his "benefit." Mr. Maclaren rather grimly explained that in his prime Dewhurst had been a secondary star in the provinces. He had "traveled," we were told, a proof that he had once been of considerable prominence. (In the days when stock companies were universal, actors of sufficient importance traveled from town to town, joining companies for a few days and acting their favorite parts.) When we learned that in his prime Mr. Dewhurst had been familiarly known as "Jaunty" Dewhurst, we were convinced that we should see one of the worst embodiments of what we regarded as the bad old school. *Othello* was in our repertoire and the title role, the part in which Mr. Dewhurst had elected to appear, would surely give him many opportunities for old-fashioned ranting.

When we met Mr. Dewhurst at the run-through on Friday morning he merely wished to be informed about his entrances and exits and to be instructed as to where he was to stand. He made only one request. He was heavy and gouty and he begged me, as Iago, to assist him to rise from his knees after the vow of vengeance in act III. He ran through the lines in a rapid mutter, giving no indication of how he would speak them at night, so we continued to look forward to the fun his performance would offer.

We went to the theatre that night to laugh and—if I may generalize from my own reaction—we left feeling much more inclined to pray. From the quiet but firm authority of "Keep up your bright swords," at the beginning to the final speech, all the verse was spoken simply and naturally, under the guidance of sincere emotion. It is true that in the more distressful scenes he wept more than a modern actor would; I can still see the tears streaming down his wrinkled cheeks. But it would be a poor spirit who saw in this a cause for ridicule.

CHAPTER 9

*J*an Maclaren's vast self-confidence did not prove to be enough capital to offset financial insecurity. There were weeks when salaries were not paid in full, and they were rarely made up later. Even worse, there were weeks when no theatre was booked and there was consequently no salary at all. After a few months the tour petered out.

My next step seems to have been a deliberate severance from my Shakespearean activities. It was important that I find work without delay, for I was now married to Mona Limerick and soon to become a father. Yet it was not to Benson that I wrote asking if he had an opening, but to Granville Barker. (He came to be known later as Harley Granville-Barker.) The fascination I had found in the New Drama had been not diminished but intensified during my Maclaren engagement. The Vedrenne-Barker season at the Royal Court Theatre (Mr. J. E. Vedrenne represented the financial aspect of the celebrated partnership) was then approaching the height of its fame, and Bernard Shaw, for whom my admiration was unbounded, was the mainstay at the Royal Court Theatre. For the first time, the general public had a chance to be startled by his plays. Shaw ceased to be merely the white-headed boy of a coterie.

Barker answered my letter by giving me an appointment at the theatre for the following afternoon. The Royal Court is a small theatre and Barker shared a crowded office with Vedrenne, so on my arrival he suggested that we go out for a cup of tea. The conversation we had together at the neighboring *ABC* Café turned out to be a fateful one for me, though not immediately. Barker was friendly and gracious. He listened with interest to all I had to say and asked me several questions. He concluded the interview disappointingly, however, by telling me he had nothing to offer at that time but he would bear me in mind. Barker suggested that I see Cyril Keightley, who was about to start a tour. I knew of Keightley as a former Bensonian, though he had not been in the company in my time. He was a polished actor who well deserved his reputation for his graceful skill in high comedy parts. (Later on he was the leading man more than once with Ethel Barrymore on Broadway, under my direction.) He was going on tour with *She Stoops to Conquer* and *The Rivals*—Young Marlow and Captain Absolute were ideal parts for him—and a rather melodramatic new play laid in the eighteenth century. One of the purposes of the tour was to try out this play with a view to a possible London production. There was no New Drama in this repertoire, but Keightley flattered me with the offer of such good parts as Bob Acres and Tony Lumpkin. Also I was to have a comic butler role in the new play and a better salary than I had previously received. I accepted with alacrity, although I was again burdened with stage management.

We opened at the Devonshire Park Theatre in the fashionable south-coast town of Eastbourne. I have cause to remember this because a disgraceful incident happened there. It seems trivial enough today, but I will tell it because of the light that its aftermath sheds on the responsibilities that the touring companies held to the local theatres and their audiences.

We sailed along in calm waters during the first part of the week with the old comedies. The trouble came on Friday with the production of the new play. Keightley played the part of a gallant highwayman beloved by the heroine. In one scene he was brought up for trial before a country squire, who used his sitting room as a court, a customary procedure in the period of the play. The squire was played by that fine character actor, Baliol Holloway, who had the amiable weakness of not being able to keep a straight face if any slight mishap struck him as funny. While struggling to hold his expression within bounds, he had a quaint mannerism of turning up one corner of his mouth in a way that was terribly infectious to the other actors. That night, at a most serious moment in the trial scene, one of the actors blundered over a line. Bay, as we called Holloway, began to splutter. I, standing by as the butler, found it impossible not to respond. There were several actors in the scene, and in a few moments the infection spread irrepressibly. We all lost control and literally shook with laughter. All of us, except one. Our manager, aided perhaps by his managerial responsibility, after first beginning to succumb himself, stamped his foot violently and bawled out the next line in an angry shout. This brought us back to our senses. We pulled ourselves together and the scene proceeded normally. But the mischief had been done. The owner of the theatre had witnessed the exhibition we had made of ourselves. He made a formal complaint and the next day we were hauled over the coals.

I was not to remain with Cyril Keightley very long. The tour took us to Ireland. There one night, in a dingy old theatre in Waterford, the theatre manager came backstage and told me that "a gentleman from Dublin" wished to see me. I was playing a part in which I had long waits between my scenes, so I suggested that he bring the visitor around. The gentleman turned out to be a tall, dark man who looked, in his coal black suit and the dim light behind the scenery, so like a priest that for a moment I thought he was one. In fact, only the rather large, loosely tied black bow tie contradicted this assumption. He introduced himself by saying, "My name is Yeats." Naively I blurted out, "Not the poet?" "Yes," he replied gravely, "I am William Butler Yeats. I suppose you might call me a poet." I later discovered that Yeats had a frank and disarming smile when he was amused, but I saw no hint of it during this formal introduction.

We made an appointment to meet after the performance at his hotel. Imagine my surprise when he then explained, over a glass of Irish whiskey, that he had made the journey down from Dublin especially to see *me*. They were looking, he said, for a stage director at the Abbey Theatre. I had been recommended for the position by Granville Barker. (This was another surprise, since the interview in the *ABC* had been my only contact with Barker up to that time.) He proposed that I travel up to Dublin to look the situation over and meet his fellow directors of the Abbey Theatre, Lady Gregory and J. M. Synge. This seemed to be a sensible suggestion, especially as the Irish National Theatre was little more than a name to me. Moreover, the time was convenient, for the Keightley company was in the unfortunate position of being "out"—that is, without a booking—the following week. It was arranged that I should go to Dublin on Sunday, meet the other directors on Monday, and see a new play that was to be performed that night.

My appointment with Yeats's fellow directors was in a sitting room at the Nassau Hotel. It was afternoon, so we were served tea and buttered toast. The Nassau Hotel was of the old-fashioned family type, with a heavy air of Victorian respectability. Later on I was to have many afternoon teas there with Lady Gregory and Yeats, for Yeats stayed in the hotel when in Dublin and shared the sitting room. I never recall those afternoon teas without imagining that I detect the odor of buttered toast. Nor do I ever smell buttered toast without thinking of the Nassau Hotel.

Lady Gregory was alone when I arrived. I thought her dowager-like manner and appearance perfectly fitted the heavily upholstered furniture of the tapestry-curtained sitting room. Her manner when receiving me, though not ungracious, was somewhat standoffish, as if she might be very authoritarian when she chose.

Synge soon joined us. He struck me as being very pale, almost wan, and his manner was so detached that sometimes it seemed as if he was not following the conversation. Lady Gregory asked him if everything was ready for the opening that night. I had read in a newspaper at breakfast that the new play was called *The Playboy of the Western World* and that Synge was the author, so I listened with interest—more interest, indeed, than he seemed to show in his own play. His very casual answer to Lady Gregory was, "All I can say is that Willie seems satisfied." I learned later that he was referring to W. G. Fay, a very important factor in the Abbey Theatre.

So much has been written about the *Playboy* riots of 1907 that I do not feel they call for much comment here. Accounts of what occurred at the first performance differ greatly, however. I was aware of no protests during the first act, but I was puzzled as I stood in the crowded foyer during the first intermission by a curious tension in the air. I also overheard some excited arguments about the merits and demerits of the play that made me conclude that the Abbey Theatre audience was very much alive. I was standing beside Synge when someone came up and remarked that everything had gone well so far. Synge sardonically suggested that he had better wait until the play was over. It all seemed rather strange. For my own part my imagination had been captured by the vitality and freshness of the dialogue, though I sometimes had difficulty in following it. Also I was fascinated by the acting, which had the unfamiliar quality of being at the same time casual and colorful.

As the play progressed I began to notice strange noises at the back of the audience—I was sitting in the front row—but I could not determine their nature. I thought at first that some man was making occasional drunken interruptions and that other people were telling him to be quiet. Then suddenly, to my complete surprise, there was an outburst of indignation, apparently from all parts of the house, and the remaining dialogue was drowned in a pandemonium of shouting. I went back to my hotel in a state of complete bewilderment.

I have a vivid recollection of my next interview with the directors. Yeats had been absent at the opening of *Playboy*, but at this meeting he was the dominant figure. Most of the talk was about the trouble at the theatre. Synge very tentatively suggested that they throw in the sponge by stopping the run of the play, though it had been advertised to last for a week. Yeats would not hear of it. His manner was high-spirited, even elated. The fire of combat lighted up his eyes as he said they must at all hazards give the play its full allotted time. If they gave way to clamor, he said, they would ever afterward be at the mercy of the whims and prejudices of their audiences. The play must go on, he said, even if they had policemen stationed by every row of seats to throw out the disturbers.

During all this, the question of my appointment was forgotten. The subject was finally brought up when Lady Gregory turned to me and expressed the hope that I was not so disgusted with the behavior of the audience that I would abandon all idea of accepting the position at the Abbey Theatre. This was the first intimation I had had that I was being definitely invited. When I assured her that I was not, my acceptance was taken for granted. A few details of my duties were discussed, and it was emphasized, as Yeats had previously made clear, that I was to have no hand in the production of the Irish folk plays. These were, as I knew by this time, numerous and vital to the work of the Abbey Theatre. From the directors' approach to the subject it was evident that they felt I would regard this as a drawback. On the contrary, I heartily approved. I knew full well that my total ignorance of Irish rural life would be too severe a handicap with plays written in such an unfamiliar idiom. We agreed that I should rejoin the Keightley company in Waterford, give my required notice, and then return to Dublin to take up my duties. But these were not, perhaps, as precisely defined as they ought to have been.

I have said that up to the time of Yeats's visit to me at Waterford in 1907 I knew nothing of the origins of the Irish National Theatre. That curious history, and its relation to the chain of events leading to my own appointment, were revealed to me only gradually. The information was given me first by Willie Fay, with whom I was soon on confidential terms, and later by Yeats. Finally I heard it from Miss A. E. F. Horniman, a character who will play a large role in these pages. Differences of opinion were more prevalent than agreements at the Abbey Theatre in those days, so the unanimity of these accounts must surely attest to their accuracy. I had best begin at the beginning.

It is universally acknowledged that Annie Elizabeth Fredericka

Horniman was a great patron of the modern theatre. She it was who, though she was English, founded the Irish National Theatre. She it was who gave Shaw his first chance in the commercial theatre. She it was who started the repertory theatre movement in England, and thus indirectly fostered the nascent community theatre in America. All these things are widely known. Yet how Miss Horniman came to be a patron of the theatre—and just what being one entailed—is less well known. Much of the story was told me by Miss Horniman herself.

Miss Horniman's family fortune had been made through her grandfather's ingenuity in being the first to sell tea in made-up packages. (Up to that time grocers had been required to weigh out the requested amount of tea and fold it into paper cones.) From him, and more directly from her grandmother, Miss Horniman inherited more than a competence. With her father, however, she was not on good terms, and it came as a surprise when she learned at his death that he had not cut her out of his will. In fact, he had left her a fairly large sum of money. In view of what their relationship had been, she was disinclined to spend this inheritance on herself. On the other hand, she had no interest in conventional philanthropy, such as the endowing of hospital beds. She decided to reserve the money for what she called "public purposes"—activities that would be valuable to society but in which she·could at the same time take personal interest. Until something suitable turned up, she would let the money "lie idle."

At this time Miss Horniman had no knowledge of, and indeed no interest in, the theatre. It chanced, however, that she became friendly with a well-known actress named Florence Farr, who is remembered today for her correspondence with Shaw. Miss Farr had as individual a turn of mind as Miss Horniman herself. She had concocted an entertainment in which she dressed in Pre-Raphaelite costumes and chanted poetry to a zitherlike musical instrument described on the program as the "psaltery"—all very original, of course, and characteristic of the avant-garde at the lag-end of the Mauve Decade. Since Yeats's poems were an important part of Miss Farr's repertoire, Yeats took an interest in her performance. So did Miss Horniman, and in this way she was brought indirectly into association with Yeats.

Miss Farr told Miss Horniman that Yeats had written a very beautiful one-act play in verse called *The Land of Heart's Desire*, which ought to be shown to the public in a regular professional theatre. When Miss Horniman pointed out that a one-act play would hardly fill the bill, Miss Farr assured her that that problem was already solved. Yeats's verse play was to be followed by a full-length prose comedy by another

Irish author. Before leaving for her annual pilgrimage to the Wagner Festival at Bayreuth, Miss Horniman gave Miss Farr a check to cover the estimated cost of the production. In doing so she asked, almost casually, for some particulars of the second play. Miss Farr replied that the title was *Arms and the Man* and the author was named George Bernard Shaw. Thus Miss Horniman came to be the great playwright's benefactor.*

In spite of an enthusiastic opening and some critical stir, the public response to *Arms and the Man* was meager. But, in Miss Horniman's phrase, it was a "fruitful failure," for it led to her meeting with Yeats. With a few literary friends, Yeats had been agitating for an Irish national theatre. They had begun by having plays written by Irishmen but acted by visiting English companies. Then they had joined forces with a small amateur group whose leading spirits were two brothers, Frank and Willie Fay. Yeats was able to induce Miss Horniman to buy a former mission hall in Dublin, convert it into the "Abbey Theatre," and give the company a small annual subsidy for a number of years.†

The programs consisted largely of one-act plays, written by the three directors of the theatre, Yeats, Lady Gregory, and J. M. Synge. Yeats found an opportunity for his verse plays to be performed; Lady Gregory's farces of Irish peasant life were amusing and well regarded by the press; and Synge, though regarded with suspicion and a kind of fearful fascination by the public, proved to be the outstanding dramatic genius of the triumvirate. Except for his one-act tragedy *Riders to the Sea*, Synge's plays astonished and irritated the Dublin public, accustomed to patriotic melodramas of sentimental romance.

Whatever jubilation there may have been on the part of the recipients of Miss Horniman's bounty, it was quenched when it was found that they had very few other supporters. The response they received from the general public was almost infinitesimal. Something had to be done to stir up wider interest. Yeats was very astute. "I know my country-

*According to James W. Flannery, in *W. B. Yeats and the Idea of the Theatre*, the events that Payne records here are essentially correct, but the order is wrong. Yeats, Miss Horniman, and Miss Farr had known each other as early as 1890, when all three joined an occult society known as The Hermetic Order of the Golden Dawn. Miss Farr's recitals to the psaltery grew out of certain rituals of this order in 1901. This did not happen, however, until 1901, seven years after Miss Horniman had backed a production of the Yeats and Shaw plays in London.

†In *Miss Annie F. Horniman and the Abbey Theatre*, Flannery reports that Miss Horniman's decision to subsidize Yeats's group was finally made only after consultation with the tarot cards. Several later decisions concerning the Abbey were also reached with the help of her highly individual combination of tarot with astrology.

men," he told me one day. "In spite of their anti-British talk, I knew they would never take the National Theatre seriously until the company had been approved by the English newspaper critics." He was convinced that they would receive that endorsement if their performances could be seen in London. Accordingly, he prevailed upon Miss Horniman to give them enough money in addition to the subsidy to cover the expenses of a brief London visit.

Nearly everything turned out as Yeats had prophesied. The plays and the acting struck an entirely new note in London. The critics acclaimed the performances as something new and refreshing in the theatre. But some of them tempered their approval with adverse comments upon the technical side of the productions. They noted that the scenery was badly constructed, with flats that did not join, that the costumes were ill fitting, and that the men wore crude wigs and beards. I doubt that either the directors or the actors paid much attention to this, but for Miss Horniman it was a major consideration. Yeats, pleased with the company's reception in London, asked Miss Horniman for an increase in the subsidy for the next three years. This would carry them over the period during which, it was hoped, support would substantially increase. Miss Horniman agreed to supply it, but with the proviso that the directors agree to have an English professional stage director at the Abbey. She would also provide his salary. I do not know what Yeats and the other directors thought of this, but they desperately needed the extra subsidy and so gave their consent.*

When the actors heard about what they called the "surrender" there was an angry explosion at the "outrage." They even threatened to strike. As W. G. Fay put it to me when we came to know each other well, "It was bad enough for an Irish Theatre to be spoon-fed by an Englishwoman, but Irish plays directed by an Englishman was too much to swallow!" In the field of compromise the English are generally reckoned to be foremost, but if the people at the Abbey Theatre can be regarded as nationally representative, I should say that the Irish are at least their equals. After much acrimonious discussion, the actors agreed to accept the indignity of an English stage director if his activities

*In fact, this was a point of contention among the directors. Also in *W. B. Yeats and the Idea of a Theatre*, Flannery says that Lady Gregory and Synge objected from the first to importing an English director and had consented only at Yeats's insistence. Some of their opposition to Payne seems to have resulted from their lack of sympathy with Yeats's desire to develop actors capable of playing the tragic and heroic roles in his own plays. In any case, by not telling Payne of the situation, Yeats placed him in an untenable position at the Abbey Theatre.

70

were limited in the way I have already mentioned: by denying him any authority over Irish folk plays.*

This resentment put me in a difficult situation, for my natural tendency was to be on the side of the actors. I should certainly have shared their feelings had I been in their position. But knowledge of their causes came to me only some time after my arrival.

On the day I took up my duties a dress rehearsal was in progress. Yeats joined me in the auditorium. The play was one of Lady Gregory's comedies. Soon the rehearsal was interrupted by an episode that turned out to be characteristic of backstage life at the Abbey. The stage, which was surprisingly small, was constructed with a considerable rake. A stage slanting upward from front to back had once been customary in all theatres—which is why actors still speak of going upstage when they walk toward the back and downstage when they move toward the audience: This is a literal description of what had to be done. As we watched the action, Yeats and I noticed that something odd seemed to be developing in the delivery of the dialogue. There were loud promptings that seemed to be ignored and continuous sotto voce interjections by the actors. After a time the act drop was suddenly lowered. Yeats went to find out what was the matter.

When he returned I could tell from his broad smile that the trouble was not serious. He explained that the brothers Fay had quarreled and Willie had struck Frank. There was nothing special about that apparently, but general indignation among the actors had turned against Willie because, in striking the blow, he had taken advantage of the rake of the stage. For a moment, Willie had been quite out of favor with his fellow actors, but Yeats had restored peace by prevailing upon him to apologize. The rest of rehearsal then proceeded without incident.

Although constant preparation of new plays necessitated daily rehearsals, I found that the actors had a most casual attitude toward them. This astonished and infuriated me, for I had always found promptness to be the rule. The actors had signed contracts that followed the long-established custom in stipulating that the actor must attend rehearsals promptly but "with ten minutes grace for difference of clocks." The English interpretation of the rule was that rehearsals began at the time they were called, but, unless an actor regularly took advantage of the leeway, he could not be censured if he arrived during the first ten

*Two other issues added to the tension. According to Flannery, "Rumours that [Payne's] salary was to be five hundred pounds per year aroused the actors' antagonism even before his arrival in mid-February." And he irritated the company still further when he cast his wife, Mona Limerick, in the title role of Yeats's *Deirdre*.

minutes. At the Abbey Theatre the actors' reading of the contractual obligation was different. They maintained that a rehearsal called for eleven o'clock should not begin until eleven-ten. Consequently, the actors generally began to arrive ten minutes after the hour. If they showed up, as they frequently did, at a quarter past, they claimed, "After all, we were only five minutes late!" When I suggested that I might call rehearsals at ten minutes to eleven I was assured that a departure from established custom would be violently opposed. After many appeals against this loss of time, I did sometimes succeed in starting rehearsals a little earlier than the previous custom, but to little avail. It seemed as if no sooner was a rehearsal in full swing—say, after about three-quarters of an hour—than one of the actresses who did not happen to be in the scene in progress appeared at the top of the short staircase leading up to the greenroom and called out, "Tea's ready!" Without an instant's delay, even to finish the sentence being spoken, the whole cast would troop upstairs for tea, cakes, and protracted conversation!

I have sometimes been asked what Yeats was like at rehearsals, or even how he conducted them. As a matter of fact, he rarely came to the theatre while I was there, except for performances. If he wished to make any comment on the acting or the staging of the plays, it was generally over buttered toast at the Nassau Hotel. When he did put in an appearance at a rehearsal, it was for one of his own plays. Even then his principal concern was the reading of the poetry—generally of one particular line or short passage. He spent most of the time walking about and intoning alternate renderings of some line or phrase in a low whisper. (Intoning, by the way, is the only word to describe Yeats's manner of speaking verse.) One day, when we were rehearsing his *Deirdre*, he was troubled about the end of one of Naoise's speeches. In the prompt script we were using it went, "Light torches there and drive the shadows out, For day's red end comes up." There was a muttered accompaniment to the rehearsal from the right aisle as Yeats paced up and down. "Day's *grey* end comes up; day's *red* end comes up; day's *grey* end comes up." His voice gradually grew louder and louder, and eventually I had to ask him to remember that a rehearsal was in progress. He apologized and asked which reading I preferred. He even said he would abide by my decision. I preferred red as the more dramatic coloring for sunset, and red it was for that production of the play. But later on he must have changed his mind, for in the final edition of *Deirdre* day's end was grey.

I have occasionally been asked whether Yeats ever talked to me about his experiences with the supernatural. He did not, but that is hardly surprising. Occultism is not a subject for general conversation and we rarely talked intimately on subjects other than those connected with the Abbey Theatre. However, one early evening we went together to the surburban house of Yeats's father. He was a portrait painter who later went to America and spent the rest of his life in New York City, where I occasionally saw him at a restaurant he frequented. I was walking with "Bill Butler" (as W. G. Fay privately called Yeats) by the side of a long field. Somehow the subject of those celebrated Irish sprites called leprechauns came up and I asked Yeats if he had ever seen one. He shook his head. Then, pointing to a house beyond the field, he added that the farmer who lived there had once caught a leprechaun. When he went to bed, he had put it into an empty bird cage. The leprechaun must have unclasped the latch, for the next morning he had disappeared. I looked around expecting to see a smile on Yeats's face. He apeared to be dead serious, so I dropped the subject.

At that time the *Playboy* riots still came up in every conversation. It was during such a discussion later that evening that the elder Yeats told us a story. The family maid, a country girl, had just returned from the funeral of her father. She told with gusto how at the wake her widowed mother had had the coffin containing the corpse stood up against the wall. Then, to the universal merriment, she had pushed an open bottle of whiskey between her late husband's lips, saying, "You shall have one more swallow before you leave us forever!" Bill Butler was outraged by the coarseness of this episode. He said that most of the rioters against Synge's *Playboy of the Western World* had justified their acts on the ground that the author, by speaking of young women clothed only in their shifts, had slandered the purity of Irish women. Yet these same persons would have been quite ready to take part in the disgusting orgy the maid had described. "This," he said, "is typical of our country's hypocrisy."

Little need be said about my work at the Abbey Theatre. In retrospect I look upon my sojourn there as a kind of interlude, for during the few months I lived in Dublin I never felt that I was striking root. I cannot say that the actors were antagonistic to my directions, but I was conscious that we were not working fully in harmony. Or rather, to put it more precisely, I felt myself inadequate in trying to express what I wanted to say in language to which they could respond. Also, I still thought of myself primarily as an actor, and obviously there was no place for me in that capacity with the Abbey Theatre company. I was in a blind alley and I knew that before long I should have to find my way out of it. Meanwhile, I worked conscientiously and, apart from producing two Yeats plays, *The Shadow Waters* and *Deirdre; Fand,* by

The setting for *The Playboy of the Western World* at the Abbey Theatre

William Poel

Miss Horniman

Wilfrid Scawen Blunt; and Maeterlinck's beautiful one-act play *Interior*, I was able, with some difficulty, to make a few improvements in the technical handling of the plays.

My work was not confined to activities behind the proscenium. Business affairs were casually conducted at the Abbey, so I was not surprised to find that, though nothing had been said about it, I was obviously expected to superintend all forms of advertising of the performances. The first independent step I took in this direction ended unhappily. Shop-window cards were customarily distributed to announce the weekly bills and the ones we were using seemed unnecessarily expensive. We were paying, I found on inquiry, nearly twice as much as the price offered by a well-known firm in Belfast, much used in the English theatre. I gave them the order for the next batch of cards. The name of the printer had, by law, to appear on the bills and, in my ignorance, I had given no thought to the fact that David Allen & Sons operated in the "black north." As soon as the new cards were exhibited there were indignant outbursts from every quarter. Why, it was asked, did an Irish national organization give work to "foreigners"? Back I was forced to go to the Dublin printer, in spite of the extra cost.

I was told that in business matters I was to have the assistance of the acting manager of the theatre. But the incumbent of that position at the Abbey, a reserved and shy man, rarely appeared at the theatre except briefly in the morning and at the performances. If I suggested that he do anything except pay salaries and enter the receipts of the performances in a ledger, he behaved like a frightened rabbit. I gathered in conversation with him that most of his time was occupied in "literary research." The research consisted in counting the number of times that Shakespeare used the words *father* and *mother*, respectively, throughout his plays. By this statistical analysis, he expected to prove that Shakespeare had loved his father a certain percentage more than he loved his mother. The balance so far as he had progressed was on the masculine side.

When I determined to arrange a second English tour for the company, I could hardly expect this scholarly manager to assist me with the booking. So I arranged it myself through correspondence with Miss Horniman. She agreed to underwrite the project. Possibly she had already had this idea herself. Beginning at Glasgow in Scotland, we worked south through some of the principal English cities and finished in London.

On our way to London the company played a few nights in Oxford. It was there that I finally met Miss Horniman. Like everyone else, on first coming into contact with this remarkable woman I was much impressed by her very individual personality. Her appearance, in fact, was equally unusual. She was of about average height and very slender, but she bore herself with dignity. Her assurance of manner was truly extraordinary. In dress, she ignored fashion completely, always appearing in clothes that were vaguely medieval in style. Her speech was direct and, in practical matters, always to the point. I soon became aware, however, that the rest of her conversation consisted of flat commonplaces. These were uttered as if they were almost pontifical pronouncements, but often ended with an amusing twist of assumed modesty. My Oxford encounters with Miss Horniman consisted mainly in listening to her complaints about the cavalier way in which she was treated by everyone in the Abbey Theatre including the directors, especially Lady Gregory. But it was against the actors, and Willie Fay in particular, that her most violent shafts were directed. She accused Fay of perpetually inventing excuses to be rude to her. It was, she explained, because of this combination of annoyances that I had never seen her at the Abbey. She had ceased to go to Ireland, she said, "only to be insulted!"

From Oxford we went on to London for a short engagement at the Great Queen Street Theatre. There was considerable tension in the atmosphere on the night *Playboy* was performed. Because of the many Irish residents in London, the company feared protests similar to the Dublin outbreak. For a few ominous seconds, scattered shouts of indignation came from the gallery. These subsided, however, when they were drowned by equally indignant counter cries. Although the police had been alerted and waited outside the theatre, there was no need to call on their help. As I had been that first night at the Abbey, I was deeply impressed by the complete air of detachment with which Synge, sitting in a stage box, gazed up at the gallery apparently with a sort of placid interest. His face, always impassive, remained as calm as a standing pool on a still day.

On another night King Edward VII came to a performance. I assume that it was considered a diplomatic necessity that the monarch patronize the Irish National Theatre. Unless his reputation belies him, ours was not the kind of entertainment that he was likely to choose for his amusement. As the King walked down the long narrow entrance hall of that small theatre, talking impatiently, I was surprised to hear that his guttural speech seemed to be strongly tinged with a German accent. I wondered what he and Queen Alexandra, who looked as handsome as she did in her pictures, thought of such unaccustomed fare as our Irish peasant plays.

Bernard Shaw, too, came to one of the performances. He shrugged his shoulders about the play and did not admire the acting. For some reason

I spoke of the players' "Irish brogue." Shaw interjected contemptuously, "It is not a brogue, it's a Dublin accent; it would do them good to be told so."

The last performance at the Great Queen Street Theatre also saw the termination of my work with the Irish National Theatre. After I had handed in my resignation I saw no more of the directors, except Yeats. He was upset and expressed regret that I was leaving them, but he understood my reasons for doing so.

CHAPTER 10

*T*he year was still 1907 and I had no idea what to do next. I should have been at loose ends, but just as the invitation to go to Dublin had come as a surprise, I now experienced another and even greater surprise. The day after I announced my decision, I received a note from Miss Horniman, asking me to visit her at her apartment. I did so, wondering why she should wish to see me. This was the first of seemingly innumerable times that I was to walk along the dark corridor, past closely shut doors, to where one was faced by an electrically lighted portrait of Yeats. There one turned right into Miss Horniman's comfortably old-fashioned sitting room, with armchairs at each side of the fireplace and a sofa facing it. This was also the first of many times that I partook of Miss Horniman's scented China tea, served with toasted tea cakes. Then, too, I first observed an endearing trait in Miss Horniman's character, her affinity with cats. Indeed, I had to remove one from an armchair before I could sit down. Later I learned just how far Miss Horniman's fondness for feline pets extended. She liked, for one thing, to have her friends call her Tabby. When anything pleased her, she said that it made her purr. On the other hand, if she was displeased, she held up her fingers, stretched out as if to scratch, and gave a low-pitched hiss.

Miss Horniman wasted no time in explaining why she had asked to see me. "I want," she declared, "to teach those impossible people in Dublin that I have other fish to fry." She said that she had decided to use £25,000 of the money she had reserved for public purposes for further theatrical activities. She would like me to undertake this project for her. As for the most effective course to pursue, that would be left up to me to choose.

At first thought it may seem that I should have been overjoyed at being offered such an extraordinary opportunity. In fact, far from being elated, I was taken aback. It was not that I feared the responsibility, weighty though it would be for a young man of twenty-six. I was too brash to feel such qualms. But I had gone on the stage because I enjoyed acting. Anything that frustrated that ambition depressed my spirits. Directing and managerial work had not been my choice; they had been thrust upon me.

One may wonder, then, why I accepted Miss Horniman's offer with such alacrity as I did. The answer—though I could not then have expressed my feelings in words—was that I saw this stroke of fortune as a step toward creating the kind of theatre that I had longed for but never found. My reading of Ibsen and Shaw, and my tantalizingly brief engagement with Madge McIntosh's pastorals, had made me eager for a chance to experience, and to help advance, the New Drama. Just how intense that eagerness had been I did not quite know myself until suddenly I was offered the chance to make the vision real.

From the first there was no doubt in Miss Horniman's mind or mine that our aim should be to build some kind of repertory company. But I pointed out, and she agreed, that it would be senseless to undertake repertory in London. A London venture would compete with what appeared to be the well-established work of Granville Barker at the Royal Court Theatre. Miss Horniman, who often spoke of her Scottish grandfather, suggested trying to found a Scottish national theatre. Glasgow and Edinburgh were talked of as possible homes for our undertaking. I maintained, however, that the Scots themselves should be the prime movers in any national venture. In view of Miss Horniman's Dublin experience, I argued, she should be leery of any enterprise that bore a nationalistic tag.

After a good deal of discussion I proposed Manchester as the seat of the new venture. I knew Lancashire well and could speak with some authority. Not only, I pointed out, was Manchester a large city, but it was centrally located among many subsidiary towns. Even more to the point, Manchester was recognized as a cultural center. It was the only provincial city that supported a symphony orchestra, the celebrated Hallé Orchestra. And then, it was situated in Lancashire, and Lancashire folk are a very colorful people with individual characteristics of speech, manners, and customs. It might even be possible, I optimistically suggested, to develop a school of Manchester playwrights. Finally, there was the *Manchester Guardian*, a newspaper celebrated for its high standard of dramatic criticism, to ensure intelligent recognition of our endeavors.

Miss Horniman proposed that I go to Manchester to look over the ground and make inquiries as to whether a theatre suitable for our purpose was available. I found, as I anticipated, that all the regular theatres in Manchester were out of the question. But a large and luxurious hotel had just been opened that was at that time unique in the English provinces. Situated at the terminus of the Midland Railway, it was called the Midland Hotel. Among other startling amenities, such as a "palm court," it had a large ballroom, furnished with stage and proscenium. Miss Horniman readily agreed to rent this hall, giving it the title of Midland Theatre, for a few experimental weeks. Arrangements were quickly made. Thus, in the fall of 1907, what became the English repertory theatre movement was inaugurated.

As these preparations were moving forward, I happened one day to be with Yeats in his little London apartment. He asked me what agreement I had signed with Miss Horniman. I had to confess that, with my usual lack of business acumen, I had not given any thought to the matter. He advised me that, when the subject came up, I should make the contract a tight one, laying down definite limits beyond which Miss Horniman should have no authority or right to interfere. "You know," Yeats explained, "she is a vulgarian." This attitude surprised me greatly for the moment. It did make me speculate, however, that perhaps there might be two sides to the perpetual rows between her and everyone connected with the Abbey Theatre, from the directors to Willie and Frank Fay. I took Yeats's advice, and learned to be grateful for it.*

My first task was to gather a company together. Miss Horniman, after consultation with me, restricted the total sum for actors' salaries to a figure that would have precluded my engaging actors with established reputations, even if I had wished to have them, which I emphatically did not. Instead I sought a group of capable actors, skillful and dedicated to their art. In this search I had the advantage of having toured in several provincial companies myself, so I was able to choose on the basis of personal observation.

As a gesture, I wrote a short letter to the Manchester newspapers announcing our coming and explaining our purpose. I stated that we would "seek to produce good plays, to revive old masterpieces and to present translations of the best work of foreign authors." In a later letter, also published in the newspapers, I added that we would keep

*Yeats's advice was based on bitter experience that is described in some detail in Flannery's *Miss Annie F. Horniman and the Abbey Theatre.*

"an especially widely open door to present-day British writers, who will not now need to sigh in vain for a hearing, provided only that they have something to say worth listening to, and say it in an interesting and original manner." Such was the simplicity and ardor of my youth.

Before our opening we held a public meeting in the theatre, under the auspices of the recently formed Manchester Playgoers' Club. The actors I had engaged sat on the stage with Miss Horniman, who was placed in the center on a stately chair. She was dressed, according to her custom on formal occasions, in a richer than usual costume of original design suggestive, as I have said, of medieval attire. For this important event its material was gold brocade, and she wore—I saw it for the first time—her famous opal-studded dragon, at least five inches across, which hung like an insignia on her bosom.

Standing by her, I again expressed the principles that I had enumerated in my letters to the press, adding explanatory riders and elaborating upon what we meant by repertory. We should not be able, I explained, to change the bill nightly, but I pointed out that the dictionary meaning of the word repertory is that it is a storehouse, and that by acquiring a store of good plays, carefully rehearsed, we should be able to make frequent revivals, thereby avoiding—what I particularly condemned—the evil of presenting the public with productions inadequately prepared.

While I worked under Miss Horniman's banners these principles were upheld. Indeed I believe they were, for the most part, as long as she maintained her company. I found it ironic, therefore, on my return to England many years later after a long absence, to be told by a friend from Manchester days that, though the name of repertory was now widespread, these companies survived by running along diametrically opposite lines from those we had originally fought for. The "reps," as they were called, put on plays whose only criterion was success at the box office, they produced them with no more than a week's rehearsal, and they hardly ever attempted an original play. But that was many years ago. It is pleasant to note that there has been a turn for the better in some, at least, of the provincial repertory theatres in Great Britain.

Little need be said about the six weeks at the Midland Theatre. We were fortunate in my choice for the opening play, *David Ballard*, because the author, Charles McEvoy, effectively struck what was then a new note in the theatre—the realistic depiction of life in an average lower-middle-class family. I had seen the play with Yeats at its only previous performance, a matinee given by the Stage Society. He was as enthusiastic about it as I was. I felt that it would be particularly suitable for our opening play, mainly because it fulfilled our demands for sincerity and simplicity in realistic modern drama, but also because the parts were particularly well fitted to the actors I was in the process of engaging. The production fulfilled my hopes. It gave us an auspicious start, and the play was revived several times in our repertory after we moved to our permanent home in the Gaiety Theatre.

Next on the list I chose—wisely, as it turned out—a play that was in complete contrast to the opener. We went from realism to fantasy with George Fleming's translation of Rostand's *Les Romanesques*, in which I had played with Madge McIntosh. Visually, I produced it in a style suitable to the author's own description of his play as "a Watteau picture not by Watteau quite." It received much favorable comment.

Then came Bernard Shaw's *Widowers' Houses*. I had regarded a GBS play as essential to our project, so it was a disappointment when he told me that all his plays were reserved for Granville Barker and the Royal Court Theatre. I asked if the ban included *Widowers' Houses*, his first play. He flatly said that the play was "no good." When I boldly told him that I disagreed with him, he replied merely, "A fool must pay dearly for his folly." So I went ahead. My persistence was most fortunate, as it turned out. The play was not only the outstanding success of the season at the Midland, but we revived it at almost regular intervals at the Gaiety for fully three years.*

Widowers' Houses was followed by a modern light comedy called *Clothes and the Woman*. This, I have to confess, was a slight—a very slight—concession to box-office considerations. I made it with many qualms, and subsequently resolved never again to compromise for financial reasons in the least degree. However, there was some satisfaction in the curtain raiser. I chose not to repeat but to build upon my production at the Abbey Theatre of Maeterlinck's *Interior*. This was a new and exciting experience, for the actors were much more responsive than those in Dublin, and it gave me a new understanding of the value of stage direction. Before this, I had had only fleeting moments of satisfaction when here and there a play, or more often a part of a play, seemed to come to life under my direction. For the first time I was conscious of an almost

*Payne played the role of Lickcheese, a cringing little man who turns aggressive with a change of luck. In *The Derwent Story* (1953) Clarence Derwent, who acted for two years with the Gaiety company and went on to a distinguished career in the United States, recalls the performance thus: "B. Iden Payne would probably be the first to deny any claim to being a great actor but his Lickcheese in *Widowers' Houses* remains in my memory as a masterpiece of ironic comedy." Shaw, unfortunately, did not share Derwent's enthusiasm.

mystical sense that there was a relationship, in a creative harmony throughout the performance, among all the elements involved, including even the absent author. I became aware that there was more in the direction of a play than I had ever dreamed.

The last play at the Midland was *The Street*, which had been recently written by Miss A. L. Williams. Though it had little importance artistically, it again contrasted well with its predecessors in the repertoire, for it was a grimly realistic picture of contemporary life.

The season had been well received by the press. The response of the public, as indicated by the box-office receipts, was somewhat less enthusiastic. In spite of this fact Miss Horniman was so pleased that she astounded everybody by buying the Gaiety Theatre. As I mentioned earlier, this was one of the principal theatres in Manchester. By this gesture, Miss Horniman wrote a page in English theatrical history. In practically all accounts of dramatic activity in Great Britain in the early part of this century, Miss Horniman's tenure at the Gaiety is referred to as a notable, and even a revolutionary, event.

CHAPTER 11

*A*s a building, the Gaiety Theatre was not exactly run-down, but it had certainly been neglected. Moreover, the auditorium was old-fashioned in construction. The dress circle, the upper circle, and the gallery were supported by cast iron columns that obstructed the view of the stage for people sitting behind them. After much debate, Miss Horniman decided that she would have the whole auditorium gutted and rebuilt on modern lines with cantilevers to replace the columns.

Miss Horniman was divided in her mind as to whether it would be best to ask me to disband the company until after the reconstruction or to let me take it on tour. Happily, it was agreed that, after a short tour during which the old theatre would have a thorough cleaning, there would be time for a six-week season there. Then I could resume touring while, under her supervision, the reconstruction was carried out. Since my main desire was to keep the company as nearly intact as possible, I was delighted with this arrangement.

For the first play to be put on at the Gaiety, I felt I must find something that would stamp upon the minds of Manchester playgoers once and for all that we were ready to experiment in any direction, provided it fell legitimately within the range of true dramatic art. I wanted to return to Shakespearean work, but, having now a greater sense of responsibility, I did not feel ready to undertake it myself. However, I had vaguely heard about William Poel's productions of Shakespeare on Elizabethan lines, and it occurred to me that these must represent a combination of both Shakespeare and experiment. So I began to wonder whether I might induce Poel to come to Manchester and produce a play for us. At the time I had no idea how close this dubious venture might come to the way I would spend much of my own life.

When I mentioned my notion to Miss Horniman, she was taken aback. She said that Poel was regarded as a crank, and crankiness was something she could never abide. But on entering into a formal contract with Miss Horniman I had not forgotten Yeats's injunction. I had stipulated that, besides having the right to select the actors, I was to have full liberty in determining the productions. She had agreed to this with the one proviso: she should be at liberty to exercise a veto on any play of which she disapproved. Shakespeare, of course, she could not object to. Indeed, she had publicly stated more than once that she hoped the time would come when Shakespeare would be given in her theatre. So here, this early in our association, her rectitude in adhering faithfully to whatever she had agreed upon showed itself. She reminded herself of our agreement, and that settled the question.

Accordingly, I found out Poel's address and wrote to him, explaining in general terms what I had in mind. This led to my having an appointment to visit him at his house in London. There I made the acquaintance of one of the most remarkable men I have ever met.

William Poel was responsible, insofar as any individual can be said to be responsible, for the return to the theatre of Shakespeare undefiled. Although a movement in that direction had already manifested itself, it was Poel who influenced it most deeply. He was the first to rebel against slavish dependence upon representational scenery in Shakespearean production, and he saw the need of returning to the original text and making it the point of departure. Soon he went further and maintained that it was only in something approximating the physical conditions of the Elizabethan theatre that a Shakespearean play could be restored to full and free expression. Fired by his desire to reintroduce these conditions, he formed the Elizabethan Stage Society in 1895. The society's performances, all directed by Poel, had little or no immediate impact upon the professional theatre, but what might be called his indirect influence cannot be overestimated. Granville Barker, the most potent force in clearing away the rubbish that encumbered Shakespearean production, acted with Poel and may be called his disciple. No doubt Poel's eccentricities, to which I shall refer later, handicapped critical acceptance of his productions. But Poel's devotion to the artistic principles in which he believed was fully recognized by everyone with whom he came into contact. As time went on, his method of putting them into practice became perverse and even absurd. Even so, no one could fail to realize that his purposes were inspired by sound aesthetic intuitions.

Poel was an idealist and quite indifferent to worldly success. He ignored criticism completely, whatever its source. If it was pointed out that something he proposed was ridiculous, he simply brushed the objection aside as irrelevant. To him it was the right way, and that settled the subject. He could never realize that there were people in the world who were less immersed in Shakespeare than he. I once found him standing with our friend Edward Garnett, the writer, on the little paved island in the middle of Picadilly Circus in London, while taxicabs and buses whirled around us in an unceasing stream. Of all this turmoil Poel was unconscious. He was totally involved in a discussion of *Hamlet* and wanted to refer to the text. He turned to me and, as another man might ask for a cigarette, said, "You don't happen to have a copy of *Hamlet* in your pocket, do you?"

But most of these characteristics I was to learn later. I must first give an account of my meeting with Poel on the Sunday when I traveled up to London. When I knocked at the door of his house in Chelsea, Mr. Poel himself opened it for me. He showed me into a rather dark and gloomy sitting room and we sat down together. I was deeply impressed by his appearance and manner. There seemed to be an aura of remoteness about him. His face was reminiscent of pictures of austere medieval saints.

My letter had merely mentioned a Shakespearean production for Miss Horniman. When I told him that it was intended for performance by her own company, he shook his head gravely. He had thought he was to choose his own actors. He said that my actors, being experienced professionals, would be too set in their ways to "take the tones." When I asked what this unfamiliar phrase meant, he explained that Shakespearean verse had to be spoken in his productions with what he called "tones" (and sometimes "tunes"), which he alone could give. He asked me to run over the names of my actors. After I had done so, one by one, he admitted that it was an advantage that none of them had big reputations. This, he thought, might make them more amenable to taking the tones. Finally I got to the last and, I thought, the least important, name on my list. This actor had then played only comparatively small parts with me; indeed, I had even been accused of hiring him because he was a good mimic who amused me with his imitations! Mr. Poel brightened considerably. "Oh, is Edward Landor in the company?" he exclaimed. "That makes a difference. He played the Duke in *The Merchant of Venice* for me. He can take the tones!"

Mr. Poel looked pleased when I told him that, if he would put on a Shakespearean play for us, I should want it to be not one of the more popular plays in the canon but one that was rarely seen. At last he consented not only to produce *Measure for Measure* but to undertake the key role of Angelo himself. I went away elated—especially since he had suggested that I play the richly rewarding part of the rapscallion Lucio. As a matter of fact, my greatest satisfaction in joining Miss Horniman in her enterprise had been that it enabled me to continue acting, which in my heart I still regarded (and shall probably always regard) as my true function in the theatre.

On the next day Poel traveled with me to the town where we were to play that week in order that he might see the company at work. He expressed unexpected pleasure at the high quality of the acting as a whole, but for the cast of *Measure for Measure* he wanted Sara Allgood as Isabella and James Hearne as the Duke. He assumed—and surprisingly enough his assumptions proved to be justified—that they would both be willing to join the company for a special engagement.* Before returning to London, Mr. Poel made arrangements with me for rehearsals, some of which had to be conducted on tour. He also agreed that we should rent the Elizabethan Stage Society's scenery and costumes for the production. It was fortunate for the venture that they were available, and I was happy in the knowledge that everything was in trim for our opening at the Gaiety Theatre on Easter Monday.

Though nothing definite was said to me directly, I could sense that the company had not been altogether happy about my engaging Mr. Poel for the production. This feeling became quite apparent when he joined us for the rehearsals. Eventually I was confidentially informed that it was his reputation for eccentricity that worried the members. The rehearsals were preceded, at Poel's request, by his reading of the play to us. Mr. Poel's unusual delivery of lines, which I shall try to describe later, made the cast exchange sly, and even overt, smiles.

We sat around a long table with pencils in hand, so that we could conveniently enter in our own scripts the cuts that Mr. Poel made in the text. The omissions consisted mainly of the numerous "improprieties" in the dialogue. This was not, as Mr. Robert Speaight states in his biography of Poel, a "surrender" to the puritanism of audiences. It must be remembered that William Poel was himself born in the middle of the nineteenth century. He genuinely regarded much Elizabethan frankness as quite unspeakable to a contemporary audience.

*In *William Poel and the Elizabethan Revival* Robert Speaight fills out the story of Poel's casting. "Poel at first tried Lewis Casson in the part of the Duke, but after three weeks' rehearsal decided that he was not sprightly enough and cast him for the Provost instead. The Duke was eventually played by James Hearne, who gave a fine performance but was not too adaptable at "taking the tones. . . . Although Sybil Thorndike was a member of the company, Poel would not accept her as Isabella." Casson later followed Payne as director at the Gaiety and went on to a distinguished career, as did Miss Thorndike, who soon became Casson's wife. Dame Sybil was one of the few actors or actresses who ultimately matched Payne's record for longevity in the theatre.

Most of the cuts were only to be expected. But I confess that I was astonished, as I am even more in retrospect, at the lengths to which Poel's puritanism carried him. He made not only omissions but alterations in the text. For instance, he changed "He hath got his friend with child"—words I had to speak as Lucio—into the flat and almost meaningless "He will shortly be a father."

I must now, to the best of my ability, explain what Mr. Poel meant by "the tones." The essence of it was that he sought to bring out Shakespeare's meaning by emphasizing the key words in every sentence. To my mind the basic idea was sound, and I ultimately found it of great service to myself. But the overdevelopment of its expression by Poel led to a most extraordinary delivery. Fortunately, the actors in Miss Horniman's company, even those who tried the hardest, did not succeed in fully effecting what he asked for.

It is far from easy to convey the full eccentricity of Mr. Poel's notion of "tones." Let me offer an example. The text at the beginning of *Measure for Measure* gives these lines to the Duke:

> Of government the properties to unfold
> Would seem in me t'affect speech and discourse,
> Since I am put to know that your own science
> Exceeds, in that, the lists of all advice
> My strength can give you.

The Poel rendering was to speak all the unaccented words with great rapidity and staccato and to draw out the stressed words in slow emphasis, with heavy inflection and with punctuation ignored:

> Of government the properties to unfold
> Would seem in me t' A-F-F-E-C-T speech and discourse,
> Since I am put to know that your O-W-N science
> Exceeds in that the lists of all advice
> MY strength can give you.

The reception by the actors of the instructions in the tones varied a great deal according to their individual characters. Some did their best—fortunately with little success—to imitate Mr. Poel. Others listened and pretended to imitate but deliberately went their own way when it came to performance, about which he said nothing. But no one at any time ventured to contradict Mr. Poel. It was soon apparent that one might as well conduct an argument with a stone wall. Happily for myself in the role of Lucio, Mr. Poel did not seem to think that the tones applied to comedy parts. Neither I nor Charles Bibby, who gave a delightful performance of Pompey, was ever called upon to rehearse the tones. Why we were spared remains a puzzle to me to this day.

I cannot mention Charles Bibby without digressing for a moment. We all know that an actor, like a poet, is born and not made. But with most actors, no matter how strong their native gift, there is generally a good deal of work to be done on every part they play. Charles Bibby was unique in my experience in his capacity for intuitively grasping a character in a flash and, without effort and apparently with instinct free from thought, creating *instantaneously* a finished picture of what he had to represent. This remarkable gift made him the finest character actor I have ever known. By "character actor" I mean not merely an experienced trouper who can routinely take on a variety of roles but an actor who can truthfully and convincingly breathe life into many and widely differing characters.

The great nineteenth-century actor Macready asserted that Edmund Kean was the only actor he knew who could clutch a character without studying it. I could use the same words about Charles Bibby. It was almost uncanny. It was my custom at the Gaiety to read a new play to the company at the first rehearsal. During the reading it was equally customary for Bibby to fall asleep. At the end of the reading the stir of moving chairs would waken him and he would come to me at the prompt table. Holding out the typed part he would ask, "What sort of a bloke is this?" I would describe the character to him. As I was doing so a point would come when his face would suddenly light up. He would interrupt me sharply by saying, "I get you!" From that moment instinct seemed to take over, and every gesture, even intonation, was perfectly in character.

Incredible as it may seem, Bibby did not always have to know the meaning of the words he had to speak. At the first performance of *Widowers' Houses*, in which he gave a perfect rendering of Cokane, I could see him, as it were, rear internally like a frightened horse when the audience laughed at a point he had made. But the laughs arose from his perfect characterization, and he received the same responses from every audience.* In this play Bibby had to answer the remark "A man must

*Shaw saw a Gaiety production of his play in June 1909. He considered Bibby badly miscast in this role and disliked his performance almost as much as Payne's own, though he recognized that Bibby was a good actor. Shaw's letter to Payne was uncomplimentary. Miss Limerick replied in intemperate terms, but it is not known whether she sent the letter. All that remains is a rough draft scribbled on the back of Shaw's letter. (Both letters are published in *The University of Buffalo Studies* for September 1939, edited by Julian Park.) Since Payne continued to produce Shaw's plays, Shaw evidently changed his mind about the quality of Gaiety productions.

live" with Voltaire's quip *"Je n'en vois pas la necessité."* Not knowing French, he learned to pronounce the words laboriously and with much stumbling. But when he came to speak them, his shrug of the shoulders and perfect intonation always assured a hearty laugh. A year later we were rehearsing the play for a revival. Again Bibby stumbled. "Oh, Charlie," said I, "haven't you got that yet?" "Well," he retorted with a note of irritation, "what does the confounded thing mean anyway?"

In addition to a unique natural talent and extraordinary versatility, Bibby had a pleasing personality. His death in action during the First World War was a serious loss to the theatre.

To return to *Measure for Measure*, the scenery and costumes arrived in due course for the first dress rehearsal. Poel supervised the building of an Elizabethan-style stage at the Gaiety Theatre. Since there was no space for a forestage, one had to be erected inside the proscenium. The set seemed small and rather dingy. Up until this time I had known nothing whatever about the construction of Elizabethan theatres. I found this one interesting, with its two inner stages, one above the other, and the projecting penthouse roof supported by the columns. But I took it for granted that Poel's reproduction of Elizabethan performances was no more than a passing curiosity, amusing to act in, but not of any particular, and certainly of no permanent, importance.

What I wholeheartedly admired were the costumes, to which Poel had always, as I learned, paid particular attention. He felt that, in Elizabethan plays, clothes should be both accurate historically and constructed as if for present-day use. He took the unprecedented step of ignoring theatrical costumers. Instead he found a regular tailor who was willing to cut out and make men's clothes to Poel's specifications as if they were up-to-date suits. In the same way, for the women's clothes he sought out a dressmaker who was glad to reproduce accurately the pictures he provided.

Poel was the proud possessor of one genuine Elizabethan belt. He regarded it as a great honor for any actor to be allowed to wear "the belt," as he always spoke of it. Edward Landor had had the privilege when he played the Duke of Venice in Poel's production of *The Merchant of Venice*, but he had hated it because it was too small and had hurt him. Fearing that he would be chosen again, he bribed the wardrobe master to hide the belt in a basket of clothes that had been rejected for our production. When it was found to be missing there was a great hullabaloo. The search lasted more than half the night before the treasure was recovered. Landor need not have worried; the belt was given to another actor.

Difficulty arose concerning the printing of the program. At Elizabethan Stage Society performances only a list of actors' names appeared, with no indication of the parts they acted. Mr. Poel wanted the same scheme to be followed, but, after much argument, he agreed to have the names of characters and actors defined. By an odd compromise, however, the list had to be headed "The Names of Some of the Actors," so that the part of Angelo and his own name could be omitted.

There was more trouble when plans were made for photographs to be taken at the dress rehearsal. This could not be allowed! Poel's contention was that Ben Greet would see the photographs and "steal" his production of *Measure for Measure* just as, so he maintained, Greet had previously stolen his production of *Everyman*. I assured him that he need have no fear, since Greet was touring with a Shakespearean repertoire in colleges in America. But Poel was adamant; he was certain that, if any photographs existed, Greet was quite capable of sending spies to Manchester to procure copies of them.

To the surprise of many of our actors, Poel's *Measure for Measure* was warmly received by the press, and to a lesser extent by the public.* C. E. Montague, of the *Manchester Guardian*, wrote appreciatively and knowledgeably about the Elizabethan setting. More surprisingly, he admired Poel's acting as Angelo. This was a relief to me, for I knew that there was a general feeling that Poel's genius lay in other areas than his acting. In spite of this reservation, Poel's Elizabethan productions had usually attracted widespread interest in the press, if not in the general public. We saw a striking proof of this interest when the Birmingham *Post* took the unusual step of sending its drama critic to Manchester for our production. His reaction was a fairly usual one, however. After expressing pleasure at the chance "to see so novel a presentation," he felt it necessary to add that "it had the interest of the museum rather than the living stage."

Most of our actors were blunter in their comments: "freakish" was the adjective they most commonly used for Poel's approach. I would not have gone so far, but at the time I certainly tended to agree with the Birmingham critic's appraisal. I was delighted, of course, that our first production at the Gaiety had attracted such generally favorable attention. But I could not have guessed at the time that much of my life, like Poel's, would eventually be dedicated to an effort to revitalize Shake-

*One reason for Poel's success in Manchester is suggested by Speaight: "Iden Payne was [Miss Horniman's] stage director and she had gathered round her a group of actors, many of whom were to become famous in the English theatre. It was probably the best team that Poel ever had to work with."

spearean production by approximating the conditions under which the plays were first seen. I am afraid that, at the time, a line from the Manchester *Courier* gave me the keenest satisfaction. Speaking of my role of Lucio, the critic called him "a roistering, swashbuckling free-liver, with a cock of the hat and a swirl of the mustache. In his voice there were late nights and amorous adventures."

At about this time Miss Horniman took a suite of furnished rooms in Manchester and began to spend a good deal of her time there. With her unusual personality, her rather eccentric dress, and the strikingly authoritative manner in which she spoke in public, it is not surprising that she soon became a prominent figure in the city. This I could understand, but, because I was very young for such a responsible position and had no knowledge of life beyond the limited experiences of a touring actor, I could not help resenting the way in which she received all the credit for our artistic activities, although she had no share whatever in them. That the whole enterprise would have had no existence without her financial support seemed to me in my ignorance to be of little importance.

Later I came to realize how very fortunate I was. I have said that, following Yeats's advice, I had insisted on a contract with Miss Horniman that gave me an almost completely free hand in the choice of actors and the selection of plays as well as in their method of production. It did not take long to discover how sound Yeats's advice had been. Miss Horniman often attributed her strong principles to her Scotch Presbyterian ancestry. No doubt these principles lent the authority that could make even her most commonplace remark seem impressive—an effect heightened by those medievally inspired costumes of brocaded silk. At first encounter I had felt almost that I was in the presence of a prophetess. It was disconcerting, then, to find, as I soon did, that there was simply no common ground on which we could discuss the artistic aspects of the work in which, ostensibly, we were both engaged.

I do not mean for a moment to belittle Miss Horniman's principles, for which I had many reasons to be grateful. She adhered scrupulously, in spirit as well as letter, to every detail of any contract she made. She had a remarkably tidy mind, in which all things were strictly regimented in their proper departments. When our theatre's financial auditor ventured to criticize our plays as not popular enough, she consigned him to his pigeonhole in a sharp letter. His function, she pointed out, was pounds, shillings, and pence; Mr. Payne's province was plays.

Miss Horniman never made so much as a suggestion regarding the life beyond the curtain. Our contract stipulated that she retained the right of veto over my choice of plays, so I regularly sent her all scripts before starting production. They were invariably returned without comment. When curiosity made me ask her opinion, she replied merely that she saw no reason for a veto.

After we had had a brief preliminary season at the Gaiety the theatre was refurbished as planned and reopened in September. The prevailing tone of the interior was white, with none of the gilded embellishments that were then considered a necessary feature of theatre decor. This innovation caused widespread comment, which was generally favorable. But we were more concerned, of course, with public reaction to the often unfamiliar activities onstage.

We did not leave this reaction entirely to chance. On Sunday nights I gave lectures in the many towns surrounding Manchester, spreading the gospel of repertory. This form of propaganda soon led to another, making what we called "flying matinees" in towns where I had lectured. Railway service was adequate and by leaving early in the morning we were able to return to the Gaiety in time for the evening performance. These incursions showed little consideration for the touring companies occupying the local theatres at night. We learned that they would have prevented them if their contracts with the theatre managers had given them legal power to do so. They must have been furiously jealous of the packed houses we attracted.

Great curiosity had been aroused everywhere with a wide orbit around Manchester. Only in one town, Oldham, though it had a fine new theatre, was there a meager audience. I asked the theatre carpenter if he could account for it. His answer, typically Lancashire in broad dialect, was, "It's only to be expected in Oudam. You wouldn't get folk to come to a theayter if you was to give 'em the Crucifixion with the original cast!"

No sooner was our autumn season in full swing than we had to give attention to a special problem, the choice of a play for the Christmas season. As it turned out, this choice had much to do with my development as a director. Christmas was not far away. At all the principal theatres throughout Great Britain the season was, as I have said, celebrated with a "pantomime." We had somehow to compete at the Gaiety Theatre with the enormously popular pantomimes at the Theatre Royal and the Princess Theatre. The Gaiety, too, until Miss Horniman bought it, had been an annual home of pantomime.

We first thought of giving a Shakespeare comedy but dismissed it as following too closely upon *Measure for Measure*. Obviously we had to find something picturesque and rich in comedy yet consonant with our purposes. I asked myself whether one of Shakespeare's contemporaries might not have written something that would meet our requirements. Beaumont and Fletcher's *The Knight of the Burning Pestle* had recently been revived in London. Reading it convinced me that even though the type of drama it satirized no longer existed, its burlesque treatment of its own period might make it the medium of jollity and light-hearted fun for the kind of audience we were trying to develop. I decided I would try it and was delighted to find that, from the first rehearsal, the actors entered with gusto into the spirit of the play.

We tried to give audiences a key to what we were driving at by announcing the production as "A Pantomine of Three Hundred Years Ago." When people entered the auditorium they found four or five gentlemen in Elizabethan dress wandering about the theatre. They occasionally talked to each other or joined in conversation with members of the audience. Some Elizabethan girls soon appeared carrying baskets of realistically constructed oranges. These were made with a withdrawable plug at the bottom and were filled with chocolates. The girls offered the oranges for sale among the audience and made a brisk trade of it. After a time the Elizabethan gentlemen ascended steps to sit on stools at each side of the stage, apparently paying extra for the privilege to attendants posted there. Then a boy came out from between the curtains with a long taper and clay pipes filled with tobacco. These he sold to the gentlemen on the stools. This attempt at an atmospheric setting worked wonders in creating the right mood of expectation for what was to follow.

The performance then swung along vigorously. To the surprise of a good many people, *The Knight of the Burning Pestle* turned out to be extremely popular. It is true that, especially at the beginning of the run, occasional protests were made by persons who had come into the theatre expecting a conventional pantomime. Sometimes a disgruntled customer asked for the manager. Mr. Heys, a dour Lancastrian with a keen sense of humor, gave them an explanation in such a way that they went back to their seats and were satisfied with the rest of the performance. Summing up, it may be said that this venture was a real triumph. One Manchester newspaper maintained that it was probably the only production of a non-Shakespearean Elizabethan play that could be regarded as a popular success since the Restoration period.

The play was fun for the actors as well as the audience, but it roused suspicion in one quarter. Our legal auditors, ever alert in attending to their business, had once had occasion to reprove me when I had been slack in letting them know the royalties agreed upon for one of our modern plays. Now they wrote me a sharp letter demanding "the present address of Messrs. Beaumont and Fletcher" and requesting information without delay about the arrangements made with them for the payment of royalties on *The Knight of the Burning Pestle.*

The play begins with the entrance of a Prologue, whose speech is soon interrupted from the audience by a Citizen, his Wife, and their Apprentice. In our production the actors in these parts walked down one of the aisles shortly before curtain time and took seats in the front row of the orchestra stalls. These intruders soon forced themselves onto the stage. The preliminaries had so well led the audience into the spirit of the play that nearby spectators frequently helped the Citizen's stout Wife to ascend the steps.

I engaged a group of dancers who specialized in English folk dances, including a Morris. Interest in these traditional dances was just beginning to be the vogue, and they were enthusiastically received. The renowned composer Granville Bantock collected the original tunes for the snatches sung by Merrythought or, where these had been lost, wrote airs in a similar style. But of all the music what delighted me most was his composition for the final chorus sung by the entire company, beginning "Better music ne'er was known, than a choir of hearts in one." It gave an appropriate finale to a production that was one of the most successful we were ever to give.

I have dwelt upon *The Knight of the Burning Pestle* because I can now see that my personal response to its hearty and unfettered vigor was an early hint that as time went on I was to become more and more interested in directing plays of an early period of our rich theatrical tradition. A year later I derived much satisfaction from producing Ben Jonson's *Every Man in his Humour.* For this play I was able to cast my former manager, Ian Maclaren, as the braggart soldier Captain Bobadil. Maclaren became a regular member of the company.

But I wrote earlier that one of my reasons for so readily deserting my acting career to direct for Miss Horniman was my desire to gain experience with the New Drama. In fact, modern plays constituted a large part of our repertoire at the Gaiety. These included works by Shaw, Galsworthy, Bennett, and Masefield, and some local playwrights whom I will mention in a moment. I was deeply impressed by the humanity of John Galsworthy's social plays, *The Silver Box, Strife,* and *Justice,* all of which I admired unreservedly.*

*In *Miss Horniman and the Gaiety Theatre, Manchester,* Rex Pogson reports that *The Silver Box* "was revived time after time at popular request." It was not only Galsworthy's

The reaction against realism in the theatre has resulted in the neglect of Galsworthy's plays. This is unfortunate, and it seems to me that the time has come for their revival—not in the commercial theatre probably, but certainly in colleges and universities. The social conditions with which they deal are lost in the limbo of the past, but the human relationships involved have the quality of universality that actors would respond to and that educationally slanted audiences would probably appreciate.

Galsworthy had a reserve of manner that reminded me of Synge. But with Synge I never seemed to penetrate the mask, whereas with Galsworthy I soon became aware of a great warmth of heart under the austere exterior. It expressed itself in generous actions, one of which deserves to be recounted. The last act of *The Silver Box* consists of a trial scene in a small police court. The set called for a boxed-in space reserved for onlookers, such as is found in all English courts of law. Normally we should have filled this space by engaging regular supernumeraries, but the police court in *The Silver Box* is supposed to be in a poverty-stricken neighborhood. Therefore I readily agreed to my stage manager's suggestion that instead he gather together a dozen unemployed men. There were many to be found at that time wandering the streets of Manchester, for the cotton-spinning trade was temporarily in the doldrums. He did so and a miserable lot they looked. At the dress rehearsal, Galsworthy was so impressed by the suitability of their appearance that he asked me where I had found our "extras." When I explained, he made no comment—indeed he showed no interest whatever. But the next day, before leaving Manchester, he shyly handed me a ten-pound note, asking me to distribute the money among them in addition to what the theatre paid. He stipulated, however, that I was to keep its source a secret even from the recipients.

Among the authors of note produced at the Gaiety, Arnold Bennett is remembered now mainly as a novelist. At that time he had a reputation as a playwright also. His *Cupid and Common Sense*, though laid, like his best novels, in the Five Towns, depicted characters so similar to our Lancastrian audiences that the play struck home. Another play of his, *What the Public Wants*, obviously satirized a well-known press magnate

---

concern with social problems to which Manchester was responding. "Payne approached even the most naturalistic play in an imaginative way. He was always probing for the imaginative and emotional essence inside the photograph and if it [was] there . . . he brought it out. . . . The acting had that perfect balance of ensemble which nevertheless gave ample scope for individuality, and formed the most striking attribute of the Gaiety company at its best."

96

and made a definite impact. A second now-neglected dramatist of that period whose plays were rewarding to produce was St. John Hankin. His very individual style of ironic high comedy is unique and his polished dialogue has an almost Congrevean quality. Though he was never a box office draw he deservedly had many admirers.

In my preliminary announcement of the opening of our company I had expressed the hope that the presence of a repertory theatre would stimulate local authors to write plays. That hope was fulfilled. Enough Lancashire playwrights responded and had their plays performed at the Gaiety that they came to be frequently referred to as the Manchester School. Their best work always dealt with Lancashire life, with its rough exterior, its aggressiveness, and its underlying kindness of heart. Harold Brighouse is perhaps the most important of these playwrights, since his *Hobson's Choice* is still very much alive. He was a prolific playwright, especially of one-act plays. Then there was Stanley Houghton, whose early death was a loss to the British drama. During my years at the Gaiety Houghton supplied us not only with one of our most popular curtain raisers, *The Dear Departed*, but with two full-length realistic comedies, *Independent Means* and *The Younger Generation*. All these plays are rich in well-observed characterizations conveyed in lively dialogue.

No English play for several years stirred up as much controversy as Houghton's *Hindle Wakes*. This domestic comedy was regarded by many as positively scandalous. It was preached against in pulpits and elicited a flood of letters to the newspapers, most of them angry in tone. The plot concerns a Lancashire mill girl who has spent a weekend with her employer's son. This escapade is unexpectedly discovered, to the consternation of both families. It is agreed by the parents of the delinquents that the only course, in spite of the social disparity of the families, is for them to marry. This solution is proposed without consulting the girl, and, to the parents' horror, she refuses to accept it. To her the weekend was no more than a lark. When she declares that she will never marry anyone except a man of her own choice, the fat is in the fire. She fights her battle for independence and the play ends with her triumph. The outcry of indignation resembled that created by Ibsen's Nora in *A Doll's House*, though of course on a far lesser scale.

The controversy over the Ibsen play was still raging at that time. In fact, I was to encounter it later yet, during my first visit to Chicago. Over thirty years had passed since *A Doll's House* had received its first performance in English—oddly enough, in Milwaukee, not far away. However, I mentioned neither the play nor its author in a talk I gave one afternoon in 1913 before a Chicago women's club. Afterward I was drinking tea, balancing cup and cake as well as I could while crushed into a corner by a phalanx of ladies three or four deep. Suddenly one woman at the back of this solid mass rose on tiptoe and, pitching her voice above the babble, literally shouted, "Mr. Payne, ought Nora to have left her husband?"

I knew at once whom she meant. What is more, so did all the ladies present. I murmured a bland reply and took refuge in my tea. But sometime later, after I had contrived to slip away, the debate was still waxing hot and strong.

At the end of our first year at the Gaiety we were not paying our way. Remembering Yeats's contention that the Irish players needed London criticism to set a seal upon their work, I wondered whether the same thing might not apply to us. When I mentioned this to Miss Horniman she was overjoyed at the prospect of taking her company to London for a brief season. In any case it would be necessary to close the Gaiety for the summer, for there would be little theatre-going public in Manchester at that time of year. Why not go to London then? Inquiry showed that, because it was the height of the London season, no centrally situated theatre was available. But Miss Horniman was able to rent the Coronet Theatre in Notting Hill, which was then described as being in the West End geographically but not theatrically. It served our purpose admirably.

Our three weeks of repertory caused a stir in London far beyond our expectations. The newspapers, while differing in their evaluation of the plays, were united in their commendation of the high quality of the acting, especially of the way the actors worked together. The general attitude of the press is well conveyed in the title of a special article by E. A. Baughan, the critic of the *Daily News*, headed "The Value of Ensemble." Baughan not only stressed the "ease and naturalness of the acting" but attacked the prevailing dominance of the actor-managers in the regular theatre.* Indeed, general press comment about the

---

*Baughan attacked "the patent absurdities" of the star system, which had "produced a style of playing in which there is very little sense of character. . . . The truth is that our particular type of star actor has been the ruin of our drama." He was obviously delighted that the Gaiety company had so clearly demonstrated the superiority of the repertory system. "I was astonished by the ease and naturalness of the acting. Each member of the company was playing his or her part entirely from the point of view of its character and its place in the scheme of the drama." Boyle Lawrence of the *Evening Standard* was equally impressed with the company's acting. "It was first remarkable for its balance and symmetry, its appreciation of the author's meaning, and then for one or two individual performances of brilliancy." Comparing the troupe's versatility with the typecasting practiced in most companies he exclaimed: "Go to the Coronet and see the company turn itself inside out from night to night so that you don't know "freshness and vitality" of repertory acting was talked about everywhere in theatrical circles. Looking back on this visit to the Coronet in 1909 and another a year later, and bearing in mind all that I have read and been told about Miss Horniman's Gaiety venture after my withdrawal from it, I believe that those first two occupancies of the Coronet Theatre constituted the high-water mark of the company's reputation.

Be that as it may, there can be no question about the high spirits with which the company resumed work at the Gaiety when we reconvened in July, nor about the enthusiasm of the audiences during the following season. Soon after it began something very unusual happened. We were plunged unexpectedly into a campaign, of which Bernard Shaw was a leader, against the official theatrical censorship. It must be explained that before a new play was produced in Britain the manager of the theatre where it was to be performed had to submit the manuscript to the Lord Chamberlain's office. There it had to be passed by an official Examiner of Plays, who, having approved it, informed the Lord Chamberlain. The Lord Chamberlain then issued a license to the theatre manager. Once the license was procured the play could be performed anywhere. This was an anomalous institution, for it had been founded in the eighteenth century merely as a piece of political chicanery to prevent the production of plays that attacked the party then in office.

In practice, the twentieth-century Examiner of Plays observed certain taboos, among which was the utterance on stage of disparaging references to living statesmen. Bernard Shaw had just written a topical satirical farce called *Press Cuttings*. Because of two of its characters it came under the official ban. One of them, called Mitchener, was depicted as the Minister of War, a post then held by Lord Kitchener. Another character, that of the Prime Minister, was named Balsquith, an obvious combination of Asquith, the current Prime Minister, with Balfour, the leader of the Opposition. The play had been submitted to the Lord Chamberlain by a manager in London and, only because of the two names, a license had been refused.

One absurdity of the censorship is that only a theatre, not an author, could submit a play for license. Shaw suggested that we resubmit his

---

which side they shine the most. . . . Is not this what the theatre should do?" William Archer, the leading critic of his day, agreed in the *Nation*. "I wish to express my deliberate opinion that this Manchester movement is the most important fact in our theatrical history since the opening of the Vedrenne-Barker campaign at the Court Theatre. . . . Judged by any standard whatsoever [the acting] was quite amazingly good. . . . The flexibility, the adaptability of the company was altogether admirable and the sense of living artistic endeavor gave excellence a new charm." All three critics are quoted by Pogson.

The company at the Gaiety Theatre, 1908. Back row: Lewis Casson, Edward Landor, Jules Shaw, Leonard Mudie, Edwin T. Heys, Basil Dean, Charles Bibby, Edward Broadley. Second row, seated: Joseph A. Keogh, Sybil Thorndike, Florence Darragh, B. Iden Payne, Penelope Wheeler, Ada King, Lilian Christine. In front: Enid Meek, Hilda Bruce Potter.

play for performance at the Gaiety with the offending names changed to the innocuous Johnson and Bones. The Lord Chamberlain was thus compelled to withdaw his objections. A license was issued to us and we put the play into immediate rehearsal, but the names Shaw substituted were kept secret until the last moment, even to the actors.

The banning of the play and the reason for it had been much publicized. Imagine, then, the reaction of the capacity audience at our first performance. In the crucial scene the Prime Minister forced his way into the War Office disguised as a militant suffragette—that being the only way in which he could safely leave Downing Street in those wild days of feminine violence. When he had removed his woman's attire, Bones exclaimed, "Great Heavens, Johnson!" When the innocuous name was heard there was a roar of laughter, followed by loud ironic applause, which was repeated when Johnson could be heard to answer "Yes, Bones."*

Among the other characters in *Press Cuttings* there is an amusing charwoman. As the play was a burlesque, I cast our best male comedian in the part. The reaction to this rather obvious device affords an instance of the change in viewpoint in half a century. The other members of the cast and the actor himself protested at the idea of a man's playing a woman's part. Forgetting that this had been universal practice in the greatest age of English drama, they alleged that it outraged decency. I pointed out that it was done in pantomimes, but they assured me that was different: pantomimes were not regarded as regular plays. There was a general feeling of relief in the company when my shocking innovation was accepted by the public.

From the beginning of our second season I had to give thought again to the question of what to do for Christmas. After some hesitation I decided that the time had come when I might venture to direct a Shakespeare production at the Gaiety. What play should I choose? I wanted to work on a play in which I had not performed myself, one on which I could exercise my own judgment and let my imagination run freely without being influenced by productions I had been concerned with. As a Christmas offering it obviously had to be a comedy. The farces were ruled out because I had played parts in them. The only comedy in the whole canon that I did not know was *Much Ado about Nothing*, so I read it eagerly. It was an exciting experience. Up to the unexpected turn of fortune that took me to Ireland I had been

*Shaw and Payne battled the Examiner of Plays not only over *Press Cuttings*, as described here, but also over *Mrs. Warren's Profession* and *The Shewing Up of Blanco Posnet*.

merely a touring actor who had played in Shakespeare with Benson. When called upon to direct the plays in Ian Maclaren's repertoire, I had handed on the traditions of the Benson company. Here was an opportunity to start from scratch with a play ideally suited to my purpose, with brilliant high comedy and the richest kind of low comedy. Even dances and a song had their allotted places.

Manchester was not well served at that time in the way of Shakespearean production. Shakespeare was known to the city in local productions only under the management of Mr. Richard Flanagan. He was the genial owner of the Queen's Theatre, the blood-tub. This custom was interrupted yearly at Christmastime by Mr. Flanagan himself, who put on what the more sophisticated called a "Shakespearean pantomime." These productions had to be seen to be believed. Mr. Flanagan, as a good professional, took care to engage actors of reputation for the leading parts and experienced actors throughout his casts. It was the scenery and costumes in which he was personally interested and to which he gave most attention. They were always rich in color and splendid in construction, but without any evidence of taste. The productions were invariably climaxed by one special set calling for elaborate scenery, in which he always tried to surpass himself. This was expected by the audience, and when the curtain rose on the climactic scene they knew their cue and applauded loudly. Thereupon Mr. Flanagan entered from the prompt corner in full evening dress but wearing his everyday brown bowler hat. This he removed and waved in acknowledgment, after which the play was allowed to proceed.*

Mr. Flanagan of course had to appeal to outside assistance for the arrangement of the texts of the plays. When he decided to produce *As You Like It* he commissioned a former actor, now turned journalist, with whom I later became acquainted. This competent editor told me how he made the conventional cuts, which included the omission, then customary, of the small part of the "hedge-priest," Sir Oliver Martext. He took his cut copy to Mr. Flanagan in his office. Mr. Flanagan put on his spectacles, sat down at his desk, and began his inspection by looking down the list of characters. On finding a line drawn through

*"Only a Hollywood publicity man could find adjectives adequately descriptive of a Flanagan production [of Shakespeare]," Pogson writes. He quotes from an article by F. Sladen-Smith in *Drama:* "Whenever anything could be real it was real, absolutely real. There were real deer, real horses, real goats, real waterfalls, real acrobats and at the least hint of a church or anything bordering on religion real incense and dozens of acolytes. . . . It was all as vigorous and fruity as it could well be, and whenever there was the faintest chance of our getting bored or unduly depressed we had a procession or a jolly dance or a troupe of acrobats or a flock of ghosts."

the name of Sir Oliver Martext, while the part of Oliver, Orlando's brother, remained intact, Mr. Flanagan became severe. It would never do to leave out an Oliver with a title. Didn't he know, he demanded of the editor, the importance of costumes? *Sir* Oliver should be restored; the untitled Oliver could go out instead. When the editor explained the situation Mr. Flanagan had to give way, but he still grumbled. He even suggested that the title should be borrowed from the priest and given to the "plain bugger"!

Whatever Mr. Flanagan's deficiencies of taste may have been, the Queen's Theatre productions were immensely popular. Special trains for the Saturday matinees were run from the smaller towns surrounding Manchester. The same cannot be said of the Gaiety performances.

But to return to my Christmas production of *Much Ado about Nothing*, at this time I still accepted all the current conventions of Shakespearean production. I took it for granted that there had to be a realistic representation of every scene shown. I determined that they should be as simple and tasteful as possible, and Hugh Freemantle, our very talented scenic artist, fortunately shared my views. His designs, charmingly depicting Italy in the sixteenth century and harmoniously according with costumes of the period, were universally admired. Though I had as yet evolved no theory about Shakespearean production, I was certainly convinced that there must be nothing to encumber what I saw to be Shakespeare's technical skill in the arrangement of the scenes from the unfoldment to the conclusion of the story.

In retrospect I can see how strange it was that never for a moment did I give conscious thought as to whether I might have learned anything from my experience with William Poel. In any case, the austerity of his production of *Measure for Measure* would have been quite unsuitable to the current requirements of a Christmas production in lieu of a pantomime. All the same there may have been some hidden influence in the deeper regions of my mind emanating from conversations with Poel. At any rate, repeated readings of the text of *Much Ado about Nothing* convinced me that there was a rhythmic flow in the unfolding of the plot—the melodic line of scene development, as I came to call it later—which would be destroyed by the customary omission or transposition of scenes to avoid many scene changes. I saw that these liberties with the text chopped up the action. It was necessary to include every scene in order to create a rhythmic progression of action. I concluded that I had to break through the illusion of locality representation to some extent. To do this I used the device of playing connecting scenes in front of neutral curtains drawn across the stage close to the proscenium.

Simple and obvious as this may seem nowadays, at that time it appeared to our company a daring and doubtful innovation! Some of the older members shook their heads dubiously, but I persisted and the experiment justified itself.*

It must be surprising, too, that having the musicians come on with Balthazar when he enters with Don Pedro to sing "Sigh no more, ladies" was another innovation. It was then customary for songs called for in Shakespearean productions to be accompanied by the musicians sitting in the orchestra pit. Every theatre, even the humblest, employed an orchestra. They were there not only to play entr'actes during the intermissions but to meet any other musical requirements such as "background" music. This was still much used, even in modern plays, though it was beginning to be regarded as out of date.

At the Gaiety Theatre we were fortunate in our orchestra. A talented Austrian conductor, Herr Dreschner, was in charge of the music at the Midland Hotel across the street, and he was able to supply Miss Horniman with a small orchestra of twelve capable Viennese performers. I sometimes wondered what they thought of our plays.

Herr Dreschner's secretary, Karl Weil, acted as intermediary with me for the choice of suitable entr'acte music for each play as it came up. He was a very friendly man and always eager to please. In fact, he was almost too eager on occasion. From time to time I asked him to fulfill some special requirement. "Karl," I would say, "I'm going to ask a favor of you." At this he would make a broad dismissive gesture, turn away, and start to leave the room, saying emphatically, "Mr. Payne, it is done!" When I protested, "Karl, you don't even know what I want!" he would move nearer the door with a still more emphatic, "No, no, no, Mr. Payne, IT IS DONE!" Finally I would have to stop him physically in order to explain what was required. But whatever was needed, the requirement was always punctiliously carried out.

The production of *Much Ado about Nothing*, though not regarded as a

---

*It was a common practice at that time to play short scenes downstage in front of flats or a painted curtain representing the setting. In writing of Poel's production of *Measure for Measure* at the Gaiety, C. E. Montague of the *Manchester Guardian* described the treatment of short scenes thus: "They are usually scurried through by actors who maintain a precarious footing on a strip of boarding between the footlights in front and a bellying sail painted with landscape, which swells out at them from behind." Often a front curtain was dropped or the stage was darkened to hide even this brief change. Payne sensed that an audience's need to adjust to a change of scene interrupted the continuous flow of action that he came to consider crucial in a Shakespearean play. His innovation was to avoid this psychological jolt by using *neutral* curtains for short scenes where specific settings were not essential. Montague's review was reprinted in his *Dramatic Values* (1910).

failure, did not have the public response we had hoped for. What troubled me most was my feeling that in some way I had failed to bring out the joyous spontaneity of Shakespeare's workmanship, which had so excited me in my preliminary readings of the play.

Ultimately I came to the conclusion that there was a certain unsuitability in the casting of the most vital characters, Benedick and Beatrice. Ian Maclaren played the former part. His performance seemed to me to be a little flat and lacking in the fire demanded by the part. Though he made a fine figure and spoke his lines clearly and with a ringing voice, I felt that there was a coldness in his personality that militated against revealing the lovableness under the surface of soldierly abruptness. However, he was the best actor available for the part in our company, so I could not blame myself for choosing him.

My biggest mistake (for which I was much criticized) was in my casting of Mona Limerick as Beatrice. She was established by this time as an actress of strange but unquestionable power in serious roles. Had Beatrice been within her range, the contrast between her serious strength and the comic role would have been all to the good. What led me astray was that she had recently proved in Shaw's *Press Cuttings* that she could give an excellent account of herself in at least one type of comedy part. That role, however, was a subtly ironic interpretation of a cold and calculating society woman at the other end of the comedy spectrum from the lively, warm-hearted Beatrice. The critics pointed out that though her emotional outburst when Beatrice declares her love for Benedick and goads him into agreeing to challenge his closest friend in defense of her cousin's honor was thrilling in itself, it was out of balance with the preponderant light passages of the part.*

*Miss Limerick's acting was often criticized for lack of control and technique, though she was praised equally often for her emotional intensity. The noted critic James Agate found more than that to admire. Of her performance in Charles McEvoy's *The Three Barrows* he wrote (as quoted by Pogson): "[Her acting] had the most amazing pictorial qualities. She took hold of you and made you believe that somewhere in the play there was a real woman. It was a piece of wonderful acting, full of intimate, half-expressed things, and made one long to see the actress in a part worthy of the art she showed herself capable of last night." C. E. Montague wrote of her performance in another role, "She played with a genius that kept the house breathless for every word she was to utter. Whatever Miss Limerick does on the stage she diffuses a sense of the tragic importance as of a whole sky darkened."

The stage of the Gaiety Theatre, 1910

Mona Limerick as Beatrice

A caricature by Ernest Marriott of Payne as Puff at the
Gaiety Theatre

*A*t about this time or not much later I began to debate whether I should remain much longer at the Gaiety Theatre. In the first place, I was feeling the strain of continuous production. Then there was the unfortunate fact that my wife, Mona Limerick, was not on good terms with Miss Horniman. This, incidentally, sometimes showed itself in a manner that caused no little embarrassment. On one occasion at a public dinner the three of us were sitting together at the high table. The subject of *Parsifal* happened to come up and Miss Horniman, in her pontifical manner, announced that she had heard it at every Bayreuth Festival for I don't know how many years. "Really?" said Mona, in her always penetrating tones. "You must be able to whistle it all the way through!" Miss Horniman was not amused. Her cheeks flushed and there was an awkward silence.

But what influenced me most powerfully was the feeling, which steadily grew stronger, that, since the theatre was losing money, Miss Horniman should have the opportunity to run her company on more popular lines if that was her unspoken desire. She never said a word to me on the subject: such was her integrity in abiding strictly to the terms of our agreement. But I was made aware from other sources that some of her influential Manchester friends were urging her to use her influence with me to select plays with more attention to their box-office possibilities. Although this worried me, it only strengthened my resolution not to lower the standard I had resolved upon from the very beginning of our venture. On the contrary, it seemed to make the time ripe for a reaffirmation of it. The opportunity came when I was asked to write an article for the *Gaiety Annual*, as it was called. This was a magazine published as a private venture by a member of the company. "The drama," I wrote, and sincerely felt, "is as important to a community as its religion. It is not, as it has been regarded for so long, a mere extraneous amusement, quite negligible in comparison with the serious things of life." I stated what I believed a repertory theatre should be, listing three requirements: "(1) The training of actors instead of automata (for only a machine could mechanically repeat the same parts for two years or more and no human being could do it and remain artistically sane); (2) performance of plays instead of machine-made exhibitions and pornographic displays; (3) restoration of the theatre to its true place as an actual part of the civic life of the community." But, significantly, I concluded by pointing out that a theatre "cannot exist without a public. Everything depends upon whether we, as a people, are ready."

Something else bothered me, less important but bothersome because there was always a shortage of suitable plays for our repertoire. There was one flaw in my contract with Miss Horniman, even though in accordance with Yeats's warning it had been tightly drawn up. This was that there was no proviso against Miss Horniman's reading and passing judgment on plays submitted to her directly. I was aware—indeed she told me so herself—that manuscripts were being sent to her and that she was finding great pleasure in dealing with them personally. It terrified me to think what plays meeting the standard of our avowed principles we might thus be missing. For Miss Horniman had a curious way of regarding the drama. She was the only person I have ever met who could see a play only from the visual point of view!

I must give examples of what I mean. Miss Horniman had traveled a good deal, especially in Germany. Soon after we began operations, when our repertoire was particularly in need of expansion, I asked her if she had not in her travels seen any European plays that might be translated for our use. After a pause for cogitation she said she could remember one play that might be useful, but all she could tell me about it was that in one scene there was a courtyard, that in the courtyard there was a well, and that when women lowered pots into it, water was seen to be dripping from their sides when they were raised. This realistic touch had impressed her deeply. It was useless to try to discover anything about the plot of the play. I did succeed in getting as far as an admission that the subject was more or less biblical, but every further question always brought her back to the dripping water pots.

A little later, the London production of a play by Mrs. W. K. Clifford was announced. Since this writer had previously had a play produced by the Stage Society, an organization noted for its modern outlook, I thought that it might possibly suit our purposes. Miss Horniman still maintained her apartment in London, so I suggested that she report on the new play. She was delighted to do so. In due course she declared that it was useless. The plot was laid in Italy in the month of October, yet there had been green grass-mat covering the stage. "Everyone knows," said Miss Horniman, "that in Italy the grass is burnt brown in the autumn!" This was the last time I attempted to procure information from Miss Horniman about the plays she had seen.*

In spite of these considerations, leaving the company was a difficult decision to make. More than a year passed before I finally made up my mind. Looking back, I can see that I must have been preparing for a severance. For example, in the Christmas season it had been our custom to engage an outside company to produce a children's play to run at matinees concurrently with the evening bill. But for the Christmas season of 1910–11 Miss Horniman readily agreed to my suggestion that Stanley Drewitt, a member of the company and a good actor with experience as a director, direct *The School for Scandal* for the evening bill, while I put on the children's play. For this, I selected *Katawampus*—by a Manchester author, Judge Parry—which had previously been produced in London. Perhaps because the central part of the play contains a satire on the English parliamentary system, it appealed to grown-ups as well as children. The production was immensely popular and played to packed houses for several weeks.

Since this is not a history of the Gaiety Theatre, I need not dwell on most of the plays that were added to the repertoire in my last year. Only later did I notice that throughout my sojourn in Manchester it was not the realistic plays dealing with contemporary life that interested me most intensely. The plays that stirred my imagination and gave me the most satisfaction as a director were, on the one hand, poetic plays and, on the other, plays of fantastic comedy. At the same time I began to read Shakespeare more or less steadily and to take an interest in what had been written about him by the commentators.

The high-water mark of my final year in Manchester was our production of Sheridan's *The Critic*. Because its satiric shafts are directed against a type of tragedy that had ceased to exist, it was feared that the burlesque humor of the play might have lost its point. This proved not to be the case. The audience reveled in the high-spirited buffoonery

*Pogson relates that Miss Horniman's habit of appraising plays solely by their appearance extended even to those at the Gaiety. After the highly successful opening of *Justice*, "when Irene Rooke, tired but triumphant, finally settled herself in her dressing room there was a knock on the door and Miss Horniman put her head into the room for one brief comment. 'My dear,' she said, 'I am *so* glad you wore a small hat!' "

as much as the actors, including myself. Mr. Puff, the childishly vain author of the burlesqued play, was the last part I played in Miss Horniman's company. Both the play and the part are pleasant to recall, and the production was enthusiastically received.*

The two other productions at the Gaiety Theatre that gave me particular satisfaction as a director belonged to a very different category. Both were tragedies. Lewis Casson, a highly valued member of the Horniman company, had played the Messenger in Granville Barker's production of Euripides' *Hippolytus*, in Gilbert Murray's translation, at the Royal Court Theatre in London. I asked him to put on the play for a series of matinees. His production was not only a fine piece of work in itself but it opened up a new world for me personally. Up until then the work of the Greek dramatists had been a closed book to me. Gilbert Murray's rendering in rhymed verse of Euripides is now regarded as old fashioned—translations of the classics must fit the taste of each successive generation—but in the early 1900s his translations spoke directly to the heart. *Hippolytus*, however, aroused my interest more than my emotions. When I read Murray's version of *The Trojan Women*, the greatest antiwar play ever written, I was deeply moved. I decided that I would not only produce it myself but take the risk of putting it on the evening bill. I felt that, with the aid of a fine cast, I was perhaps achieving as much of the classical spirit as was possible in a small interior theatre. But the financial outcome troubled me. Though the cheap seats in the pit and gallery were well filled, the more expensive ones in the stalls and dress circle—our mainstay from the box-office viewpoint—were almost deserted.

This was also the fate of the other poetic tragedy, *The Cloister*, by the Belgian poet Emile Verhaeren. Partly, perhaps, because of its all-male cast, the play has been neglected. Its action, as the title suggests, is laid in a monastery. A script in which every character is a monk ought to have warned me what to expect. Perhaps it did, but I was obstinately determined to adhere to the policy of producing British or foreign plays of true artistic merit whenever they came our way. I never regretted adhering to it.

I was able to persuade William Poel to come to Manchester again to play the principal part in *The Cloister*, that of a man who has killed his father before becoming a monk. Though he has been absolved,

*Payne had good reason to be pleased with the part, and so, it seems, did Manchester. According to the *Courier*, "No actor has a finer sense of burlesque nor tears a passion to tatters more flamboyantly or with better grace." The *Manchester Guardian* agreed: "As an actor of burlesque Mr. Payne is incomparable."

his conscience prompts him to demand that he shall make a "public" confession of his crime. He is an aristocrat by birth. So is the abbot, an old man who has been grooming him to take his place in fear that a new type of monk, more worldly and aggressive, will take command of the monastery on his imminent death, unless he has a forceful successor. The abbot first begs, then commands, the protagonist to be silent. But nothing can stop him from carrying out his threat. After his public confession in the chapel of the monastery he is physically thrown out.

Poel, who had a supreme capacity for getting deep into any part with religious emotion, gave a penetrating and poignant delineation of a difficult character. But though the play was well reviewed by the critics, it was another financial failure.

Poel's eccentricities, sometimes annoying but nevertheless amusing, were again in evidence. When he had read the play and accepted the part I went up to London to discuss the details of the production with him. He was distressed to learn that the place of action was to be a Dominican monastery. The Dominican habits are white with black hoods. Poel pointed out that white stands out strongly on the stage. Of this I was well aware and I thought to allay his fears by assuring him that we had already decided that the whiteness should be toned down into a pale coffee color. He appeared to give way, and everything else met with his approval. As I rose to leave, however, he casually remarked that he already had his wig. Now I knew from a Dominican brother with whom I had consulted that no formal tonsure was required and the bald patch in Poel's own hair was sufficient. This pleased me, since Poel's everyday appearance was perfect for the part. I told him so and took my departure.

A couple of weeks later, after the first rehearsal in Manchester, Poel came over to me at the prompt table and said with a beatific smile that he had "brought his habit with him." I told him I trusted it was Dominican. He pretended to be surprised, but there was a characteristic slyness in his eye as he said, "Oh, no! You told me the monks were to be Franciscans." Instantly the wig came back to my mind and I asked sarcastically if he had brought that too. He had. After much argument we reached a compromise. He agreed to be a Dominican monk, but I surrendered my objection to the wig, provided that I could have it dressed. As he showed it to me it was unkempt and rat-tailed, a condition that he thought of as being suitable to the part.

There is an aftermath to the story of the wig and the gown. One of our actors discovered Mr. Poel one day in our rehearsal room at the top of the theatre. The habit was spread on the floor and Poel was walking back and forth on it in the hope that this would further tone down the white! Then, Esmé Percy, who shared the dressing room with Poel, noticed that he took his wig home every night in a little black bag. Esmé asked him why he did this. Mr. Poel explained that I didn't care for the wig and he feared I would get into the dressing room after he had left and steal it. He added that *he* would certainly do so in my situation!

My severance from the Gaiety Theatre was a drawn-out process. For some time I was partly engaged in other activities. In the summers of 1910 and 1911, when Miss Horniman's company was not operating, I kept the theatre open with a company of my own, which I also sent on tour. It was not until 1911 that I formally handed in my resignation. It was accepted reluctantly.

Before I left Manchester, supporters of the Gaiety Theatre organized what was called, rather oddly, a Recognition Dinner for me at the Midland Hotel. It was a large gathering under the chairmanship of Miss Horniman and was attended by many prominent citizens and by most of the dramatists whose plays I had produced. John Galsworthy was the principal speaker.*

I had rarely seen Miss Horniman except at the theatre and on matters pertaining thereto. Since on business affairs she had left the running of the theatre entirely in my hands, we had always been on good terms. We never ceased to carry on a sporadic correspondence after I left her. The last time I saw her was in 1937, when I visited her in her apartment shortly before her death.

*Pogson ends his account of Payne's tenure at the Gaiety thus: "Without Miss Horniman's financial support, Payne would never have been given his opportunity; without her unswerving loyalty during the first four years nothing could have been done. That must never be forgotten, but it is nevertheless true that the Gaiety and consequently the repertory movement in this country was very largely the creation of Payne. He it was who founded what might justly be called the Gaiety tradition in acting, production and choice of repertoire. He started with a clear perception of what he wanted to do, and he was largely successful in putting it into practice."

CHAPTER 13

I will pass lightly over the next eighteen months except to record that I had two companies on tour. One was formed in partnership with a Manchester friend. It performed a single play, *The Younger Generation*, a light and very competent comedy by Stanley Houghton, which had been a popular production at the Gaiety. Miss Horniman generously surrendered her touring rights. With the other company I may possibly have made theatrical history by making an author, other than Shakespeare, the star feature of the billing! Although B. Iden Payne and Mona Limerick were cited on the bills as managers of the company, it was announced in very much larger type that we were presenting PLAYS BY BERNARD SHAW.

Bernard Shaw's reputation had grown enormously during the last few years. I was surprised, therefore, to learn from the managers of one or two of the theatres we visited that they had received puzzled inquiries as to who he was. And as I was in the kitchen of one of the houses where I lodged on tour, the landlady's husband, who was sitting by the fire smoking his pipe, asked me what the company was playing. When I told him plays by Bernard Shaw, he immediately showed interest. "Bernard Shaw?" he said. "Why I knew him years ago in Australia. He was a middleweight boxer then. I never thought *he* would be able to write plays!" Nothing could convince him that he had known a different Bernard Shaw. "Bernard Shaw!" he said, "Yes, that's the man and no mistake. Well, I really am surprised!"

Whether the anonymity of the plays on the bills was a wise move, the plays were undoubtedly enjoyed. Business always rose rapidly from the beginning to the end of each week in the towns we played. Before long we had to change the billing. No longer did Shaw's name star. *Man and*

Superman so far exceeded the other plays in popularity that we decided to have two companies, one performing only that play, the other giving a repertory of modern plays that included the other Shaw plays.

I began too to toy with the idea of looking for a new script that had never been produced. I read and thought highly of a play by Cicely Hamilton, the author of a recent success on the London stage. It required one more woman than I had in the company, but since the addition was only for a very short housemaid part, it would not add much to the salary list. When I happened to mention this to Edward Broadley, the stage manager at the Gaiety Theatre, he told me of a young woman who was badly down on her luck. He asked me to help her if I could, so I arranged an appointment for her. This lady, whom I shall call Miss Smith, seemed at first sight to be quite suitable and I engaged her. She told me that she was very grateful, but when I showed her to the door she gave me the first of a long series of shocks. Looking me squarely in the eyes she pointedly remarked, "I'm particularly pleased *you've* engaged me because I know *you* will not let the socialists persecute me." I was so surprised that I could only mutter something like "Certainly not!" She went away convinced, I am sure, that my manner of response was due not to embarrassment but guilt! When she arrived at the theatre for rehearsals I happened to be standing on the stage. Emerging from the dressing rooms she came straight to me and said, "You've wasted no time, have you, putting me to dress with a notorious socialist!" I told her, of course, that I didn't know what she was talking about, and that in any case the stage manager, not I, allocated the dressing rooms. Only later did I learn that the lady who happened to be chosen to share her dressing room was in fact a contributor to the *Clarion*, a socialist newspaper. Incidentally, this culprit soon abandoned the stage and became a leading figure in the literary world.

I was already thinking that the actress who played the maid in the *Man and Superman* company, then playing in the Midlands, was more mature. Thus she was better suited to the maid's part in the Hamilton play, and I determined to switch actresses. A few days later I received a postcard from Miss Smith saying that she admired my ingenuity in instructing the ladies of the new company to make fun of her poor little guinea navy-blue costume. Navy-blue suits happened to be fashionable that year, and each of the ladies had been wearing one at the run-through of her two-line part on the afternoon when she joined the company. Miss Smith apparently was convinced that this uniformity of apparel was arranged by my instructions. One of the ladies confirmed this cruel plot by remarking on the curious coincidence that they were all dressed alike!

Although Miss Smith left the company after a time, I had not yet had my last contact with her. This turned out to be another puzzling postcard, informing me that her virginity had been attested at the homeopathic hospital in Liverpool. She said that she had sent copies of this proof to Miss Horniman and the Archbishop of Canterbury. Moreover, unless I inserted an advertisement in the *London Times* averring that she had not played in my company at Brighton, she would commit suicide outside the Houses of Parliament with a paper pinned to her bosom stating that she was the victim of snobs in navy-blue suits. Apparently she had learned that the name of the actress playing the maid had been quickly changed on the programs of the Hamilton play, and the lady who had taken her place was somewhat broadly constructed. Therefore it might appear—or so Miss Smith imagined—that she was pregnant. Happily this was the last I heard from this poor woman.*

Neither of these companies was a bonanza, but each of them paid its way. Indeed, they brought in enough to enable me to make, with some financial help from an author and one or two friends, a modest attempt at a London production. This was a venture in the field I had come to love best, that of romantic, poetic drama. Under my own management I put on a play derived from the early Spanish classic *Celestina*, by Fernando de Rojas. The original is immensely long and perhaps was never intended for performance, but my friend Edward Garnett, two of whose plays I had produced at the Gaiety, had fashioned a play called *The Spanish Lovers* out of the central episode. In it a cunning old bawd, Celestina, beguiles an innocent and unwary young girl into a situation that, according to the strict code of Spanish honor then prevalent, leads the way to a tragic denouement. Although I chose the play primarily because it seemed enthralling when I read it, I also

*Dame Rebecca West, who was at the age of nineteen the "notorious socialist" in this strange tale, recalls it differently in some respects. The incident of the blue costume is essentially accurate, she writes, but in fact the paranoid actress remained with the Hamilton play throughout its engagements in Eastbourne and Brighton. On the last night of the run she locked Miss West in a dressing room. Other members of the company had to rescue her in time for her scene. The play would have gone on to London, but for the collapse of a balcony in the theatre into which it had been booked.

Miss West's next, and last, theatrical engagement, also with Payne, was in a D'Annunzio play that never saw its first night because its producer—Strindberg's second wife, Frieda Uhl—ran out of money. It is perhaps not surprising that Miss West forsook her theatrical career. It was less easy, however, for her to end her acquaintance with the mad actress. She continued to receive postcards and telephone calls off and on for the next fifteen years. Dame Rebecca records an ironic twist to the story: before the engagement with Payne the actress had herself been the mistress of a well-known socialist. This once passionate affair had been ended by her tragic psychosis.

thought it would provide a good part for my wife. I made a mistake in both respects. When it came to performance, literature seemed to predominate over drama. And the always strikingly individual acting of Mona Limerick had more power and tragic intensity than was required for the gentle character she was portraying.

The play failed and I was nearly penniless, but there was no reason for alarm. After all, I could fall back on provincial touring to ensure a livelihood. But that had lost its glamor. Then, as unexpectedly as my summons to the Abbey Theatre and Miss Horniman's offer to inaugurate a repertory theatre, an alternative presented itself. It seems that every change in my life's course has been unexpected and unsought!

Again Miss Horniman asked me to see her. The Chicago Theatre Society, a small group of businessmen who were interested in the New Drama, had approached her with a proposal to bring a company to Chicago. They wished to guarantee a season of a few weeks at the Fine Arts Theatre there. Miss Horniman was not interested, but she wondered whether I would care to undertake it instead. She told me that she had already mentioned this as a possible alternative and they had readily agreed to the suggestion. I was immediately drawn to the idea and accepted.

My eagerness perhaps calls for explanation. I had a particular reason for wanting to discover what America was like. Like many Englishmen of my generation, I found the poetry of Walt Whitman a powerful influence. In addition to its deeper significance, its profound sense of the brotherhood of all humanity—not as a theory but as an actuality —stirred me. Not surprisingly, then, Whitman's passionate love of his native country aroused my curiosity about it. I can illustrate how I felt about Whitman by relating an episode that occurred soon after I reached Chicago. For publicity purposes I had to speak at an afternoon meeting of a woman's club. In the course of my remarks I mentioned that great poets are a rare phenomenon in history and that it was greatly to the credit of a new country to have already produced one. I took it for granted that everyone present would understand to whom I referred. But when at question time I was asked for the name of the one great American poet, my emphatic "Whitman, of course!" obviously surprised my audience. The combination of incredulity and disapproval on the faces of many of my auditors surprised me as much as my reply apparently shocked them. It was the first time that I met with the vestiges of the puritanical spirit in America. I reminded myself that in Whitman's time it had been so strong that friends had begged him to exclude *Children of Adam* from publication in his *Leaves of Grass*.

The arrangements made with the Chicago Theatre Society were simple. In fact, it was merely agreed that there should be a series of payments sufficient, with due economy, to cover the cost of an eight-week experimental season. As the nucleus of the company, I took with me from England two good character actors, as well as my wife. Whitford Kane, a fine character actor who had worked with me in both Miss Horniman's and my own companies, was already in New York and was eager to join the enterprise. He was in touch with a number of English actors there. With some of these, and others suggested by his press representative, Dixie Hines, who later became my own agent, we were able in a few weeks to make a good selection. It included Walter Hampden, whose training as an actor had been in England. It was a stroke of fortune to secure Walter, because he was already well known as a leading man and his style of acting fitted in well with the rest.

On arriving in Chicago in 1913, I was surprised but not greatly disconcerted to find that the Fine Arts Theatre was very small—not much more than a long hall with a stage and a proscenium at the end. Its name was derived not from the quality of its fare but merely from its situation in a corner of the enormous Fine Arts Building.

Since I knew that the Chicago Theatre Society was most interested in the new type of repertory play, our programs consisted mainly of the works of Shaw and Galsworthy and other English plays of the New Drama. I entertained a slight hope that local dramatists might arise, as they had in Manchester, when they had the opportunity for production. This hope was partially fulfilled, though none of the manuscripts I was able to produce made any attempt to deal with local Chicago life. This was only to be expected, for the community revolved around no central axis but was divided into separate ethnic groups. No play was offered from any of these. Kenneth Sawyer Goodman, whose name is preserved in the Goodman Theatre in Chicago, furnished us with some useful curtain raisers. One of them, *The Game of Chess*, is a well-constructed and effective melodrama that for some years was a favorite with amateur groups all over the United States. I need not give details of the repertoire, but I should dwell for a moment upon one production in a different key from the rest.

My deep-seated urge to meet the challenge of Shakespeare rose to the surface again, and I set to work upon a production of *Measure for Measure*. I must confess that I was influenced in my choice of the play by the enjoyment I had felt when acting Lucio, and I had great pleasure in acting that role again. But once more, I gave no thought at all to what

Whitford Kane with Payne: a long friendship

Walter Hampden as Hamlet

Kenneth Sawyer Goodman about 1913

I might have learned from Poel's production in Manchester. I stuck to the conventional method of Shakespearean production, except in my strict adherence to the scene pattern of the play, avoiding the transposition or omission of scenes. I met the short-scene problem by the method I had used for *Much Ado* in Manchester, placing them in front of neutral curtains drawn across the stage near the proscenium.

What amazed me was that the puritanical spirit I have already mentioned so permeated the social atmosphere that even Shakespeare was not immune. There were accusations even in the press that the play was immoral! One critic struck at me personally by saying that "only a man with a dirty mind would have raked out this Elizabethan sewer." However, this had no effect on our takings, and business was neither better nor worse than for our other productions. It used to be said that a charge of impropriety was helpful to the box office. This is not necessarily the case, but there have been instances when even the misunderstood title of a play attracted the prurient. St. John Ervine's *Mixed Marriages* is concerned with the matrimonial difficulties arising through religious bigotry in Northern Ireland between Protestants and Roman Catholics. It was produced by Whitford Kane for a series of matinees in a theatre in New York while another play was on the evening bill. Unexpectedly it played to crowded houses. In the lobby I overheard a man who was booking seats for the evening show. "*Mixed Marriages!*" he said to a friend who was standing by. "That must be hot stuff; I'm sure going to see it." That, I was told, was a common notion. About the same time a play called *The Unchastened Woman* owed its success in large measure to the fact that many, ignorant of the word *chasten*, took the title to mean "the unchaste woman."

Terminology may have lain behind the fact that, though we had more than a few enthusiasts who enjoyed our plays during the Chicago season, there were not nearly enough to fill houses. A regular supporter of our productions once told me that he had been chatting with an acquaintance before leaving for the theatre. His friend considered going along until he learned that the play was at the Fine Arts Theatre. He sank back in his chair, saying, "I don't care for amateur acting." When our supporter assured him that we were all professional actors, and good ones at that, his friend was puzzled. "Then why on earth," he asked, "do they give it a name like Fine Arts?" He decided to give us a trial and actually became a convert to our repertory. I suspect that the Fine Arts name was a serious detriment, though probably at that time the Chicago public was not ready for our kind of theatre in any case. Nevertheless, though we never drew the general public, business was good enough to induce the Chicago Theatre Society to extend the original eight-week season to twelve. However, the society faded out of existence at the end of that period.

Again the unexpected. One day—the year was still 1913—Kenneth Goodman looked in at rehearsal and asked me to have lunch with a friend and former colleague of his the next day. He did not even tell me his name, but he mentioned that he had come from Pittsburgh for a short visit to Chicago. I took it to be no more than a casual social invitation, but it turned out differently. For me it was a fateful meeting, initiating a long friendship and partnership in work. Even more than that, it opened the door to a gradual change in my whole professional outlook and ultimately diverted the whole current of my career into a new channel.

But this is to anticipate. The beginning of the luncheon engagement puzzled me. Kenneth Goodman merely introduced me to his friend, Mr. Thomas Wood Stevens, in the lobby of the hotel and immediately disappeared. Feeling somewhat bewildered, I was led to the restaurant and presented to a Dr. Arthur Hammerschlag, who, Mr. Stevens explained, was the president of the Carnegie Institute of Technology in Pittsburgh (now Carnegie-Mellon University). We sat down, luncheon was ordered, and I was able to take stock of my companions. Mr. Stevens appeared at this first meeting to be a very quiet-mannered, reserved gentleman completely overshadowed by the talkative, forceful, and even flamboyant personality of Dr. Hammerschlag, who monopolized the conversation. The president explained that he had sought to meet me because he was then in the process of adding a department of drama to the college of fine arts and he had engaged Mr. Stevens to organize it. He was well aware that a drama department at the university was a daring innovation but, he said with unnecessary truculence, he was determined to carry it out. He wondered whether I might be able to give him any advice as to how it should be constituted. It was such a new idea to me that I could do very little besides wish him good luck.

The general attitude of the theatrical profession toward the whole notion of teaching drama in a school was one of scepticism, if not ridicule. When a few years earlier Beerbohm Tree had started a school of drama, most actors had sent up a hoot of laughter and asked scornfully, "Can acting be taught?" Mr. Stanley McCandless, the distinguished expert on theatre lighting, had a similar reaction. He had picked up his knowledge of the craft empirically by lighting plays for Dr. George Pierce Baker at Harvard University in Baker's extracurricular little theatre. When Dr. Baker left Harvard to start a full-scale drama department at Yale he asked McCandless whether he would join his faculty to teach stage lighting. McCandless's immediate reaction, he told me, was to ask incredulously, "Can lighting be *taught?*"

Some people had been sympathetic but dubious about an acting school. It was to that group I had belonged and I said so frankly. Mr. Stevens took the wind out of my sails by pointing out that practitioners in the other arts—painting, music, and architecture—had to acquire technique in schools or colleges. Would I exclude acting from the same category? he asked. It will be noted that, though we spoke of it as drama, everything revolved around acting as the center and soul of its activity. All technical requirements such as scenery and costumes were mere auxiliary appendages.

It is hardly necessary to mention that Dr. Hammerschlag and Mr. Stevens were not aware that in creating the first university department of drama ever to exist, they were planting a seed that would proliferate throughout the length and breadth of the country and ultimately spread abroad.

As we rose from our chairs to separate, much to my surprise Dr. Hammerschlag asked, as if the notion had suddenly flashed into his mind, whether I would put on a play at the Carnegie Institute when I was free from other engagements. To the best of my recollection I was a little hesitant in my reply, though I thought it might be interesting to find out how the new idea was shaping up. I told him that I doubted whether a professional approach would be acceptable to the students. I was assured that, on the contrary, it was exactly what was wanted, since the purpose of the department was to train actors for the professional stage. I therefore agreed that we should complete arrangements for a visit as soon as we found a mutually convenient time.

In spite of my doubts, within a year I made my first visit to the Carnegie Institute of Technology. It came as a surprise to find that the number of students was very small. But what astonished me much more was the discovery that one of the students had unquestionable acting ability. When I mentioned to Mr. Stevens that I had not expected this, he offered a convincing explanation. He pointed out that the theatrical profession was still regarded by many as not altogether respectable. A much larger number of people regarded acting as a precarious calling that it was foolish to adopt in a land of opportunity. Consequently, students in anything as novel as a university drama department had had to fight their way through a brier hedge of parental opposition. They had succeeded in doing so only if they had a powerful urge in the direction of a stage career.

It was exhilarating to find a group so enthusiastic and eager. I could not but compare their fervor with the matter-of-fact and often blasé approach generally shown by professional actors at that time. However, it is necessary to add that this happy state of universal enthusiasm was not permanent. This intense eagerness among students became less prevalent when drama, or speech and drama, departments came to be almost a matter of course in any university or college curriculum. Undoubtedly that initial eagerness was a powerful—indeed the principal—factor in my interest in educational theatre. This interest grew year by year as I was invited to return to Carnegie Tech. Before long it became a settled custom for me to produce a Shakespearean play each spring, the run to include a performance on Shakespeare's birthday, April 23. Of all the evidences of student enthusiasm, there was one that never failed to move me. As we neared an opening date it was sometimes necessary to call a rehearsal on a Sunday, a much needed day of relaxation for our busy students. I would find to my surprise that one or two who were not in the cast had come to watch. As the rehearsal continued I would notice out of the corner of my eye that other students, one or two at a time, had slipped in quietly and unobtrusively until practically the whole department had assembled.

I had no difficulty in finding a competent cast for Shaw's *You Never Can Tell*, the first play I directed there, selected by Stevens from the list of suggestions I had given him. I found that not only the vigor but the actual polish of the acting was positively exhilarating.

During the work on this play my feelings of regard for Thomas Wood Stevens—TW, as the students called him—blossomed into friendship, and it was not long before I was on confidential, though less intimate, terms with President Hammerschlag also. As was to be expected, he was very proud of his initiative, and even courage, in being the first to add a department of drama to a college of fine arts. He chuckled as he told me how he had not dared to tell Andrew Carnegie, the man to whose bounty the university owed its existence, until the very day when he came on an official visit to inspect all the completed buildings.

There was a mischievous twinkle in Dr. Hammerschlag's eye as he described his introduction of Andrew Carnegie to the drama department. He had instructed TW to have a rehearsal in progress at the hour when Carnegie would be inspecting the fine-arts building. At the right moment Dr. Hammerschlag threw open the door to the theatre—with a flourish, I am sure, for flamboyant gestures were part of his makeup and he was proud of the little theatre with its rich, warm paneling. Carnegie was impressed; he admitted it was a "very fine lecture hall." But he inquired what those people were doing on the stage? Assuming as casual an air as possible, Hammerschlag explained that they were the drama students at work. Carnegie was startled and shocked. He asked what legitimate grounds there could be for such a department. Hammerschlag was prepared. Knowing that commercial practicality was always foremost in Carnegie's mind, he called his attention to a fine, upstanding young man who was delivering a Shakespearean soliloquy. "You see that young man?" he asked. "Acting is the only capacity God has given him, but if he went onto the stage without preliminary training he could make no more than a few dollars a week, whereas he would earn twice as much if he had a college degree." Mr. Andrew Carnegie immediately acknowledged the utility of a drama department. "That is quite all right," he said.

Dr. Hammerschlag knew that he was exaggerating the financial benefits of a college education to a beginning actor. But he surely never anticipated that drama graduates who went to New York seeking work on Broadway would find to their mortification that a college degree, far from being helpful, was actually prejudicial to their chances of finding employment. The theatrical agents they approached learned of their college training with hostility. The growth and influence of educational theatre is such that this is not the case today. A young aspirant for work on the professional stage is no longer advised to "keep it quiet" that he holds a college degree.

A different kind of problem arose in regard to the first group of graduates. There were two young women in the drama department who had no acting capacity. TW consulted me about what appeared to be a serious situation. These two girls had the highest grades in all academic subjects, so that it seemed they had to be graduated. Yet TW thought that it would be a disgrace for the department to be represented by people who were unable to act. He had, however, received letters from some high schools asking whether he could supply directors for their annual play productions. Stevens wondered whether he might dare to recommend these girls. After all, they had worked like all the other students on the technical side of productions and, though not in the casts, had been observers at rehearsals. My advice to TW was that, as long as they did not have to act, by all means he should take the chance. He decided to do so.

On my arrival in Pittsburgh the following spring I asked for news of the two girls. I cannot remember ever seeing TW look more pleased than when he described the success of his recommendations. He had received letters from the principals of the schools the graduates had gone to, filled with profuse thanks and especially praising the girls' drama work. "You would have thought they were geniuses," Stevens said. Amusing proof of how even a little technical knowlege can help to give form to dramatic productions! Thus, unwittingly, was the first step taken in the educational theatre toward the creation of the innumerable professional technical workers now to be found there.

When I took the engagement in Chicago I expected to return to England to resume work in the regular way. But while I was taking the Chicago company on a short tour of one-night stands I was approached by Mrs. Jay, a lady from Philadelphia, who owned a little theatre there. It had been used only for occasional performances, but she said that she would like to make it the home of a professional repertory theatre. There was still magic for me in the mention of repertory. When, at the end of the tour, she offered a substantial weekly guarantee for the following fall and winter, it seemed too good to be true. We made an agreement accordingly and I returned to England for the spring and summer. There I toured again and, by arrangement with Miss Horniman, ran a four-week season at the Gaiety Theatre. I then returned to America to complete and rehearse the Philadelphia company. Whitford Kane and Ian Maclaren had already been engaged, and the rest of the company was selected, with the help of Dixie Hines, from among actors the three of us knew.

We opened in Philadelphia with high hopes, but, to put it mildly, Mrs. Jay turned out to be extremely impractical. At the end of the second week she confessed that she was unable to meet the guaranteed salaries. She said that she had hoped to raise it from her friends during the summer, but even those who had made promises had failed to fulfill them.

After much discussion among the members of the company we decided that, rather than close the season, we would continue to run the company ourselves on sharing terms with Mrs. Jay. The men in the company formed a "commonwealth" (as it used to be called theatrically) of an unusual kind. Out of the company's share of the gross takings the first portion went to the actresses, who were paid the full salaries stipulated in their contracts. What was left over was distributed among the men in proportion to their salary arrangements with Mrs. Jay. We hoped for an increase in public support. To some extent it came, but it was variable and altogether too gradual for the men's share, which sometimes was not enough to meet our hotel bills. After a few weeks we decided to close the season after our next production, *The Critic*, which had already been announced. So indeed we did, but once again chance opened for me a door into the future.

At that time legitimate theatres throughout the country were monopolized by two huge syndicates, the Shubert theatres forming one group and the Klaw & Erlanger theatres the other. Just after *The Critic* opened, Mr. J. J. Shubert, who happened to be in Philadelphia, was taken by a friend to see our production. He was puzzled but felt that his brother, Mr. Lee Shubert (the head of the organization), should be the judge of its possibilities for New York. Accordingly, Mr. Lee Shubert came down to Philadelphia to see our production. He was so well impressed that he engaged us to play the Princess Theatre in New York for a regular run. As ill luck would have it, one of the worst blizzards New York had experienced for years began the day before and snow continued to fall steadily throughout the opening day. Although it was well received, the play never recovered from this misfortune and the run was short.

The closing of *The Critic* might have left me at a loose end, but I most opportunely received from Harold Brighouse the manuscript of his yet unproduced Lancashire play, *Hobson's Choice*. I liked to fancy myself the godfather of this play, which had been a long time in gestation. In my Manchester days I had been chatting with the two local authors Stanley Houghton and Harold Brighouse in the American bar at the Midland Hotel. Neither had approved of the acting of one of the principal parts in the play then running at the Gaiety Theatre. One of them asked me why I had cast the part as I did. My retort was that it had been a case of Hobson's choice; there was no one else available who would have been any better. (The expression "Hobson's choice" comes from an old story that tells how a livery man named Hobson would tell a customer as they went to the stable that he could have any horse he liked. However, he regularly maneuvered the customer so that he had to take the one nearest to the door.)

No sooner had I said this than it occurred to me that the phrase would make a good title for a play. I said so and Houghton and Brighouse agreed. A friendly argument arose as to which of them should be the author of the hypothetical *Hobson's Choice*. I suggested that they toss a coin. This they did and Brighouse won. A curious inception of a successful play!

I was able to interest Lee Shubert in *Hobson's Choice*, and it not only had a good run at the Comedy Theatre in New York in 1915, but two companies toured the country with it the next year. The play has deservedly been called a "minor classic." When the National Theatre began work in London, *Hobson's Choice* was the only modern English play to be selected for its first repertoire. It was one of the plays taken by the company's director, Sir Laurence Olivier, on an official visit to the U.S.S.R. Charles Laughton played the leading role in a movie version, and a musical version had some success on Broadway in 1966. Thus Brighouse became the most widely known product of our Manchester School. But it should not be imagined that these triumphs were lightly achieved. *Hobson's Choice* almost vanished from the American stage before it had a chance to show its quality. The story points a moral.

Everyone knows that chamber music cannot be heard to advantage in a vast auditorium. But the general public does not seem to realize that the same principle applies to plays—indeed, to plays more drastically than to music. Even experienced professionals have often seemed to me obtuse on this point. *Hobson's Choice* was booked to open in New York at the Comedy Theatre, a small playhouse that no longer exists, after only one preliminary week out of town. For this week, we were sent to a very large theatre. The reception was unencouraging. The local critics were puzzled by the Lancashire dialect, but, more seriously, audiences were cold in their response with both laughter and applause.

Our producer, Mr. Lee Shubert, instantly wrote off the play as a total loss. He ridiculed my contention that the basic trouble was the size of the theatre, and another play went into the Comedy Theatre. Fortunately for us the substitute play proved a failure. After much persuasion, Mr. Shubert allowed us to open there after all, though he frankly stated that he expected our tenancy to be merely a stopgap. As I have said, the play was enthusiastically received by both press and public, and we occupied the Comedy Theatre for months. But when I reminded Mr. Shubert of what I had said he still scoffed at the notion that the size of the theatre had anything to do with the matter. "No," he declared, "it is just that New York audiences are different."

In fact, the crucial factor involved is the distance of the actors from the audience. Eugene O'Neill's tragedy *Desire Under the Elms* had a great success in New York at the Criterion Theatre and was then sent on tour. The company manager, a friend of mine, anticipated a long tour, as did everyone else. When I expressed surprise at meeting him in New York a few weeks later, he explained that the tour had been abandoned. He had a theory about the failure, however. The setting of the play shows both the inside and the outside of a farmhouse. "Before opening on Broadway," my friend recounted, "scenery was built in which the house was placed well back from the footlights so as to leave plenty of room for the exterior action. To the great disappointment of everyone, however, the only theatre available was the Criterion, where the stage was so shallow that they had to bring the house downstage near the footlights."

Although the actors hated playing so close to the audience, there was no alternative. When they went on tour, however, they played in large theatres. Everyone, especially the actors, rejoiced. At last they were going to show the play in an adequate setting. The discarded wings were brought out from storage. "But somehow or other," my friend said, "the actors lost all contact with the audiences. The big tragic scenes inside the farmhouse went for nothing. Anyway, in both Philadelphia and Buffalo, the only two towns we visited, the play failed to draw."

My friend was convinced, and I have little doubt that he was right, that this all-important loss of contact was mainly to blame. But it was useless to beg the management to revert to the New York setting. They pooh-poohed his argument, convinced, like Mr. Shubert, that it was all because of a fancied difference between New York and provincial taste. "So," my friend concluded, "a fine play was thrown to the winds."

CHAPTER 14

*A*t this point—it was 1916—the direction my career was to take was again determined by chance. But exactly how it came about I do not know even now. Perhaps either *The Critic* or *Hobson's Choice* or both were seen by Mr. John D. Williams when he was about to produce Galsworthy's *Justice*. However, there was a story to the effect that when Williams applied for the right to the play, Galsworthy, knowing I was in New York at the time, replied that he would grant permission only provided that Williams could secure my services as director. In any case, Williams approached me with the request that I direct the play. Naturally I was interested, as I would have been in any Galsworthy play.

John D. Williams had held a most unusual position as press agent for Charles Frohman, who was then the leading American theatrical manager, with interests in both America and England. Frohman was said almost to monopolize the star actors in both countries. He was, however, largely dependent upon English dramatists for his American attractions and he habitually invited them to New York when one of their plays was in rehearsal. Like all the other managers, he employed a press agent, but he required a particular type of representative, one who could also look after and entertain his foreign playwrights. He found just what he wanted in John D. Williams, a Harvard graduate with charming manners and widespread interests. But the limitations of his work irked John D, as his friends called him. He had decided at this time that he would strike out for himself by becoming his own manager.

In discussing the casting of *Justice*, John D asked me what I would think of John Barrymore in the leading part. I had to admit that I knew nothing about his work or even his reputation. He told me that John Barrymore had been associated entirely with comedy parts but that he had aspirations toward serious work. Barrymore was perfectly willing, John D assured me, to read the part with me so that I might judge his suitability. Accordingly I spent two afternoons with Barrymore in his apartment. Even at the first meeting I came to the conclusion that he had all the qualities for the part and I so reported. To my surprise John D did not look altogether happy about my decision. He silently acceded, however, and we went ahead and started rehearsals with Barrymore in the leading role.

After a couple of days, John D came to see me and asked if I was quite sure I had not made a mistake in prevailing upon him to have Jack Barrymore in the part. I assured him that rehearsals had done nothing to change my opinion. He shrugged his shoulders but made no comment. When he repeated the question a day or two later I asked him to tell me frankly what was troubling him. He explained that some of his friends had told him he was jeopardizing the whole enterprise because Jack Barrymore under other managers had on several occasions not turned up at performances. He dreaded that the same thing might happen with him, in spite of their friendship. He feared, in short, that he was taking too great a risk. I replied that it was entirely a matter for him as manager to decide. As the director, however, I still approved of the casting and I hoped he would not change it. John D again shrugged his shoulders and rehearsals continued. The upshot was that *Justice* was a great success in every way, and John Barrymore especially won acclaim. Falder, in Galsworthy's *Justice*, established him as a leading actor of star quality.*

Many times I have been asked what John Barrymore was like in rehearsal and performance. Possibly because he realized what his friend John D was risking during the run of the play in New York, he was as accommodating and reliable as any leading actor could be. When the play went on tour I heard of certain eccentricities during performances, but then I was no longer with the company. In later productions much was reported, of course, about his extravagant behavior on the stage.

---

*Barrymore wrote in his *Confessions of an Actor* (1926) that his friend the playwright Edward Sheldon urged him to "play a part without a bit of comedy in it." Barrymore was reluctant, fearing that a serious role would force him to sacrifice his moustache, "a thing not to be lightly parted from." Sheldon persisted and "arranged with the producers" that Barrymore should star in *Justice*. Payne makes it clear that the "arrangement" was not quite so simple as Barrymore chose to recall it.

129

My own view is that John Barrymore was instinctively a wit and, belying his classical features, temperamentally a clown. He had a powerful instinct to play the fool. Examples of his wit are manifold. One afternoon during the run of *Justice* I had to see him at the end of the matinee and I arrived at the theatre while the last act was in progress. The business manager told me that Jane Cowl was out front and he had given her a stage box. He added that she seemed to be enjoying the play, for he had noticed that she wept during all the pathetic passages. This did not surprise me, for Jane Cowl was a leading actress notorious for playing lachrymose parts. Tears may be said to have been her long suit. At the end of the play I went around to see Jack. When I asked him how he was he gave me one of his baleful looks and replied, "Never better, I have achieved one of my ambitions; I have costarred with Jane Cowl!"

There was an amusing aftermath of my experience with Barrymore. Years later, when he was well established in motion pictures, a movie-struck student of mine who was graduating asked me for an introduction to the famous actor. Later I had a letter from this student (whom I shall call Beau Hopkins) saying that he had met Mr. Barrymore and that he had spoken beautifully of me, declaring that I had saved him from wasting his life. Later I heard a somewhat more exact account of the incident. Another student had since encountered Beau. "You know Beau was determined to meet Barrymore," he said. "He got a walk-on in his latest movie and as Barrymore was leaving the lot, Beau intercepted him. 'Excuse me, Mr. Barrymore, but I have a message from Mr. Iden Payne.' Barrymore swung around and faced him. 'What, that blankety-blank so-and-so? Why, he saved me from being a bum.' " The next time I saw John's sister, Ethel, I told her the story. She was delighted. "You know," she said, "I think that is the nicest thing Jack has ever said!"

Encouraged by the results of his venture with *Justice*, John D. Williams prevailed upon John Drew, Barrymore's uncle, to undertake the title role in a dramatization by Langdon Mitchell of Thackeray's *Pendennis*. The play was called *Major Pendennis*, since the major was the principal role. I was pleased when Williams again engaged me as director.

John D had shown discrimination in his choice of John Drew, though I quickly realized that he was a perfect example of Bernard Shaw's "case-hardened actor"—if one well chosen for the part. Shaw used the term "professional case-hardening" to describe what happens to actors who have been too long cast to type. I spoke earlier of my admiration for the extraordinary versatility of Charles Bibby, who played with

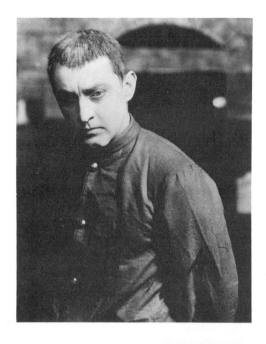

John Barrymore in *Justice*, 1916

Ethel Barrymore in *Embezzled Heaven*, 1944

Brandon Tynan and John Drew in *Major Pendennis*, 1916

me in Manchester. On the professional stage, unfortunately, such versatility can actually be a detriment to an actor. At least, it is a gift that he is seldom allowed to exercise, so he suffers a perpetual sense of heartbreaking frustration. Typecasting flourishes because producers want to know exactly how an actor will play a part before they engage him. As a result actors can scarcely avoid repeating themselves. They speak scornfully of the practice of typecasting, but they have to succumb to it.

Once an actor has made a reputation for himself in a particular kind of role, not only producers but audiences as well identify him with it and are unhappy to have their expectations disappointed by any change. The actor himself may grow content with this role and the audience response he can count on it to bring. This is the process of which Shaw was thinking. I will have more to say about typecasting later on.

As for John Drew, the case in which he was encrusted consisted of an unyielding, rather square figure, abrupt but very clear speech, a dominant but kindly manner, everything betokening all that is best in the word *gentleman*. All of this well befitted the retired military officer he was to play. Rehearsals revealed that Mr. Drew did not have to act. He was exactly the same both off and on the stage, always Major Pendennis.

Nevertheless I have pleasant memories not only of John Drew but of all the rest of the cast, especially of the well-contrasted ingenues, Helen MacKellar and Helen Menken. Brandon Tynan, too, was excellent as young Pendennis.

The play, however, appeared to be too literary for the Broadway taste of the time. It was well liked by those who attended, but they were too few in number to give the play more than a comparatively short run. Still, my Broadway productions were both pleasurable experiences for me, and both were highly praised. As a result I think that I succumbed temporarily to overconfidence. Evidence of this came when Mr. A. H. Woods offered me the direction of *The Guilty Man*, a play translated from the French. At the time the salary seemed very large, and I imagined that I could make the play artistically worthwhile even though the script, though not entirely melodramatic, showed little psychological penetration in its characterization. My delusion introduced me to yet another kind of theatrical experience.

Mr. A. H. Woods, generally known as Al Woods, was a very different type of manager from John D. Williams. He had made a good deal of money as the owner and manager of what were known as the tentwent-thirts, cheap theatres specializing in melodrama, where the prices of admission ranged from ten cents to thirty cents. They were situated on the Lower East Side of New York. It is not surprising that their good financial return had given Mr. Woods the stimulus to carry his activities into the larger field of Broadway. There he did so well that by this time he had been able to build his own theatre, the Eltinge. It was named for the actor Julian Eltinge, especially known for female impersonations, who had been the star in the first of his profitable Broadway productions. Before his miscalculation with *The Guilty Man* Woods had been generally fortunate in his choice of plays, though he scored the suggestion that luck had had anything to do with it. He boasted that he followed a very simple plan for finding the box-office value of a manuscript. He read it, then asked himself whether he would give three dollars to see it performed. If the answer was "yes" he bought it. Other producers knew that such a naive formula could never be relied on. Possibly when Al Woods began his Broadway producing, his own particular taste corresponded with the general trend, but a streak of good fortune must have favored him also. Later on, as the current veered into another channel, what had seemed like his oracular power faded away and he rapidly lost ground. Already at this time, if Mr. Woods had used his three-dollar test with *The Guilty Man*, it had failed to operate. Though not exactly a failure, the production was far from the moneymaker he had hoped for.

Al Woods was neither tall nor short, nor could he be described as stout, but he was stocky and broad, so he gave a general impression of being a large man. His manner was frank and jovial. He called everybody, male or female, "Sweetheart," but he gave one the feeling that his bonhomie might overlie a hard kernel of unfeeling harshness. He had a very ready and colorful tongue. Words poured out of him in spates of almost Elizabethan richness. I recall an instance when he was persuading an actor to join the cast of *The Guilty Man*. This young man had recently received fine notices for an emotional role and had just received an offer for a similar part in a moving picture. Al Woods tempted—and secured—him by saying, "Don't waste your talent in movies, where you'd have to downgrade your emotions. Come to me and I'll give you a part that'll make your guts do a tango on the ceiling!"

No sooner had I signed an agreement to direct *The Guilty Man* than I received the first of many shocks the Broadway theatre was to give me. In Manchester, Chicago, and Philadelphia—in short throughout my repertory work—I had been the organizer as well as the director of the companies. The choice of actors had been entirely in my own hands.

So it had almost been in the casting of *Justice* and *Major Pendennis*. John D. Williams, for the most part, engaged actors already known to me or those whose acting was familiar to me. In short, I assumed that casting was wholly or mainly in the hands of the director. I took it for granted that the same plan would be followed by Mr. Woods. Imagine then my consternation when he handed me a sheet of paper, saying, "Here's your cast." His surprise when I protested appeared to be equal to my disquietude, and I was soon to learn that he was only following the custom among Broadway managers at the time. He mollified me to some extent by assuring me that I could make any changes I wished during rehearsals, but the thought of having to tell an actor he was unsuitable appalled me. I went to the first rehearsal expecting and fearing that Mr. Woods had probably made many mistakes in his selection of the cast. It was a relief to find that I was wrong. With only one exception the actors were capable and well fitted to their parts.

The exception was a man with a small role but one with a well-defined character that was obviously unsuited to the actor Mr. Woods had engaged. After rehearsal I ascended by a diminutive elevator that led to Mr. Woods's roomy office high up in the front of the theatre. I found him sitting in a barber's chair set up for his use in a tiny annex at the back of the office. The visiting barber was just completing a shave. Mr. Woods asked me to take a seat. Soon he joined me and sat at his desk. When I told him that one miscasting would have to be remedied, he asked me to describe the type of actor required. When I did so I had a second shock. Mr. Woods said he had exactly the man I wanted in one of his touring companies that was closing in a couple of weeks, and he could join us then. He casually said, "Don't tell the man we have now that he won't be wanted; just use him at rehearsals until the other fellow comes." Astonished, I told him that this would be brutal. I refused to keep the man rehearsing if he was to be dismissed later on. At first Mr. Woods was amused, but soon his tone changed. He said quite sharply that this was the regular thing to do. I stuck to my point, however, and the next day the actor was "let out." The stage manager read the part until the new man arrived. It was this kind of unfairness, not to say inhumanity—an actor could be dismissed at any time during rehearsals—which led to the foundation of the Actors' Equity Association and the actors' strike in 1919. Since then there has been a contractual limitation of time when cast changes are permissible during rehearsals.

I had had some doubts about undertaking *The Guilty Man*, for I did not think very highly of the script. I should certainly have refused the offer, except that I was subject to financial pressure from England, where my wife continued to reside with my two daughters. This pressure, which was to continue for a considerable period, overcame the much greater hesitation I felt when, immediately after the run of *The Guilty Man*, I was offered the position of general stage director to the Charles Frohman company.

Charles Frohman, one of the most successful producers in England as well as America, had been drowned in the sinking of the *Lusitania*, but the firm continued with the same name under his partner, Alf Hayman. He carried on the policy inaugurated by Frohman of employing star actors and actresses to head all the companies. Their names were printed in the largest type in all the advertising, much larger even than the name of the play in which they were appearing. After a week or two of out-of-town tryouts, the productions were always housed in the very handsome Empire Theatre, where the managerial offices, including my own, were located. After the run in New York every production went on the road. The provincial tours were by far the most profitable part of the enterprise. The road was a dependable gold mine.

It was 1917, and I had spent eighteen years in the theatre. I accepted my appointment with the Frohman firm with a bitter sense of shame. It meant identifying myself with the "star system," which I had always condemned as a soul-destructive shackling of the art of the theatre.

My state of mind was not helped by my relationship with Alf Hayman. There were times when he reminded me of a woolly English sheep dog, but they were rare. These moments generally came when I spent a weekend at his home in the country. There he was a friendly host who loved to tell anecdotes about his early days in the theatre. He would sit slumped down in his big armchair until, at some trifling annoyance, he would heave himself up looking like a sea lion emerging from the waves. And he would then roar like a sea lion. In fact, he was always so ready to roar that he was often referred to by the actors and stagehands as "the big noise."

The conductor of an English musical comedy that Hayman produced described how, when he had just arrived from London and was happily rehearsing the orchestra, they were suddenly interrupted by a loud bellow from the back of the theatre. He stopped playing and looked around to see Hayman storming down the aisle shouting stentorian curses at the musicians for being an incompetent lot of boobies. Naturally the conductor was terribly upset by this—so much so that it was hard

Alf Hayman

Payne as a Broadway director

for him to continue the rehearsal. Later, when he joined Hayman in his office, the producer asked whether he had chosen a good moment for the interruption. He had made it, Hayman blandly explained, in order to stimulate the efforts of the musicians.

In his sheep-dog mood Alf Hayman sometimes told me interesting anecdotes concerning the origin and early days of the Frohman company, when they were touring the newly sprung-up, and at the moment very prosperous, mining towns in the West. I enjoyed most his account of their first great success. The firm was brought to birth in a bold venture that made nationwide headlines in the press.

Both Hayman and Frohman, working separately, had had ill luck with small theatrical ventures around New York, so they were both badly off for money. They mutually agreed that it was time for a bold stroke, although their sole asset was a few dollars that Frohman had stashed away in a savings bank.

William Gillette, already a big star, was about to close the successful run of a play in New York. Presumably he had no immediate plans. Hayman had once met him, so Frohman suggested that he make the unprecedented offer of taking the whole company of Gillette's play, lock, stock, and barrel, to San Francisco. Alf Hayman's brother, Al Hayman, was the manager of the Alcazar Theatre there and would naturally be delighted.

The first step was for Alf Hayman to see Gillette. He did so and made the daring proposition. Gillette's immediate response was to say that he knew Hayman did not have the money for such an undertaking. Hayman countered by affirming that his friend Charles Frohman could and would finance the venture. Gillette was dubious, but he agreed to meet Frohman that night after the show in the Knickerbocker Hotel bar.

Frohman had prepared for the situation by withdrawing all his money from the bank in the form of two ten-dollar bills and a small stack of ones. Between each two one-dollar bills he placed a slightly smaller piece of wrapping paper. The two ten-dollar bills were on top, thus giving the appearance of an enormous roll of money. There was no reason for Gillette to suppose that the ten-dollar bills were only window dressing. This gesture turned the trick and an agreement was signed.

The problem now was to transport the company to San Francisco. A high official of the New York Central Railroad, known to Hayman, agreed to transport the company to California without prepayment, assuming that Alf Hayman's brother would meet the cost of the journey on their arrival. There were naturally many small expenses to be met along the way. They arrived in San Francisco literally penniless. There they received the catastrophic news that the Alcazar Theatre had gone bankrupt!

The receivers informed them that they would gladly lend them the theatre, but they refused to advance money for the preliminary expenses, including the payment due the railroad company. Since their only recourse was to confess their dilemma to Gillette, they went to see him in his hotel. Sitting in his room talking of this and that they kept urging each other with nudges to speak out, but both were afraid to do so. Eventually, Gillette, as a hint that they should leave, withdrew his watch from his pocket. He looked at it closely, shook it, and then expressed surprise at finding that it had stopped.

Now, this watch was famous. It had been presented to him by his fellow townsmen on some notable occasion as an expression of their pride in his achievements. It was a particularly fine timepiece, well known as the result of much publicity. Seizing the opportunity, Hayman almost snatched the watch out of Gillette's hand, saying that he knew the only watchmaker in San Francisco who could be safely trusted with such a treasure. They rushed to a pawnbroker and with the money borrowed on the watch they managed to make the opening and the success they had counted on. The famous Frohman company was established.

Hayman told of another episode with particular relish. A company he managed was touring pioneer towns in the West with *Camille*, starring Maurice Barrymore, the father of Ethel, Lionel, and John. They arrived at a newly developed mining town where it was impossible to engage extras for the gambling scene. The town was so flourishing that the money they could afford to offer was laughed at. The only thing to do was for Hayman himself and the company's advance agent, who chanced to be in town, to supply the place of the usual ten or a dozen guests representing the gambling party. It will be remembered that, at the instigation of Armand's father, Camille pretends to be unfaithful to her lover to save his reputation. The distracted Armand calls in the guests and demands, "Do you see this woman?" They reply that they do. Armand then asks, "Do you know what she has done?" They answer, "No"—whereupon he denounces Camille. The two "supers," who did not have to appear until late in the play, boosted their nerves by having several drinks. The result was that, when they were summoned with "Come in all of you," they almost staggered onto the stage. Asked if they saw the woman, neither of them could speak for several seconds, but eventually the press agent managed to articulate a feeble "No!" Maurice Barrymore, after an angry glance at them, topped the audience's laughter by shouting the second question, "Do you know what she has done?" Hayman was still speechless, but his companion gave a hiccupy "Yes!" This was too much for Barrymore and he called out to the stage manager in the prompt corner, "Oh, what's the use? Ring down the curtain!" And so the act was ended.

This was a company with a star. Hayman told me, however, that in those days smaller companies did not book theatres in advance. They moved from town to town according to the state of their finances. It was not unusual, he told me, for the manager to go to the railroad depot (he had often done it himself), spread out all the money he had in the exchequer, and ask the booking clerk how far it would take them. On arriving at whatever town they were able to reach, they found local printers to provide the bills announcing the night's performance, and the actors would post them.

My five years with the Charles Frohman firm on Broadway make a dispiriting story of almost continuous frustration. If it had not been for the financial pressure I mentioned earlier I like to think that I should have had sufficient strength of character to abandon my position with the Frohman company. I quickly realized that I was myself committing the crime that I had so strenuously condemned in my Manchester days, that of letting financial considerations dominate artistic ones. To tell myself that I was forced into this compromise by circumstances I did not choose was a paltry excuse. I felt that I was selling my birthright for a mess of pottage. I was very unhappy and, though I went about my work conscientiously, I felt it placed me in the position of a glorified stage manager rather than a director.

Any attempt to direct the star actors beyond plotting movements or giving the broadest possible suggestion of an interpretation of some scene or passage was obviously misunderstood. After all, it was upon an individual technique that an actor's reputation had been fashioned. It was his stock-in-trade. As for the lesser actors, they too seemed to belong to a different genre from those I had known in repertory companies. Even the actors of secondary parts were in most cases as crystallized in their methods as the stars. They were bewildered by anything in the way of direction other than physical placement. I had to couch any suggestion about the expression of emotion in carefully chosen terms, or a blank look of incomprehension froze their faces.

Once I asked a talented actor why he became cold and distant in manner throughout rehearsals, whereas he was friendly and convivial outside the theatre. He told me that it was because I was the director and the director was the enemy of an actor. When I asked him to account for this attitude he explained that the director had to think of the good of the whole play, while it was the actor's task to look after himself and make the most of his part. I challenged him as to why the actor should not be concerned with the artistic worth of the play. Laughingly he replied that to the actor the part comes first. It reminded me of the old stock-company days before the arrival of the stage director. Actors would retort to any suggestion from anyone with a stern, "Sir, I know my business!"

Another cause of my frustration at the Empire Theatre was the method of casting. One could understand Mr. Hayman's preference for employing actors who had already played in Frohman companies because he was familiar with their work. But he was not content with that safeguard. He always wanted to be sure that their parts belonged to exactly the same category as those in which they had previously appeared. Typecasting was carried to the extreme limit by Alf Hayman. When interviewing an actor for a part, his only consideration was whether he had acted similar roles.

Once I persuaded him, with some difficulty, since he did not know the actor's work, to engage an old friend of mine from the Benson days, Thomas Louden, for the small part of a butler in a play with Ethel Barrymore as the star. Louden gave, as I knew he would, a satisfactory account of the part. The play ran its course and we were again casting Ethel Barrymore. In this play there was no butler, but there was a short role of a family lawyer, for which Louden was particularly suitable. In fact, he had actually practiced as a barrister in Ireland before taking to the stage. When I mentioned Louden's name for the part, Hayman looked at me with almost apoplectic amazement. "What's the matter with you, Payne," he demanded. "Are you crazy? Louden plays *butlers!*"

In speaking of professional case-hardening, I have already remarked on how widespread in the professional theatre was this practice of typecasting. Another manager than Hayman put it succinctly enough. The director's main task, he thought, was casting a play. "Choose the right types," he said. "As far as possible pick known actors that the critics like, and everything falls into place."

To the imaginative actor who hopes to grow in his profession this attitude on the part of managers is destructive to talent, as well as disheartening. Perhaps its saddest aspect is its effect on actors who have an unclear sense of their own potential. For the Players Club in New

York I once directed a production of Congreve's *The Way of the World*, a play in which the polished diction demands a particular speech rhythm. One of the actresses spoke her lines with very clear enunciation but so rapidly that her scenes were out of focus. When I asked her to slow her tempo, I was puzzled to notice that this routine request seemed to worry her. She continued rehearsing at the same breakneck pace, so I had to speak to her again. She looked more distressed than before. The gallop was slightly reduced for a time, then returned to full speed. On my third protest the young woman burst into tears. After years of struggle, she complained, she had finally scored a success in her last play when several critics praised her for her clear and rapid diction. "And now," she cried, "you want to take it all away from me!"

Speaking very generally, there seem to me to be four kinds of actors on the professional stage. There is, very rarely, a purely instinctive character actor like Charles Bibby. At the opposite end of the spectrum there is the technical actor of the sort of John Drew. Thoroughly case-hardened, he is always the same from the first rehearsal to the final performance. For his casual air and complete confidence, the more sensitive actors both scorn and envy him. But he is known for a certain type of part, and he is always sure of an engagement when there is a part open that fits him. He is not vain, and he is inclined to speak disparagingly of his profession.

A third type of actor is the self-exploiter, who loves to demonstrate his charms to the public. Once he has been accepted for leading roles, he is secure with that public. Let me quote a remarkably accurate description of one such actor from a letter written me by a former student who was trying to break into the theatre in New York. "He has achieved his position by the expansion of his interesting self. His charming personality warps every role to fit itself. He is never unconscious of the audience. All through rehearsal every piece of business, every gesture, every reading, is weighed on the scale of his personality before it is accepted for delivery. 'How will this make *me* look before *my* public? Charming? I must expand it. Ridiculous? Then I must either force the director to drop it by playing it poorly or, if that is not possible, so underplay it that the audience will never know it is there.' I am sure that, if he were asked the road to success for an actor he would say, 'Never read plays, read mirrors. Polish not thy cultural knowledge. Instead cultivate social grace, an easy smile, good manners. This is what makes you an actor.' " This is, of course, the antithesis of art.

Finally there is the essential creative artist, the actor who works from within, consciously and deliberately, instinct alert but controlled by intelligence. He is generally slow in development and often does not give his best until he has played a part many times. There is great danger in store for such a person. Because he works slowly managers are understandably afraid of him. But, if he can escape case-hardening, it is just this actor who will get the greatest satisfaction from his work. Moreover, he will make the most lasting appeal to the public. He is the true actor, the artist.

Before I leave the subject of actors and casting I should perhaps speak of something that was practically a corollary of typecasting: the acting tradition. Until fairly recently the notion of "tradition" used to impress all but the most resolutely individualistic of actors. My own feeling for it was influenced more than a little, however, by two experiences of my own.

When I directed a dramatization of Blasco Ibáñez's Spanish novel *Blood and Sand*, starring Otis Skinner in a Frohman production, I had another contest over casting with Alf Hayman. For the role of the journalist who interviews the hero, a matador, I persuaded Hayman, with much difficulty, to engage a certain actor in spite of the fact that he had a stiff knee that made him limp. The disability had been earned in the First World War, so I was eager to give the actor a chance. And I saw no reason why the journalist, a fan of bullfighting, might not have once been in the bull ring himself and received a wound there. In any event I overcame Hayman's resistance. A year or two later I met an actor acquaintance who told me that he had played in *Blood and Sand* with a Boston stock company. I asked what role he had played. "Nothing much," he replied, "only the journalist who limps."

Sheridan's *The Critic* contains a burlesque rehearsal of a tragedy. In this scene the part of the heroine's confidante is small but immensely effective. When I revived this play after many years I discovered that the original stage business had apparently been lost. One day the young lady cast as the confidante came to rehearsal with a severe cold, sniffing atrociously. She was filled with apologies, but I noticed that the sniffles had a very funny effect. I asked her to retain them in performance and she made quite a hit. A few years later the play was done in London. Although I did not see it, a friend told me that one of the funniest things in it—something that he would never forget—was the fact that the confidante's role was played with a bad cold. He asked me if this device was "traditional." A fine word. The way in which it is commonly used reminds me of the tale of the old lady who said that of all the beautiful things she heard in church her favorite was "that blessed word Mesopotamia."

I do not want to give the impression that, in the days when the revival of old plays was the rule instead of the exception, there were no genuine stage traditions. There were—and some of them were bad. We read, for example, that it was traditional for the First Gravedigger in *Hamlet* to begin his exertions by shedding several waistcoats. That sort of unhistorical and inept clowning has caused a revolt against stage business handed down as traditional.

It does not follow, however, that what is clearly implicit—and sometimes explicit—in a text should be avoided. King Lear, in his madness, taking shelter in a hovel from the violence of a storm, imagines that his cruel daughters, Goneril and Regan, are present. Summoning both to trial, he says, "Arraign her first; 'tis Goneril." The Fool responds, "Come hither, mistress. Is your name Goneril? . . . Cry you mercy, I took you for a joint-stool." Obviously there is a stool in the room and the mad king has fancied that Goneril is sitting on it. Without a real stool onstage, the Fool's words are meaningless. Yet, so extreme is the desire to avoid the traditional that I have seen a production of *King Lear* in which no stool was provided for this scene. Shakespeare himself was never so afraid of the obvious. Yet who knew better the scope and power of the imagination? Listen to Theseus in *A Midsummer Night's Dream:*

> The poet's eye, in a fine frenzy rolling,
> Doth glance from heaven to earth, from earth to heaven;
> And as imagination bodies forth
> The forms of things unknown, the poet's pen
> Turns them to shapes, and gives to airy nothing
> A local habitation and a name.

The scenery for productions of the Frohman company was of the highest quality money could buy. The scenes were invariably realistic, but it would be a mistake to despise them for that reason. Realism in the theatre was the fashion, and the sets were designed and painted by talented artists, not mere craftsmen. Apart from suggesting their general style, my function was merely to indicate physical necessities, such as the placing of doors and windows. And when the designs were submitted by the scene painters I could suggest improvements if necessary. The designs were then shown to Mr. Hayman. Invariably he complained about the cost and tried to reduce the estimate, but he made no comment on the designs themselves.

It was only in the lighting of the plays that I felt I could let the reins of imagination loose. There were no lighting experts in those days;

stage illumination was part of the director's job. At the Empire Theatre, the head electrician was ever ready, even eager, to supply whatever was required, and the head carpenter was most cooperative. Uninterrupted at night, when rehearsals were done with for the day, I had the great satisfaction of creating visual effects that I still believe to have been as good as those produced with complicated switchboards and specialized instruments. Above all, the effects were unhurried in their execution. In interior scenes, as in well-lighted productions today, intensifying the light on one part of the stage while diminishing it elsewhere in order to concentrate the spectator's attention was so subtly done that the spectator felt the result of the change without noticing that it was being made. We could also use lighting effectively to create mood in exterior scenes. For a dawn scene in a forest we were able to make a very slow development of light with the changing sky seen through forest trees. The characters entered only when there was sufficient illumination for the speakers in the dialogue to be recognized. Possibly a modern audience would be impatient, especially as there was no background music. That ornamentation was then despised as cheap and melodramatic.

As for my directorial relationships with the actors, having accepted the limitations of casting that I have described, there was nothing to prevent my being on amiable terms with the actors. There used to be a prevalent idea that star actors (or more often actresses) were in the habit of taking liberties, such as arriving late at rehearsals or even of absenting themselves altogether. This is something I never met, except with Ethel Barrymore. Though it would be wrong to call it a habit, there were occasions when she strolled in quite calmly as much as half an hour late for a rehearsal.

But Miss Barrymore's worst shortcoming was that she was still holding her book three or four days from our opening out of town. She worked hard enough at her lines *after* the opening—thus necessitating daily rehearsals of her scenes—but she was never verbally at ease until after several performances. This did not seem to worry her. The audience apparently meant nothing to her, and she was equally oblivious to the disconcerting effect she had upon the other actors. When there was a complete "dry-up" she used to stare her fellow actor full in the face and imperiously inquire, "Well?" as if he were the one who had forgotten the lines. In this way she generally succeeded in directing the onus away from herself, but once or twice she met her match and got no help. Then the prompter's voice, audible to the audience, gave the situation away. This annoyed Miss Barrymore considerably.

Away from the theatre, as for instance on our many railroad journeys, Ethel Barrymore was often companionable. Everyone enjoyed her lively conversation, which was sometimes salted with caustic remarks about well-known actors, not excluding her brothers, John and Lionel. At other times she sat alone and read a novel. One day while chatting in her dressing room I mentioned that one of the actors in the company had, for me, a Dickensian personality. Her face lit up immediately. She told me that she read Dickens regularly. *Our Mutual Friend* was her favorite novel and she read it once a year at Christmastime.

Another of our popular stars was Otis Skinner. Vitality was the keynote of his acting, and he was most effective in parts that had something of the quality of a dashing buccaneer. Off the stage, too, he was the hearty good fellow. I found his high spirits infectious, and indeed he was generally on good terms with everyone. Unfortunately, after his vigor abated, he still continued to act. When long after I had ceased to work with him he came to Pittsburgh on tour, the weakness of his performance depressed me. Several of our students went to see the play especially because of its celebrated star, and I overheard a group of them discussing the play. They were unanimous in disparaging Mr. Skinner's performance. Understandably, they thought that there must have been something very wrong with acting and popular taste in the old days if flat, dull acting was regarded as worthy of stardom. Joining rather sadly in the conversation I explained how time had brought the decay of Skinner's powers. I assured them that no one at any time achieved lasting renown without showing outstanding ability in one direction or another.

The most refreshing oasis in what for me had become the desert of Broadway was the production in 1918 of J. M. Barrie's *Dear Brutus*, with William Gillette as the star. There were several reasons for this. In the first place, this holiday from realism brought me once more into the enchanted world of fantasy. It made me realize that my imagination was becoming parched and craved sustenance. By good fortune we were happy in the whole company, especially in what I regarded on first reading the play as the most difficult part to cast, the dream daughter in the magical forest. I wondered whether any actress could be found to do it justice. I would not have been afraid if I had known that the whole enchantment of the forest was destined to come to life in the performance of one of the finest American actresses, Helen Hayes. It was her first major success among her many memorable performances on Broadway. By the time of the performance I had the experience of wishing that the part were longer. During the rehearsals I had been very obtuse at first in worrying about what I afterwards learned to be her Southern accent in an English part. But the beauty and vitality of Miss Hayes's performance completely obliterated my shortsighted qualms.

A second delight was the presence of Mr. William Gillette as the father in the play. Gillette was in my estimation the First Gentleman of the American theatre. He was somewhat aloof in manner, and strangely enough he never appeared to take much interest in what he was doing. Nevertheless he carried out his task with undeviating efficiency, and with his fellow players he was always considerate and gracious. In William Gillette, I saw exemplified once more the old-time theatre etiquette. I regarded it as valuable as well as charming, but it had so nearly disappeared from the theatre that I had almost begun to forget that it had once been universally practiced. Gillette had not forgotten. He would never interrupt a scene to approach the prompt table. If he had some real reason to speak to the director, he would choose a suitable moment between scenes or when the action had temporarily ceased.

At the Empire Theatre I had managed to reintroduce an old and now neglected stipulation that the auditorium remain clear throughout rehearsal, even of the actors in the cast. The purpose of this was to safeguard the concentration of the actors. It was so understood and well observed. Still, no other star of the first magnitude would have unobtrusively come to the prompt table, as Mr. Gillette did one day, to ask if he might slip through the front of the house. He had to see the manager on business and was not concerned in the scene about to be rehearsed. He added that he would certainly have gone out by the stage door and around the outside of the theatre, but it was pouring rain. Such courtesy can never be forgotten.

It was not long after *Dear Brutus* that Hayman told me we were to produce another Barrie play called *Mary Rose*. He had not read it, nor did he see any reason for me to do so prior to casting. The author's name and the fact that it was running in London were enough for him. I awaited the manuscript eagerly but was somewhat disappointed on reading it. I should have thought better of it perhaps if it had preceded *Dear Brutus*. Barrie again attempted to create the paradox of an unreal world in the midst of a realistic setting, but I thought that he did so less convincingly. Considering the spell he had cast with *Dear Brutus*, it seemed to me this time his fantasy had failed to take wings. This feeling carried over into the rehearsals. Although we had a capable cast on the whole, most of the acting lacked that inspired quality that I had found in *Dear Brutus*.

To my mind, there was a striking instance of the weakness of the star system in the choice of Ruth Chatterton for the title role. She was, I saw at once, a very talented actress, but her personality had too earthbound a quality for the wistful Mary Rose. It was a case of the wrong instrument being destructive to an orchestral effect, no matter how well it is performed. I told Hayman so after the first rehearsal and I well remember the expression of astonishment mingled with contempt with which he retorted, "Good God, man, she's the star!"

Typecasting, in Hayman's estimation, did not apply to stars. Once he gave me a script to read that had been recommended to him for production. I asked him for whom he had it in mind. He answered it would be for either William Gillette or Otis Skinner. This seemed odd, and odder still when I found on reading it that the leading part was that of a Corsican bandit. Next day I told Hayman that I would not recommend the play for production but that in any case it was obviously suited to Skinner and would be absurd for Gillette. He looked as if he was on the point of explosion as he said, "What's the matter with you, Payne? They're both stars!"

Hayman's curious attitude of mind disclosed itself in a similar way when we were discussing the scenery for *Mary Rose*. I proposed to make a slight change from the ground plan used in the London production. Hayman was horrified. Here was a play, he said, that no one could make head or tail of, yet it was making money in London and was done with the author's approval. To make any change from that production might destroy whatever incomprehensible thing it was that made it a success.

There were times when we were neither preparing for nor working on a production. Then Mr. Hayman sometimes "loaned" me out to put on a play for another manager, as long as he belonged to the Klaw & Erlanger syndicate in which the Frohman firm was included. I did this three times for David Belasco, when he wanted to see performances of new plays out of town so as to judge by the reactions of the audiences whether he would be wise to produce them in his New York theatre. He decided against all three of them, even *The Romantic Young Lady*, by the Spanish playwright, Gregorio Martínez Sierra. That time I was disappointed, for the play had a delicate charm that might have served well at the Belasco Theatre. But probably Belasco was right; he was a shrewd judge of what the public wanted.

The most interesting of the loan engagements was for *Caesar's Wife*, by Somerset Maugham. It was produced by Florenz Ziegfeld, with his wife, Billie Burke, as the star. The production brought me one of

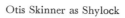

Otis Skinner as Shylock

Billie Burke in *Caesar's Wife*, 1919

Helen Hayes and William Gillette in *Dear Brutus*, 1918

the least burdensome of my experiences on Broadway. Billie Burke, who at that time reminded me of a delicate Dresden china figurine, was as friendly and warm offstage as she was charming on it, and Ziegfeld was lavish and free-handed in supplying every technical requirement. The latter trait was a pleasant change from the reluctance of Hayman, who, apart from the cost of scenery, was positively cheeseparing. He seemed to revel in checking and arguing about expenditures on even the most trivial items.

I tried to make the best of things throughout my Broadway experiences. But the most discouraging aspect of my situation was that, tied as I was to the Charles Frohman company, I could be no more than a sympathetic onlooker at a time when the American theatre was beginning to shake itself free from the shackles of outworn theatrical convention. It was heartbreaking to face the fact that instead of being a pioneer in the theatre, as I once had been, I had been turned into a laggard in the forward march.

CHAPTER 15

*E*ven with our own productions and those I made for other managements, there were intervals, sometimes of several weeks, in which nothing required my presence in New York. This happened more often when I left the Frohman firm on the death of Alf Hayman in 1922 and became a free-lance director. It became habitual with me to fill in the gaps by going to Carnegie Tech, where I was always in demand. At first, each visit to Pittsburgh had supposedly been for a special occasion, particularly the annual celebration of Shakespeare's birthday. Now the time came when I oscillated regularly between the two cities. I became aware that I took increasing satisfaction from what Pittsburgh afforded and less and less interest in my work in New York. Gradually I developed a positive aversion to commercially sponsored production.

At Carnegie Tech the numerical strength of the drama department increased year by year. It was evident that the barrier of parental objection to acting as a career was being lowered. As this happened the proportion of students with outstanding acting ability markedly declined. But there was as yet no falling off in enthusiasm. I could not begin to compare the eagerness of the students with the lack of interest shown by professional casts during rehearsals. Of course professionals were businesslike in carrying on their work, but, except on a first night, there was little of the heartwarming excitement that filled the atmosphere throughout a production at Tech. There was something contagious about this. It pervaded the whole drama department, not merely the cast involved at the moment.

Another change was that more students were joining the department whose principal interest was not in acting but in the technical side of production. Others discovered that they lacked acting talent but still retained an interest in theatre work. Nevertheless, the problem of mounting plays increased step by step with the ever-growing number of productions. At first all students had to share in the technical work, even those who were actually rehearsing. But this did not prove satisfactory. A solution was found in a very simple device. Throughout their freshman year students attended acting classes but were excluded from acting in the major productions. They had to work on the technical side of all productions, however, under a professional technician employed to direct this work. Thus freshmen, though eager to act, had to begin with what they regarded as a sort of penal year. Many could hardly have endured it if they had not been able to look forward to release from bondage in their second year, when they would never more be called upon to wield a hammer or turn a screwdriver. It became the custom for students to celebrate their enfranchisement by painting a list of their names and the year of their servitude within a decorative frame on the wall of a backstage area.

At about this time my interest in Shakespeare both widened and deepened. William Poel came to Pittsburgh at the invitation of myself and T. W. Stevens. His production of Ben Jonson's *The Poetaster* created much excitement among the students and playgoers.* I was greatly disappointed to be unable to attend either rehearsals or performances because of commitments in New York. My regret was somewhat allayed, however, when I learned that Poel had not relied on his usual quasi-Elizabethan setting. Nevertheless, my renewed contact with him made me all the more eager to experiment with a production of this kind myself.

On my next visit to Carnegie Tech I decided to produce *Richard II*. I hoped to take this opportunity to try my hand at Poel's approach. Stevens, however, talked me out of it. He wanted me to use his own scene designs. They were ready when I arrived from New York, and I found them simple and charming. Stevens readily agreed to my use of neutral curtains for intermediate scenes to avoid breaking the flow of action.

I had several reasons for choosing *Richard II*. For one thing, it was a kind of test. I wanted to find out what I could make of a history play that

*Speaight records that these performances were so successful that they were repeated at the University of Detroit. The impression they made was not soon forgotten. Neither were Poel's rehearsal methods. "American students, though they are docile to ideas, are not amenable to discipline; and they began to tell gloomy stories about rehearsals from ten to five without a break for luncheon. At five they were dismissed for a cup of tea, with instructions to return at five thirty. Poel held that nobody could begin to act until they were on the point of collapse, and he himself had a fakir's capacity for going without food."

Thomas Wood Stevens in 1913

Mementoes of the backstage crews at Carnegie Tech

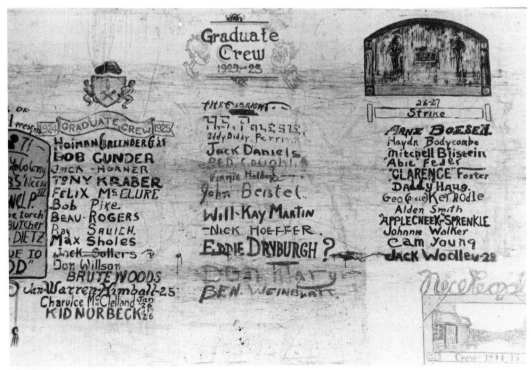

I had not done under any other management. I had walked on in this play during my trial engagement with Benson, but my memory of that production was too dim to count. *Richard II*, moreover, held a strong personal appeal for me. Finally, I had a purely practical reason for choosing it. The role of the king is a risky one to entrust to young actors, but there was at Tech a young man in his senior year whose experience and skill led me to believe that he could be relied upon to meet this challenge. I had confidence in him, and though he portrayed the weak, tyrannical side of the character a little more convincingly than the poetic side, he fulfilled my expectation.

Sadly, it was this talented and sensitive young actor who taught me that tragic waste of resources is not confined to the professional theatre. Otis Skinner happened to be in Pittsburgh during the later rehearsals and attended one of them. He was so impressed by the acting of my young student as the King that he invited him to come to New York for an interview after graduation. The young man did so and joined Mr. Skinner in the fall. During rehearsals, however, he was summoned back to Pittsburgh by the serious illness of his mother. She soon recovered and he went back to New York, where he was fortunate enough to get another engagement. Rehearsals had hardly begun when another telegram demanded his return to Pittsburgh. Another recovery and another venture in New York brought no more than a repetition of the same ill luck. This was too much for the young man. He threw in the sponge and returned to Pittsburgh permanently. His friends were disgusted, feeling that his mother's illnesses were more imaginary than real. Whether they were right or wrong, he gave up his acting career and went into business. Many years later, while I was rehearsing a production at Tech, I noticed that a short and very stout middle-aged man had slipped in unobtrusively and taken a seat. At a break in the rehearsal he introduced himself as my King Richard, but he refused to talk further, saying that he had to leave. As we shook hands I could not help detecting a wistful expression in his eyes. He lingered for a few moments and I hoped he would say more, but he abruptly turned and left the theatre.

While I am on the subject of actors in our production, I must add that *Richard II* provides an outstanding example of Shakespeare's extraordinary ability to give full and rich characterization even to a minute part, when his imagination is aroused in depicting one. This is in the role of the groom who visits the King in his prison shortly before his assassination. The groom indirectly shows his love for his former master by lamenting the fact that the usurper, Bolingbroke, has ridden upon "roan Barbary," the horse that he had so carefully groomed for Richard.

I was deeply touched by the true, sincere feeling that an actor named Mulligan infused into the part at Tech. Sometime later I found out that I was not alone in this. Recalling the *Richard II* production with the dean of our college of fine arts, Glendenning Keeble, I mentioned how good the actor had been in the King's role. Keeble agreed but added that he always remembered first the wonderful performance given by William Mulligan as the groom.

Mulligan's performance was effective because he was so completely absorbed in being the King's groom that all self-consciousness disappeared. Paradoxically, there is a sense in which, with the cessation of conscious self, true acting begins. This fact was demonstrated in reverse, as it were, by an episode that happened when I was putting on Ibsen's *An Enemy of the People* in Manchester. We were rehearsing the town-meeting scene. Before the dialogue began, citizens came in one by one or in couples and greeted friends in dumb show before taking seats in the rows of chairs provided for them. Sometimes they waved to friends seated some distance from them. Charles McEvoy, the author of a play I was to produce a little later on, arrived just after the rehearsal of this scene began. I asked him to take a seat until we finished. Quite by chance, in the midst of the rehearsal a porter came in carrying his trunk on his shoulders. He set it down and looked about for someone to sign a receipt. Suddenly my arm was seized and I looked round to find McEvoy quite excited as he whispered, "That man with the trunk! How good he is, isn't he?"

But I must return to what I learned from this, my first production of *Richard II*. For quite some time I had regarded Shakespeare as greatly more than a source of magnificent acting opportunities or even an exciting challenge to a director's ingenuity. My reading of what scholars had written about him in comment and exegesis had become a fascinating pastime. But as yet my interest was too unguided and unsystematic to be dignified with the name of study. It was ardent, nonetheless, and the outcome was both revealing and enlivening. With the production of *Richard II*, I was for the first time able to put the knowledge I had attained to practical use. It provided me with helpful suggestions to give the actors, the overtones needed for the full expression of their characterizations.

One part of what I learned was the historical background of the plays. Let me give an example of how this affected my production. What does the audience gather from the first scene? The King has summoned two factious nobles, Bolingbroke and Mowbray, to his presence. They challenge each other to mortal combat, each accusing the other of treason. The King attempts to pacify them but fails. He is compelled to assert his authority by summoning them to a formal trial at arms on a specified future date. That is all that happens. But since it is dramatic in itself, it arouses curiosity as to what the result will be when the combatants meet.

But how much more meaning the actors can instill into the lines if they understand the full significance when Bolingbroke, the King's first cousin, accuses Mowbray of having plotted the assassination of the King's uncle, the Duke of Gloucester. Rumor—and possibly more than rumor—has it that the King himself was implicated in the crime. This complication adds daring and even a hint of subtle ambition to Bolingbroke's asseverations. It gives tremendous weight to the King's aside, "How high a pitch his resolution soars!" Moreover, it indicates exactly the manner in which it should be spoken to reveal that there is a hidden purport in Bolingbroke's insinuations. The effect is enhanced if, when Bolingbroke makes the accusation, everyone present in the court tightens up. This adds an electric tension to the air, and there should be an ominous pause before Bolingbroke resumes his speech. Although, admittedly, the audience as a whole does not get the point of such readings, emotions expressed on the stage are dramatic and contagious. There is a responsive heightening of interest in what is happening and possibly the consciousness that there is much more going on than appears on the surface.

In the following scene the fact that the King is implicated in Gloucester's murder is clearly stated. His widow fruitlessly appeals to her brother-in-law, John of Gaunt, Bolingbroke's father, to avenge her husband's murder. He refuses to assist her in five lines of great significance. Not only does he definitely accuse the King, but he introduces an idea that is vital to the understanding of the purpose of the whole play: A king is God's anointed representative on earth. For this reason Gaunt abjures all personal responsibility:

> God's is the quarrel; for God's substitute,
> His deputy anointed in his sight,
> Hath caus'd his death; the which if wrongfully,
> Let heaven revenge; for I may never lift
> An angry arm against his minister.

In undertaking a panoramic history play, I feared that the smallness of the theatre would prove to be detriment. On the contrary, I was pleased to discover that the small size actually encouraged a feeling of intimacy with the actors and of reality in the action. It may well have created something of the spectator's participation that must have characterized the Elizabethan theatres.

During the next seven years my almost annual Shakespeare's birthday productions at Carnegie Tech included *A Midsummer Night's Dream*, *Romeo and Juliet*, *King John*, *Richard II*, and *The Merry Wives of Windsor*. They were all done in the general manner of *Richard II*, as was Dekker's *Shoemaker's Holiday*, with which in 1922 I broke the Shakespearean cycle. Earlier on I had made and produced a condensation of Fletcher's *The Elder Brother*, but that was in addition to the annual Elizabethan production.

Each year I had the same argument with TW about my desire to try the Elizabethan method. This desire was particularly strong when we came to Dekker's play. While doing preparatory work on this charming and gentle comedy I had a strong feeling that its simple-hearted spirit would manifest itself most tellingly on Elizabethan lines. But whenever I tried to argue the point TW was obviously so distressed at the possibility that his designs would be discarded that my heart melted.

CHAPTER 16

By 1925 Thomas Wood Stevens had become in some respects at odds with the administration of Carnegie Tech. Growing restive, he resigned and accepted the management of the newly founded Goodman Theatre in Chicago. I had left the Frohman firm, and my only remaining connections with Broadway were sporadic free-lance productions, in which my interest steadily diminished. Consequently, I was pleased to accept the suggestion that, for the time being at any rate, I undertake the chairmanship of the drama department at Carnegie Tech.

Here was the opportunity I had been hoping for. I was free to make my next Shakespearean production in the style that I had so long wished to try. And I could take ample time about it. With nearly eight months on the spot I could cast it in September and work with actors individually until March, when full rehearsals could begin. The time seemed unlimited in comparison with past productions. *Hamlet* was the first play I undertook to produce in this manner.

Before describing my approach to it, however, I should remind my readers of the kind of Shakespearean production that was then prevalent, and which I had so long found unsatisfying. During the Restoration, Shakespeare's plays had been "improved" upon by producers such as William Davenant. In addition to rewriting extensively and introducing, for example, songs and dances for the witches in *Macbeth* or a happy ending in *King Lear*, they often rearranged the plays to fit the spectacular scenery that pleased the audiences of the time. David Garrick, in the 1700s, did much to revive respect for Shakespeare's own words, as well as a natural style of acting, but the tradition of realistic scenery continued. In the Victorian period Henry Irving, though a Shakespearean actor of great seriousness, was sometimes criticized for subjugating the plays to elaborate scenery.

Shakespeare's plays, because so much of the action is carried forward in short scenes, are especially vulnerable to tampering. As long as it was assumed that each scene required an entire stage set the expense was prohibitive and the time needed for scene changes disrupted the flow of action. For very practical reasons there was a strong temptation to drop many scenes, to rearrange their sequence, or to combine them into longer scenes. Occasionally this was done to build up leading roles into vehicles for stars. More often, however, it was an attempt to solve the physical and financial problems presented by multiple scenes. Whatever its purpose, however, its effect on the logic of the plot was likely to be disastrous.

An example of this sacrifice of plot and sense to the demands of the scenery—one that dates from as late as 1931—was a production of *The Merchant of Venice*, with Maude Adams as Portia and Otis Skinner as Shylock. The play begins with a series of scenes in which Shakespeare cunningly interweaves the casket theme and the Shylock theme by making the action oscillate between Venice and Belmont. In this production, however, because the elaborate scenery was difficult to set up and strike repeatedly for the two locations, they played all the Venice scenes first and followed them with all the Belmont scenes. This made the play difficult to follow. Worse yet, it completely destroyed what I call the melodic line of scene development. The result could be compared to playing all the appearances of the first theme in a Beethoven symphony consecutively and following them with all those of the second theme.

Up to the time when I began work on my fateful *Hamlet* production at Tech my only solution to the practical problem of short scenes had been to play them in front of neutral curtains drawn across the whole stage. This device had not proved entirely satisfactory. Complete continuity of action, I had come to realize, was absolutely essential to the appreciation of a Shakespeare play. But the spectator's subconscious association of closing curtains with the idea of one thing ending and another being about to start destroyed the melodic line. I wished to see whether the all-important sense of continuity would be preserved in an Elizabethan setting. But before describing how I came to the conclusion that that was indeed the ideal milieu, I must say something about what that setting was like.

It would be absurd to claim authority on a subject that is almost entirely a matter of speculation. Very little is known about the structure of the Globe Theatre, Shakespeare's "wooden O," for which he wrote so much of his work, and still less about the earlier theatres and innyards where he tried his wings. My sole contention is that if one accepts what are widely regarded as the main elements of an average Elizabethan stage structure as the basis for the production of Shakespeare's plays —while always observing the universal principles of stage production— certain possibilities become probabilities, if not certainties. At the very least they shed light on Shakespeare's problems in constructing his plays to meet the requirements of Elizabethan stages, and also, sometimes excitingly, on the artistic use he made of the facilities of that stage.

When Shakespeare left his native Stratford-upon-Avon and came to try his fortune in London, playgoing in buildings exclusively devoted to playacting was an exciting and comparatively new development. For some time there had been companies of professional actors touring the country. They had to make the best of any place where they could put up a stage, or "scaffold," as it was often called. Of all the makeshifts they had to contend with, the most convenient by far were the inn yards. Certain London inns, such as the Cross Keys and the Bel Savage, added to their income fairly regularly by playing host to companies of players.

A typical inn was built about a central yard, open to the sky. Galleries overlooking the court, with doors opening into the bedrooms, were reached by outdoor staircases. When arrangements had been made with the landlord about sharing the receipts, the players could erect a stage at the end of the court opposite the arched entrance to the yard, or at one of the sides. The eminent scholar Leslie Hotson has claimed that the audience surrounded the stage on all sides. Most other scholars, however, believe that the audience stood on only three sides, with the back of the stage against the building. This arrangement seems to me far more plausible. Not only would it have given the actors easy access to the stage, but they could have used the adjacent galleries as needed for additional playing space whenever an actor was required by the plot to appear on an upper level, such as a balcony.

At performances, "gatherers" carried boxes in which they collected money paid for admission to the yard. There most of the spectators— the groundlings, as Shakespeare called them—would stand, unsheltered from the elements. Other, more affluent spectators sought the shelter and relative comfort of the galleries. Some parts of the first gallery, provided with seats, were known as the "lords' rooms." Needless to say gatherers stood ready at the entrances to the galleries to collect extra admission. When the audience was fully assembled, the gatherers took their boxes to an office where the landlord divided the takings with the actors. A vestige of this practice survives today in the term *box office*.

In spite of the many advantages of inn yards over earlier accommodations for plays, they were not completely satisfactory. To begin with, the receipts had to be shared with innkeepers. Moreover, many inns were within an area that fell within the jurisdiction of the City Council, which was inimical to theatrical performances. This prejudice arose not only because its members were predominantly puritanical in their outlook—though that had a good deal to do with their attitude—but because apprentices frequently played truant from their work in order to attend performances, which took place in the daytime. Then, too, it was claimed that pickpockets and women of ill repute plied their trades among the crowds attending the plays.

However much justification there may have been for these complaints, the council could point to one unquestionably valid objection to performances, at least at certain periods. Every summer there was an outbreak of the plague, and the crowding of the spectators was something to be avoided. For this reason, performances were forbidden whenever the plague broke out, and theatres remained closed until the disease abated as the summer heat declined. The performances would doubtless have been suppressed altogether if the Privy Council had not insisted upon their continuance. It pointed out that Queen Elizabeth liked to see plays, and the players had to be kept in training for the times when they were summoned to give performances at court. In taking this stand the Privy Council was no doubt carrying out the direct orders of Her Majesty.

The drawbacks of the inn yards apparently did not, in the view of the actors, have much to do with their physical characteristics. They considered their shape and structure well suited to dramatic presentations. Consequently, when James Burbage in 1576 hit upon the revolutionary idea of erecting a building especially for the public presentation of plays, he took the inn yard as his model.

Borrowing money, as well as investing his own, Burbage built his new structure outside the city limits, where it would be beyond the jurisdiction of the city fathers. He called it simply the Theatre. The name was not so presumptuous as it sounds. At the time, no other building existed in England—or indeed in the world—that was built for and devoted solely to play production and open to anyone who paid for admission. Burbage little expected, we may be sure, that his enterprise was to spawn such a vast progeny throughout the world!

Although not much is known of the structure of the Theatre, it is clear that it incorporated the main features of the inn yard. The central area was open to the sky. The stage projected into this open space. Later Elizabethan playhouses, if not the Theatre, added one convenience that the inn yard could not offer: a roof covering part of the acting area. In back of the stage was the "tiring house"—that is, the attiring house, or dressing rooms. The roof, sometimes known as the shadow, was supported by two columns, placed toward the forward corners of the stage but leaving plenty of space in front of them. Above the roof in some theatres (though probably not the Globe) was a "hut" containing machinery for raising and lowering actors in scenes calling for gods to appear from heaven, or other spectacular effects. In fact, the roof was sometimes called the heavens. At the Globe the underside may have been painted with stars on a blue background. It has been suggested that Hamlet refers to it in his line, "this brave o'erhanging firmament, this majestical roof fretted with golden fire."

Another feature of the inn yards that was copied in the theatres was the galleries. Most theatres seem to have boasted three tiers of them. Obviously Elizabethan theatre owners could count on far larger audiences than those that patronize the theatre today: the Globe is thought to have held about two thousand people. It seems certain that a modified gallery crossed the back of the stage. It would have been used, for example, for the balcony scene in *Romeo and Juliet*. Some researchers have suggested that a third tier, above it, held the musicians that some plays required. Whether there was also an adaptation of a gallery at stage level has been a main subject of controversy, so I will reserve my own views on that question until later.

My purpose in introducing these details of Elizabethan play production is, of course, to point out that the physical limitations to performance that the actors encountered in the inn yards and then perpetuated in their theatres can tell us much about their manner of presentation. Since there was little artificial light available, performances were always given in daylight. Audiences not only stood on three sides of the stage but looked down on it from the upper galleries, so curtains were of no use in concealing the stage. Therefore a change of place or time could not be indicated by either of the usual modern devices of closing the curtains or dimming the lights. It is evident that the action had to be completely continuous. This being the case, and taking into account the great number of scenes in Elizabethan plays, it is also obvious that players and playwrights could not depend upon representational scenery to define where the action was taking place.

Shakespeare and his contemporaries must have taken these conditions entirely for granted. They did whatever was needed to make the action clear. The problem of how to identify place they met in much the same way as do writers of radio drama. Locality could often be ignored altogether. When it could not, an actor mentioned it. In moving, between scenes, from one place to another, actors simply told the audience where they intended to go and then announced their arrival when they got there.

An instance of this device occurs in *As You Like It*. The usurping duke's niece is banished from his court with her dearly loved cousin Rosalind. They decide to join Rosalind's father in the Forest of Arden, taking Touchstone as an escort. Time has to pass before they arrive, so three scenes intervene. The weary travelers then reenter. So that the audience shall be in no doubt as to their whereabouts, Rosalind says flatly, "Well, this is the Forest of Arden." To drive the point home to the less attentive members of the audience Touchstone continues, "Ay, now am I in Arden, the more fool I. When I was at home, I was in a better place; but travelers must be content."

This is an obvious example of how Shakespeare coped with what modern audiences until recently would have seen as a disadvantage imposed upon Elizabethan playwrights by the conditions of production. Only when I began to work on a stage that incorporated the main features of Shakespeare's own did I gradually come to realize that those conditions were in fact advantages for those plays that had been written to fit them.

To set the stage, as it were, I must first describe what I came to call "modified Elizabethan staging." I should emphasize that in developing it I was not concerned with accurately reproducing the stage of the Globe Theatre, interesting though the many hypothetical reconstructions of it can be. At best, little is known about the Globe, except that it presumably contained most of the features I have described as typical of Elizabethan theatres. My intention was simply to adhere to what Poel's production of *Measure for Measure* had taught me: that the fundamental quality of a Shakespearean performance should be complete fluidity of action.

I need hardly say that my conception of modified Elizabethan staging was further modified over the years. What I will describe here is an advanced stage of its evolution that differs in some respects from that first experiment at Carnegie Tech.

The most prominent feature of the stage I used was undoubtedly the *penthouse*, a more prosaic term than the heavens for the roof over the central part of the stage supported by two tall, sturdy columns. (This roof may, in fact, be dispensed with where it is impractical to construct,

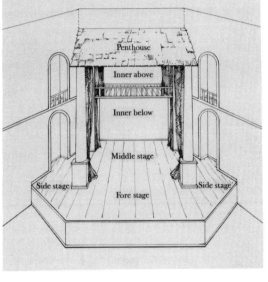

Alice Hecht

Diagram of a modified Elizabethan stage

The outdoor theatre at the Oregon Shakespearean Festival, Ashland

Hank Kranzler

but the columns are essential.) The penthouse divides the main stage into four sections: the *middle stage*, beneath the roof, is the largest area; the *fore stage*, a fairly narrow, apronlike area, lies in front of it; two *side stages* extend on either side of it, with a door giving onto each from the tiring house.

Behind the middle stage are two shallow, curtained inner stages, entered from either side. I came to call them the inner above and the inner below. The inner above corresponds to the modified second gallery of the inn yards as it was almost certainly perpetuated in Elizabethan theatres. The inner below is more problematic. There is little doubt that there were at the back of Elizabethan stages doors through which the actors could enter, and also a curtained area used for "discoveries." A discovery space, as the scholars call it, was needed for many scenes, such as those in *The Merchant of Venice* where Portia reveals the caskets. But there is little agreement as to whether this space was an inner stage at the back or some sort of booth set against the back wall.

If only because the inner stage is a far more practical and flexible arrangement, it seems to me the most likely answer to this question, and I used it to great advantage. For similar reasons I have contended that the side stages must have been broader than they are generally made in models of the Globe Theatre. There are places in the text where it is obvious, to me at least, that short scenes must have been acted on these side stages, sometimes alternately.

The six sections of the stage—middle and fore stage, two side stages, and inner above and below—I shall call zones of interest. This term emphasizes their practical use in the theatre, which was of greater interest to me than questions of historical accuracy in reconstructing an Elizabethan theatre. In referring to them I shall follow the standard practice in the theatre of defining right and left from the standpoint of the actor, not the audience. I might mention here that, for some obscure psychological reason, entrances made on the left side of the stage (the audience's right) make a more dynamic impact on the audience's attention than do entrances on stage right.

Although it is highly unlikely that Elizabethan players ever hung curtains from the penthouse, I found it advantageous, as William Poel often did, to employ them. To open and close them I used two boys (or boyish-looking girls), one for each column. After opening the curtains to the middle stage they retired simultaneously by the nearest doors. Near the end of a scene they would enter unobtrusively, again at precisely the same moment, and close the curtains on cue. This practice

164

seemed to me more appropriate than using some mechanical and impersonal device for working the curtains.

Another significant modification of Elizabethan custom was my use of artificial lighting. Shakespeare, whose actors played in theatres open to the afternoon sky (at least until they moved from the Globe to the Blackfriars theatre), had no need of such a device. He represented darkness or moonlight in the dialogue, or by having the actors carry torches or lanterns. His language, properly spoken, could go a long way to set the mood. However, for performances given in roofed auditoriums, usually at night, artificial light is necessary. I saw no reason, therefore, not to enhance the language with the use of our efficient modern lighting instruments. Nevertheless, I took pains to keep lighting effects well within bounds, and used lights merely to suggest the time of day or indicate changes of mood.

Still other modifications of the Elizabethan stage were variations on the side entrances and the occasional use of scenic vistas at the back of the inner stages. One might imagine, as I did at first, that, when the curtains to both the inner above and inner below were open and revealed different levels of the same backdrop, the bridge, or horizontal platform, that separates them would seem an illogical impediment to the spectators' vision. Surprisingly this never seemed to be the case. As for the side entrances, when an Elizabethan stage is built on a modern one, these can be varied considerably. Doors can be set at any point up- or downstage, and can be raised, to be approached by steps. Alternatively, open wings can be substituted for doors.

Finally, in describing my modified Elizabethan staging I should give an example or two of what I discovered in practice about the special character of specific zones of interest, and even of such specific features as the two columns.

It gradually became evident to me that Shakespeare conceived the fore stage as entirely unlocalized. I found that it was most useful, when the penthouse curtains were closed, for six types of scenes: (a) short scenes used mainly to indicate a lapse of time between previous and following scenes, (b) scenes in which characters are on their way somewhere, (c) long soliloquies, particularly when they are expository, (d) processions, which move from one side door across the fore stage and out the opposite side door, (e) expository scenes of plot development, and (f) low-comedy scenes. Nothing but the direst necessity would keep a comedian upstage. His natural instinct is for the closest possible contact with his audience. And that is what, above all, the fore stage offers. Together with the side stages it also provides the longest space for a continuous movement. Finally, when the penthouse curtains are opened, the fore stage becomes a forward extension of the middle stage.*

The two columns at the front corners of the middle stage serve many purposes for an ingenious actor. One can be the tree trunk on which Orlando nails his verses in *As You Like It*. In another play it might become a scaffold. When Antipholus of Syracuse mistakes Dromio of Ephesus for his own servant in *The Comedy of Errors*, the unfortunate fellow naturally takes refuge from his supposed master's blows behind the nearest column.

> *Antipholus*. What, wilt thou flout me thus unto my face, Being forbid?
> There, take you that, sir knave!
> *Dromio*. What mean you, sir? For God sake hold your hands! Nay, an
> you will not, sir, I'll take my heels.

But the greatest dramatic value of the columns, as Shakespeare must have known well, was that they could convey a feeling of separation between actors or groups of actors. Even with other players close by, an actor can deliver an aside most convincingly if partly shielded by a column. In the first Cyprus scene in *Othello* Iago comments at length on Cassio's gracious behavior to Desdemona as Cassio assures her that her beloved husband will arrive safely. Think of Desdemona and Cassio as just inside the column at the left, perhaps seated on a bench. Iago stands just outside the column and peers malevolently around it: "Ay, smile upon her, do! I will gyve thee in thine own courtship." As I experimented with a modified Elizabethan stage I soon learned that the sense of separation created by a single column can be extremely effective.

In time I was to learn that each zone of interest, singly or in connection with other zones, was particularly fitted for one or more types of scenes. Together they permitted the continuous flow of action that is essential to Shakespeare's melodic line. When it seemed appropriate, the action could overlap slightly, with, for example, the actors of one scene entering while those in the previous scene were still walking off the stage. I

*Payne spoke earlier of the problems created in a large theatre by the distance between audience and actors and he has much to say in the pages to come about his use of the fore stage. Some of his views were anticipated by C. E. Montague in his review of Poel's *Measure for Measure* quoted above: "The essence of the Elizabethan theatre was the fusion or interpenetration of stage and auditorium and the essence of the modern theatre is their separation by the proscenium arch." Montague went on to speak of other advantages of Poel's stage, even though it could not escape from the proscenium at the Gaiety. "With Mr. Poel's arrangement the short scenes and the long ones flow into one another without the slightest jolt or scrappiness. The use of the upper stage, too, was surprisingly effective and undisturbing. . . . As for scenery, one did not think about it, either in the way of missing it, or of being glad it was away."

learned these lessons gradually, however, and they only began with my first *Hamlet* production at Carnegie Tech.

It may seem strange that I should choose the longest and one of the most demanding of all Shakespeare's plays for my first experiment with modified Elizabethan staging. In spite of its length, however, *Hamlet* requires fewer changes of scene than most of the plays, so I expected—rightly, as it turned out—little difficulty in allocating the zones of interest.

There were other reasons for choosing *Hamlet*. I had played no fewer than six parts in it with various professional companies and I knew that it was expedient for me, as both a director and a teacher, to free myself from the almost hypnotic effect of previous productions by trying to approach the text as though I were meeting it for the first time. Finally, I was confident that among my students I had a talented young actor who was well fitted for the great leading role. I have never made a sounder judgment in casting. Hardie Albright's Hamlet lives in my memory as one of the finest of many good performances given by student actors in the universities where I have taught.

For our production at Carnegie Tech, it was essential to reduce the playing time. I had long been used to cutting plays, but it was not merely the exigencies of time that had caused professionals to make changes in the script. It was usually the desire to build up the star part of Hamlet, however destructive that might be to the central purpose of the play. This had resulted in the complete omission of Fortinbras, which was not only detrimental to the play but made the references to him quite meaningless. Polonius's scene with Reynaldo used to be cut, in spite of the invaluable change of mood it provided after Hamlet's encounter with the Ghost. Another serious omission was the whole account of Hamlet's adventure with the pirate ship, without which his return to Elsinore was unexplained. Though condensation was inevitable I resolved that no blue penciling should interfere with the artistry of the play's construction. Therefore, every scene had to be included, and I was determined that the lines omitted should be only those that were definitely inessential and that they should not be of high poetic value. I took care also that the cuts never distorted the metrical construction.

It is not my intention to describe in detail my first *Hamlet* production. I will merely use short scenes from it and from certain later productions to illustrate how I learned to use a modified Elizabethan stage effectively, and in so doing discovered its marvelous adaptability.

In the very first scene the appearance of the Ghost demonstrated that mysterious effects can best be achieved by simple means. Horatio, Marcellus, and Barnardo were crouched on the ground at the right before the black penthouse curtains. They huddled together for warmth as Barnardo recounted what had happened on the two preceding nights. As the audience's attention was focused on these three figures in the near darkness, the Ghost slipped out between the curtain and the column on the left. Stalking with unhurried dignity past the terrified soldiers he disappeared again between column and curtain on the right. The Ghost's entrance and exit both took place within full view of the audience, yet I was asked many times how it was done.

The change of scene shortly after the Ghost's second appearance was a persuasive example of the almost cinematically fluid effect offered by the slight overlapping of scenes, as I mentioned earlier.* Fortunately, Horatio's lovely lines

> But look, the morn, in russet mantle clad,
> Walks o'er the dew of yon high eastward hill.

gave reason to increase the light slightly. Otherwise the sudden coming of full daylight in the next scene would have been too hard on the spectators' eyes. As Marcellus finished the last line of the scene, "I this morning know / Where we shall find him most conveniently," the full stage lighting came on instantly. At the same moment the penthouse curtains were quickly opened, revealing the council chamber. The dialogue of scene ii followed without a second's pause, even while the actors of scene i were walking off the stage. The spectators were so accustomed at that time to breaks between scenes that the transition was greeted with an audible gasp of astonishment. Throughout the rehearsals—even at the dress rehearsal—I had not fully realized how effective complete continuity would be.

I might put in a word on a characteristic of Shakespeare's plays that no doubt resulted from the paucity of furniture on his stage. Seldom does he tell his characters to sit. When he does, and sitting is not absolutely required by the logic of the situation, he always has a sound theatrical reason for it. Before the Ghost's first appearance, for example, Horatio says, "Well, sit we down, and let us hear Barnardo speak of this." The fact that they are seated at the advent of the "dreaded sight" makes their fear more graphic as they leap to their feet.

Shakespeare uses this device for comic effect in act III, scene i of *A Midsummer Night's Dream.* Quince says, "Come, sit down every mother's

---

*In the words of Payne's student Angus Bowmer, who himself became a Shakespearean director, Shakespeare invented the lap-dissolve.

son, and rehearse your parts." Now, it might seem more practical to rehearse Quince's short and very active playlet while standing. But if the artisans were not seated when Bottom appears with his ass's head, they could not scramble to their feet in such an amusing display of consternation.

The scene in the council room is followed by one in which Laertes takes leave of his sister and then his father. The question of which zone of interest to employ here required careful consideration. Scene ii had filled the middle stage and extended onto the fore stage. Although the quartos and folio give merely act and scene divisions, later editors, in their eagerness to define localities, have chosen to place scene iii in "A room in the house of Polonius." This suggests a change of zone. But in the following scene Hamlet meets the Ghost, and this obviously must take place where the Ghost had previously appeared three times. The futility of letting oneself be hypnotized by editorial locations—as one is unconsciously inclined to be—became clear when it struck me that Polonius, as lord chamberlain, would probably be quartered in chambers within the royal palace. In our production, as Hamlet left the stage by one door Laertes and Ophelia entered by another. This kept the action pleasantly continuous.

The two scenes at the end of act I—in effect one long, solemn, and dramatically crucial scene—in which Hamlet talks with the Ghost, are soon followed by another long scene, equally crucial, in which Rosencrantz and Guildenstern spy on Hamlet for the King. In between, however, falls a short scene between Polonius and his servant Reynaldo. In the professional productions that I had known, there had been an intermission between the two major scenes to allow for a change of scenery, and the Polonius–Reynaldo scene was omitted entirely. I was delighted at Tech to see how perfectly, when the flow of action was not broken, the short scene served the purpose for which Shakespeare intended it. It harmoniously relaxed the tension after the harrowing confrontation of Hamlet by the Ghost. At the same time, in showing Polonius's gloating pleasure in his scheme for having his own son spied upon, it prepares for the court atmosphere of the next scene, in which intrigue is piled upon intrigue. I think, too, that it was in the playing of this scene that I became fully aware of Shakespeare's skill in placing what I am sure were always fore-stage scenes between two major scenes of wider dimension and deeper importance. They are invaluable for changing a mood and introducing expository matter that must engage the attention of the audience.

In the long following scene, learning the uses of the inner below accidently taught me something also about the play. For this room in a castle where there is so little sense of privacy I opened the curtains to the shallow inner below, which thus became a passageway at the back of the middle stage. During this scene Polonius proposes to the King and Queen his plan for using his daughter as a decoy so that they may spy on Hamlet. At one of our rehearsals the actor of Hamlet, walking along the rear passage to prepare for his next entrance, happened to glance at the other actors as Polonius was revealing his scheme. It struck me that this accident might be incorporated into the performance. I had always been dissatisfied with the traditional business in act III, scene i, in which Hamlet discovers the eavesdropping scheme on catching Polonius peeping through the curtain. This usually happened shortly before his unexpected question, "Where's your father?" halfway through his conversation with Ophelia. Having Hamlet learn of the plot even while it is being hatched increases the dramatic tension and also helps to account for Hamlet's harsh treatment of Ophelia throughout their scene.

I had chosen to place the performance's one intermission just before this scene, at the end of Hamlet's long soliloquy of self-condemnation as a "rogue and peasant slave." His last line, "The play's the thing / Wherein I'll catch the conscience of the King," represents a crucial decision in the unfolding of the plot that rouses suspenseful expectation. Moreover, the next scene makes a good resumption after the break.

Act III, scene i, also contains the most famous of Hamlet's soliloquies, beginning "To be, or not to be—that is the question." I had long felt that the convention of pronouncing the entire speech slowly and ponderously, as if in deep contemplation, was contrary to Shakespeare's intention. I maintained that Hamlet should speak it swiftly and furiously as if he seriously considered suicide and was held back only by "the dread of something after death." When Hardie Albright carried out my conception at Tech I was convinced by its success that I had been right. Much later I had the gratification of learning from Dover Wilson that my contention had textual support. In the second quarto, which is believed to have been printed largely from Shakespeare's holograph copy, the soliloquy has very light punctuation. This is tantamount to a direction for rapid utterance.

In staging the scene in which the Players perform I was unfortunately less free of past influences. I made the conventional cuts in *The Murder of Gonzago*, including the entire dumb show—a mistake in judgment that I corrected in later productions. Also, I followed custom in working up the point at which the King stops the play to a noisy as well as a high dramatic pitch, with all the courtiers shouting "Lights for the king!" The temptation to do this is great, but it should be resisted as contrary to Shakespeare's intention and an anticlimax to Hamlet's excitement at the success of his trap. After all, the point of the scene is not the King's reaction per se but what it proves to Hamlet.

Throughout the rest of the production I became increasingly aware of the flexibility of the stage. In later productions I partially restored some unwise cuts and made different decisions here and there about the most effective zones to employ for particular scenes. For over half a century I continued to experiment with this style of staging and felt that I was growing constantly surer in my use of it—and constantly closer to what must have been the practice at the Globe Theatre. Never again, however, was I to match the excitement of discovery that I felt during that first *Hamlet* at Tech.

And I found that I was not alone. Up to the dress rehearsals, apart from the necessity of giving all possible attention to the actors and their interpretations, I had been chiefly concerned with technical considerations. At the dress rehearsals I did begin to think that I had made no serious mistakes in allocating the zones of interest. But only when it came to the performance was I able to see the production more from the point of view of a spectator. Then I was made forcibly aware of the truth of the old saying that a play is a play only when it is being performed. The audience reacted with unquestionable enthusiasm, an enthusiasm different in kind from anything I had experienced in the past. It was obvious that the play had a more living impact upon them than I had ever known. It was *The Tragedy of Hamlet, Prince of Denmark,* unimpeded by anything extraneous. The quality of audience reaction to the modified Elizabethan production is impossible to describe, but it is unmistakable. As this was my first experience of the phenomenon, I found it almost breathtaking. Among other things, the comments of individual spectators, so often repeated that they have become almost monotonous, expressed surprise at the *swiftness* with which the action moved along. But for me, by far the most exciting result of the production was a resurgence of feeling that can be described only as a kind of illumination—an ineffable stirring of aesthetic dynamics, as it were—which I remembered from the early days at the Gaiety Theatre in Manchester during productions of Ibsen, Shaw, and Galsworthy plays.

Yet another personal reaction made this production memorable for me. Immediately after the first dress rehearsal I had a strange and wholly unexpected experience. Probably because I felt that I might be subject to ridicule I have preserved silence on the subject until the present moment. I realize that my response may have arisen out of my own unconscious. But putting aside all consideration of its origin, the fact remains that I was suddenly transfused—I can find no other word capable of describing it—with a feeling that Shakespeare himself was present and expressing approval and even pleasure at what we had just completed! I was sitting alone in the dark auditorium of the theatre, and so I remained until the silence was broken by the chatter of actors crossing the stage on their way out of the theatre. I rose immediately and set out on my solitary walk to my lodgings with the strange mood still continuing, though with diminishing intensity, until it faded away altogether.

Hamlet at Carnegie Tech in 1926, with Hardie Albright, F. Leon Ford, and Clarita Stevens

Measure for Measure at Carnegie Tech in 1928, with Don Wilson, Irene Tedrow, and Neuton Cowan

*J*t seemed obvious that a comedy should follow the *Hamlet* production. My choice was *Much Ado about Nothing*. I had a desire to compare the response to a modified Elizabethan presentation of this play with what I remembered of my Manchester production, in which representational scenery, though very simple, had been employed. The outcome firmly convinced me that the staging at Tech was by far the more effective medium. Even though the actors were less experienced than in Manchester, there could be no question that the spectators' response was far greater, and I could only attribute this fact to the method of production.

This was gratifying in itself, but there was even greater satisfaction in the conviction it brought me that Shakespeare was being better served. With this production I finally decided that Shakespearean comedy as well as tragedy (and I later found that the same applied to the histories) should be unencumbered by scenic devices, and that nothing but some form of Elizabethan setting can fully meet this requirement.

If the melodic line is broken, the symmetry of the plays cannot be conveyed to the spectators. Even a "unit set," a single setting devised to illustrate the play as a whole, with or without indications of special localities, does not serve. The spectator is made conscious of the setting at the outset, and as the play progresses, his attention is distracted by speculating why this or that section is being used to indicate a particular locale. Again, if single changes are made, such as lowering and raising set pieces, they invoke curiosity, so the spectator is still less able to concentrate upon the dialogue and the action. The artistry of the performance is sacrificed to extraneous gadgetry, whereas such minor scenic changes as were made behind the penthouse curtains during forestage scenes were accepted as merely illustrating the action and did not divert the attention.

In our quasi-Elizabethan production of *Much Ado about Nothing* I found that the play came out almost as a domestic tragicomedy, though with the comedy predominating. The criticism frequently heard that the plot is unduly artificial was shown to be invalid. It may appear to be so when the resplendent scenery nullifies the tone and feeling Shakespeare intended for the play. Indeed, I found this out to my cost later when I made a scenically beautiful production in Stratford-upon-Avon.

The *Much Ado* production taught me much about the possibilities of the inner above, especially when a removable staircase connects it with the middle stage. I had used such a staircase to dramatic effect in the scene on the battlements between Hamlet and the Ghost. The inner above had mainly served, however, as background to action taking place in other zones. In *Much Ado* I discovered how the inner above and the staircase could be fully integrated with the action elsewhere and lend it, quite literally, another dimension. Also, the inner above, shallow though it was, provided space for decorative touches that could add scenic variety and lightness. In act II, scene i, for example, lighted lanterns and festoons were hung there to give an atmosphere of nocturnal merrymaking. In another zone they might have impeded the action, and their placement and removal would have presented a problem.

The scene known as act II, scene iii, gives an amusing illustration of an Elizabethan playwright's problem of identifying the setting of a new scene, and the somewhat bald way in which Shakespeare sometimes solved it. There is nothing to suggest where the plot that Benedick and Beatrice's friends have concocted two scenes earlier is going to be set afoot. When Benedick appears alone in scene iii, Shakespeare wanted the audience to know immediately where he is, without waiting for the other characters to appear. Evidently he did not wish to clutter Benedick's soliloquy with extraneous detail. His only alternative was to introduce another character solely to identify the setting. Here is how he did it:

Enter Benedick alone.
Bene. Boy!
[Enter *Boy.*]
Boy. Signior?
Bene. In my chamber window lies a book. Bring it hither to me in the orchard.
Boy. I am here already, sir.
Bene. I know that, but I would have thee hence and here again.

The book is never brought. If this had been a realistic play, such an apparent oversight would be regarded as careless workmanship. But

Shakespeare has no use for the boy except as a signpost announcing a locality. When he has served that purpose Shakespeare cavalierly dismisses him from the play, knowing well that the audience will quickly forget the quest for the book.

By this time I had concluded that modified Elizabethan production was the right course for me to follow. I decided, therefore, to make *Measure for Measure* my next experiment so that I might compare the result with my recollections of my previous, more conventional productions. Although I tried to recall Poel's Elizabethan production of the play in Manchester, I had little success. My attention at that time had been almost entirely concentrated on my performance of Lucio. I remembered a few details of individual performances, especially Poel's as Angelo, but everything else was lost.

I was fortunate in having, in Irene Tedrow, a young actress capable of playing Isabella. However skilfully the part is performed, if the actress does not have a fervent spiritual quality in her personality, turning against her brother when he begs her to save his life by the sacrifice of her chastity seems either implausible or outrageous and can even arouse antagonism to the play. But if an actress possesses that rare quality of innate spirituality she can persuade an audience that she is following the only possible course both for her and for Claudio. To Isabella it is obviously a thousand times better that her brother should lose his mortal life than that he as well as she should be thrust into eternal damnation. Frankly, I would say to anyone contemplating a production of *Measure for Measure:* Be sure you have an Isabella such as I describe or abandon the project.

Again with *Measure for Measure* I was persuaded of the advantages of an Elizabethan-style stage. At one point, however, my choice of a likely place for an intermission collided with one of my firmest convictions about the appropriate use of the zones of interest. The Duke's rhymed summing up of the situation at the end of act III seemed the obvious place to break the action. The speech falls at the end of a scene that takes place on a street and is obviously suited for the fore stage. But that zone is not normally the place for a climactic scene. I solved this problem at Tech by recourse to a device that Shakespeare could not have used: a dramatic lighting effect. When the Duke was left alone he was standing center. As soon as his soliloquy began—"He who the sword of heaven will bear / Should be as holy as severe"—the lights were unhurriedly dimmed, except for a spotlight on the Duke himself. When he reached the line "Craft against vice I must apply" even the spot began to dim, until only his head was visible. On the final line it faded out entirely. Part One ended in total darkness.

In a later production, at Statford-upon-Avon, I took the liberty of transposing the Duke's rhymed passage to the end of the preceding scene. It seems peculiarly appropriate both to the action and to the prison setting. The alteration worked so well and led so forcefully to an intermission at that point that I highly recommend it.

In this Stratford production I also found a solution to a problem that still plagued me at Tech. There I felt, as I had at previous productions, that the long scene which constitutes the last act, though admirably articulated, was in some indefinable way a little disappointing. I have heard that other directors have had the same experience. When this sort of thing happened to me in a Shakespeare play I always felt that the fault might be my own—that I had failed to find the clue to something that was missing. At Stratford-upon-Avon I found that clue, and I confirmed its effectiveness at a later production at the University of Texas. The solution lies in the use of the crowd of citizens. They must be rehearsed to express themselves freely throughout the scene, but especially when the supposed Friar Lodowick is brought on and defies the judges. At that point their indignation rises almost to a riot. Tension then remains wrought up to a high point, and the sudden silence when he is revealed as the Duke makes a fine dramatic climax. Everyone kneels to the Duke, there is a long moment of complete silence, and then, on a gesture from the Duke, everyone rises. From this point there is no falling off of interest in the action. The play concludes with a processional exit led by the Duke and Isabella.

My next two choices for production were one of the latest and one of the earliest plays in the canon, *Cymbeline* and *Love's Labour's Lost*. Although *Cymbeline* may have been written mainly with the Blackfriars stage in mind rather than that of the Globe, both plays worked equally well on the stage at Tech.

During a later production of the second play, at the State University of Washington, I was approached by the young actor who played "honey-tongued Boyet," the Princess's attendant. He told me that he was so impressed by the effectiveness of the production that he thought I ought to write a book about the modified Elizabethan approach. I replied that production was something that should be done, not written about. The conversation had a fruitful outcome. The actor, whose name was Angus Bowmer, graduated soon afterward and went to Ashland, Oregon, to accept a position at the local college. There he found, well situated near the center of that pleasant little town, the oval-shaped, roofless walls of what had been the home of a Chautauqua in the flourishing days of that now defunct amalgam of entertainment and instruction. He has told me how, when he found it, neglected and disregarded, he instantly recalled what I had said to him. It spurred him on to make a single Shakespearean production the following summer. From this modest beginning, thanks to his enterprising spirit, his gift as an administrator, and his skill as an actor and stage director, Angus Bowmer has developed an annual Shakespeare festival in an elaborate theatre constructed on Elizabethan lines. Attendance has steadily grown year by year until now the theatre, which seats over a thousand spectators, is filled to capacity for scores of performances every summer. This is surely a most notable achievement.*

My next Shakespeare production at Carnegie Tech—it was now 1931 —provided further evidence to support my belief that mysterious effects are the more telling when they are simply achieved. The play was *Macbeth*. On the last note of the third trumpet that preceded our performances almost all the lights were instantly extinguished, to a loud clap of thunder. The penthouse curtains were opened and a dim illumination revealed the three Witches, apparently poised in the air. This effect was created simply by having them crouch on black painted boxes placed in the inner above. They spoke the lines of the short introductory scene to the accompaniment of rumbled thunder, varying in volume. The line "There to meet with Macbeth" was interrupted on the word "with" by a loud owl hoot. This completed the line metrically and at the same time made it sound dramatically as "There to meet with—whom?—Macbeth!" The fateful name was uttered violently, with great volume. There followed the squalling sound of a cat's cry, to which the First Witch responded with "I come, Graymalkin." Then came a loud frog's croak, which was answered by the Second Witch's "Paddock calls" and the Third Witch's "Anon!" Finally, as the three Witches together spoke the concluding couplet,

> Fair is foul, and foul is fair.
> Hover through the fog and filthy air.

they rose to a standing position on the elevated boxes. To the astonished audience they appeared to rise high into the night sky.

In the appearance of the Witches to Macbeth and Banquo a large

*The Oregon Shakespearean Festival flourishes today, under the direction of Jerry Turner. Shakespearean plays are given in the outdoor Elizabethan theatre that Payne mentions. Other productions are offered in the new Bowmer Memorial Theater.

rock formation dominated the middle stage. In addition to its pictorial value its function was twofold. First, the Weird Sisters were able in their opening dialogue to race up it into a commanding position. Macbeth was similarly raised high later in the play as he listened to the fatal prophecies. Second, it served an important practical purpose by solving the problem of the Witches' disappearance "into thin air." There was no possibility at that time for a trapdoor at Tech to carry them into the bowels of the earth. Anyway, I was doubtful whether such a contrivance might not seem rather ridiculous to a modern audience. What I decided to do was to let Banquo carry a rather dimly lighted lantern. As he said, "Stay, you imperfect speakers," Macbeth took the lantern from Banquo and, holding it high, partly illuminated the rock. At "Speak, I charge you," he lowered the lantern and descended, then turned as if to approach the Witches and force them to stay. This movement of the light attracted every eye in the theatre, thus directing the line of vision away from the Witches. Bending low they ran behind the high part of the rock. Banquo then crossed Macbeth, taking the lantern from him, before uttering his amazed

> The earth hath bubbles, as the water has,
> And these are of them. Whither are they vanish'd?

In the *Macbeth* production I borrowed a practice that Frank Benson had used—and had perhaps himself borrowed from earlier custom. When Shakespeare introduces a minor character only briefly and to advance the plot, he often gives him no name but merely specifies his function. There are several instances of this in *Macbeth*. A Messenger announces that King Duncan will stay at Macbeth's castle. Servants carry messages, an Attendant brings Banquo's murderers to Macbeth, another Messenger warns Lady Macduff of her danger. Later a character named Seyton performs a similar function. Benson used the actor of Seyton for all the other roles, and also for the Third Murderer at Banquo's death. In addition, he played the character who speaks the lines inappropriately attributed to Lennox at the end of the cavern scene. Whether this device is justified or not it tends to make Seyton an interesting and sympathetic character. He becomes a cord threaded through the action that helps bind it together.

The most interesting sidelight on Seyton's character appears when he gives Lady Macduff belated warning to escape. This scene, exciting and moving though it can be, never played in the days when each locality was thought to require a separate setting. As I continued to work with modified Elizabethan staging it was borne home to me how little a setting need be identified with scenery, yet how vital to the whole structure of Shakespearean plays is clearly established movement from place to place. Whether consciously or not the spectator wants to feel that each separate place is indeed separate. No mere localizing of light on a unit set can give a fully persuasive sense of place. A chief virtue of our stage was its capacity for conveying this feeling strongly and naturally, yet by simple means.

Two years after the *Macbeth* production I felt that the time had come to do another history play. I decided on *Henry VIII*, though I feared that the pageantry, an essential clearly indicated in the text, might suffer from the restricted scale of the Tech theatre. It was a needless apprehension. What seemed to be a hampering limitation turned out to be advantageous. The processions, the court and trial scenes, and the grand climax foretelling the glory of Queen Elizabeth's reign, were all so impressive that they gave a concentrated atmosphere of grandeur that would have evaporated in a large auditorium.

After this play I would normally have turned to a comedy or a tragedy. However, I had a promising student to whom I wanted to give a good role in his senior year. It occurred to me that Franklin Heller had both the capacity and the necessary physique to play Falstaff. This fact made me decide to choose for our next production *Henry IV*. But which part should it be? I had played the small role of Mouldy in Frank Benson's *Henry IV*, Part Two, but I had never even seen Part One performed. Partly for that reason I was inclined to try it, but on reading the play, though I was intensely interested throughout and delighted by the Falstaff scenes, I found the end tame and anticlimactic. It was almost as if there were more to come. And of course, there was. As soon as I had gone on through Part Two, I was convinced that *Henry IV* was in fact a single, long play and, moreover, a masterpiece of form. The inconclusiveness of Part One now seemed a deliberate anticipation of what was to follow.

In the very last speech the next stage of the action is clearly announced by the King:

> You, son John, and my cousin Westmoreland,
> Towards York shall bend you with your dearest speed
> To meet Northumberland and the prelate Scroop,
> Who, as we hear, are busily in arms.
> Myself and you, son Harry, will towards Wales
> To fight with Glendower and the Earl of March.

More remarkable, however, is the way in which Prince Hal's soliloquy at the end of act I, scene ii points the way to his rejection of Falstaff at the conclusion of the double play. Although it seemed a gigantic undertaking I determined to do both parts of the play at alternate performances. This I did, and the satisfaction of the audiences more than confirmed my conviction.

Of the many Shakespeare plays that I produced at Carnegie Tech through the years, one of the most demanding on a director's ingenuity in using a stage was *Antony and Cleopatra*. In localizing the scenes the editors of the plays had reached a reductio ad absurdum, with thirteen scenes in the third act and fifteen in the fourth. Some of the scenes had no more than four lines. It is evident that the absolute continuity of action necessary to the shape of this complex play requires a stage with many distinct but flexible playing areas. This requirement was perfectly met by our quasi-Elizabethan stage, but it was questionable whether the grandeur and panoramic sweep of the play could be encompassed by such a stage as well as by a larger, more open, stage.

Before producing *Antony and Cleopatra* at Tech I had accepted the offer to be the director of the Stratford-upon-Avon Festival Company at the Shakespeare Memorial Theatre in England. But in doing so, I had made provision that I return to Pittsburgh to do one more Shakespeare production at Tech. Reluctantly I had agreed that only some of the productions at Stratford should be modified Elizabethan. *Antony and Cleopatra* was to be produced there with scenery designed by Aubrey Hammond, a fine artist with a high reputation. Doing *Antony and Cleopatra* at Tech as well as at Stratford offered me a chance to compare the results of the two methods. And my resolution to undertake a student production of a play that demands so much of its two chief actors was spurred by the fact that in Arthur Kennedy and Polly Rowles I had an actor and actress of great ability. I knew that they would give outstanding performances. My confidence in them was fulfilled not only at Tech but in their later work in the professional theatre.

My belief that *Antony and Cleopatra* could best be performed on the modified Elizabethan stage despite its scale proved true. Even though at Stratford I went back to my former use of a neutral curtain for intermediate scenes to produce continuity of action, there is no doubt that the uninterrupted Tech production had far more grip on the audience. In spite of the austerity that, at my request, characterized Aubrey Hammond's designs, his charming pictures interfered with the overall harmony of Shakespeare's creation by diverting attention from the language and action to themselves.

Henry IV, Part One, at Carnegie Tech in 1934, with Franklin Heller as Falstaff

Antony and Cleopatra at Carnegie Tech in 1936, with Arthur Kennedy and Polly Rowles as the lovers, Jane Francey and Mary Cheffey as Iras and Charmian

Even more than in the case of *Antony and Cleopatra*, this was demonstrated for me with *The Taming of the Shrew*. While I was at Stratford, the latter play was produced in two different seasons. One production was staged by a truly brilliant director, Theodore Komisarjevsky, with scenery that, taking advantage of the rolling stage available in the Stratford-upon-Avon theatre, unfolded different aspects of a long hall. The other was my own Elizabethan modified production. The difference in reception by the audiences was beyond all question. The laughter and applause—in short, the enjoyment—was unquestionably far greater when the play was unhampered by extravagant scenic devices.

Here I must backtrack a bit. Before going to Stratford-upon-Avon, I joined Tom Stevens at the Goodman Theatre in Chicago for three years, though by special arrangement I continued my annual Shakespeare productions at Tech after giving up my academic classes. He had gathered a repertory company around him, among them now-experienced actors who had formerly been students at Tech and my old friend Whitford Kane, who was his leading character actor. One thing that attracted me in making this move was that it gave me the opportunity to act again in most of the productions. But I also continued to direct, and one of the first plays I directed was *Romeo and Juliet*, in which I also played Mercutio, a favorite part from my earliest Shakespearean performances. The stage at the Goodman Theatre did not permit the complete modified Elizabethan method, but it did manage to retain its principal features.*

In the summer of 1934 I went to England for a summer vacation. I took with me several photographs of my Tech productions, knowing that I should have an opportunity to renew my acquaintance with William Poel. He asked me to call on him at his home. Though the day turned out to be very inclement, I decided to fulfill the appointment. I was glad afterward that I persisted, for he died later in the year.

Poel's peculiar way of regarding everything concerned with theatrical production was never more characteristically manifested than on this occasion. He was enthusiastic about the photographs and calmly suggested I find some rich man who would build a theatre for me! He said that I could suggest to this hypothetical donor that the theatre could be used for "pictures" when it was not in use for plays. I took it, of course, that he meant moving pictures. This seemed so contrary to all

*The Goodman Theatre, at the Chicago Art Institute, is known primarily for its productions of contemporary drama, though Elizabethan dramas are occasionally performed there.

I expected of him that I could only exclaim that he surely did not mean it seriously. "Yes," he said, "they could have the pictures displayed on easels around the stage and admission might be charged to see them." I had hardly time to recover from my surprise at such a naive suggestion before he changed his mind and said emphatically, "No, that would never do. It might make money and then they would want to keep the exhibition open every day and that would interfere with rehearsals."

Later on, Poel told me that he now saw the mistake he had made when producing Elizabethan plays other than Shakespeare's. The mistake had been in charging admission! I asked him if he could possibly mean what he said. He put it this way. "You decide you want to produce some play like Ford's *Broken Heart* or Massinger's *Duke of Milan* and how much money does it draw? Only four or five pounds. That's all you lose and if you make admission free, you are saved all the annoyance of bookkeeping!"

A little later, I visited Stratford-upon-Avon, where I was introduced to Sir Archibald Flower, the chairman of the Shakespeare Festival Company. I happened to tell him about my recent meeting with Poel, and he asked me to show him my photographs. Soon after my return to America I was surprised to receive a letter from Sir Archibald inviting me to return to Stratford with all expenses paid to consider an offer to become the director of the festival company. I accepted and found myself once again crossing the Atlantic to look over a new possibility. It was made clear that various forms of production would be desirable. This did not deter me, for I had no desire to be entirely bound by the modified Elizabethan method.

I will say little here about my work at Stratford-upon-Avon. In the eight years it continued, the festival season ran for twelve to sixteen weeks. The annual repertoire always consisted of eight plays, of which I always directed from three to five myself. The whole repertoire was required to be running at the end of the first three weeks of the season, yet it was never possible to have more than six weeks rehearsal. As may be imagined, the period of rehearsal and opening nights was one of great strain. I found to my disappointment that only comparatively rarely was I able to put on a modified Elizabethan production. But whenever I did I found that this style could be relied upon to draw an enthusiastic response from the audience. I was confirmed in my conviction that Shakespeare for a modern audience can be a living experience if both the limitations and the advantages of the Elizabethan theatre are observed. It is also necessary to be faithful to the author's intention and not to encumber the text with extraneous fanciful notions. The director's duty is to interpret a play faithfully and never to show off his personal ingenuity. Worst of all is to deliberately distort the author's purpose and intentions.

Perhaps the inclination to embroider unnecessarily is particularly strong when dealing with Shakespearean farces, and none is more susceptible to such treatment than *The Taming of the Shrew*. The most egregious—and, alas, usual—form this takes is in making Petruchio treat Katherine with violence bordering on brutality. Such cheap, farcical action is entirely contrary to Shakespeare's intention as clearly expressed in the dialogue. In my own productions of the play at the University of Texas, Stratford-upon-Avon, and elsewhere I was careful to avoid the temptations the play offers for directorial display. On the other hand, I did take an unusual liberty with the text. This requires a bit of explanation.

My first acquaintance with *The Taming of the Shrew* had been in the Benson company. There, following the custom of the period, the induction was dispensed with. This was a great mistake. The induction is full of character comedy of high order, which it is a pity the audience should miss. More important, the farcical elements of the play proper are set in focus, as it were, when it is presented as the work of a company of strolling players. This is especially the case when the framework established in the induction is retained throughout the play.

In the play as it was printed in the First Folio, Sly, the drunken tinker of the induction, disappears from the text after making only one comment on the play: "They sit and mark." There is, however, a surviving play called *The Taming of a Shrew* which, though very different, is also furnished with an induction by a drunken tinker. He remains onstage throughout, sometimes making interjections, and at the end he is featured in a short epilogue. Sly's one interjection convinced me that Shakespeare had originally retained him throughout *The Taming of the Shrew*. It seems to me that his disappearance from the Folio can be explained if it is assumed that *The Taming of the Shrew* was printed from the script of a touring company with limited personnel in which the actor who played Sly had to double a part, probably that of Grumio, also a tidbit for a low comedian.

However this may be I have felt justified in borrowing the interjections and epilogue of *A Shrew* in my productions of *The Shrew*. Although the writer's diction for the most part lacks Shakespeare's pungency, it is fully in harmony with Sly's character. Sly's part works effectively in the theatre, and the epilogue rounds out the play perfectly. Indeed, the whole play is enriched with an additional dimension when Sly is thus integrated into it throughout.

In the Stratford-upon-Avon production the role of Sly was played by Mr. Jay Laurier, a popular performer in English pantomimes. Since his comedy routines were always very broad, a good many doubts were expressed that his work would fit Shakespearean comedy when I engaged him as my regular clown. But my instinct was right. Laurier was a great success and always fully in character not only as Sly but in such parts as Bottom the Weaver and Launce in *The Two Gentlemen of Verona*.

In this last role, however, Laurier met his comic match. I procured a really odd-looking dog—a regular mutt—for Launce's dog, Crab. He seemed to have an instinct for getting in touch with the audience and a way of sharing his master's character touches. Strangely enough, Jay was jealous of his dog's success. I had the greatest difficulty in persuading him to take his dog on with him when he took his curtain call at the end of the play. But when he was forced to do it he made a graceful gesture toward the dog as if all the credit belonged to him.

CHAPTER 18

*A*fter the engagement at Stratford-upon-Avon, I devoted most of the remaining years of my career to The University of Texas. There, after 1946, I taught and directed in the drama department. During those years and earlier, I made visits to other universities including Washington, Iowa, Missouri, Michigan, San Diego State College, and Banff School of Fine Arts, Alberta, Canada. Texas, however, remained my home.*

Shortly before going to Stratford I enjoyed a unique experience. Thomas Wood Stevens had designed a hypothetical reconstruction of the Globe Theatre for the Chicago World's Fair in 1934. During the fair season I directed a company of young professionals in greatly shortened versions of Shakespeare's plays. The year after the Chicago fair closed, the theatre was rebuilt at the Pacific National Exposition in San Diego. The abbreviated productions were played there for two years. They were so popular with audiences that this "Old Globe Theatre" later became the center for the San Diego National Theatre Festival. I had the pleasure of directing the first production of the festival, *Twelfth Night*, in 1949, and I returned many times in the years that followed.†

*Mr. Payne came to the end of his manuscript in his ninety-first year, and some aspects of the latter parts of his life were not as fully written out as he had planned. But the records show that, after almost sixty years as a vagabond, he found that the ambiance, associates, students, and facilities at The University of Texas gave him much satisfaction and pleasure. Before his retirement in 1973 as Professor Emeritus in Drama he had directed no fewer than twenty-four plays from the Shakespeare canon at Texas, as well as six modern or classic plays.

†This organization, which has been under the direction of Craig Noel since 1947, produces a regular series of modern dramas in the winter months as well as its summer festival of Shakespeare's plays.

Payne as Squire Hardcastle with the Goodman Repertory Company on tour in St. Louis in 1927

Payne with the cast of *Twelfth Night* at the Old Globe Theatre in San Diego in 1949

Bill Reid

The enthusiastic response of audiences—even of those casually sampling attractions in the carnival atmosphere of world's fairs that also boasted a nudist colony and a midget circus—once more confirmed my faith in the style of staging I had chosen. Although in the mid-1940s I twice returned to Broadway to direct productions, one of them *The Winter's Tale*, I never again—with one last exception—could be content with the conventional staging of Shakespeare.

To those who have not experienced the extraordinary fluidity of an Elizabethan stage its physical limitations seem restrictive. To confine a production to it can appear, as Poel's *Measure for Measure* first did to me, a somewhat pedantic archaism. Skeptics say, "If Shakespeare had had a modern stage at his disposal he would have leaped at the chance to use it." This seems to me a half-truth. Shakespeare was a practical man of the theatre—indeed, he was inspired in his use of his stage far beyond any of his contemporary playwrights. He would almost certainly have welcomed and quickly employed any innovation, such as modern stage lighting, that became available, provided that it served his dramatic purpose.

What was Shakespeare's dramatic purpose? He had many purposes, of course, and some were suited only to the play in hand. But if any intention was constant and everywhere visible it was his determination to maintain the uninterrupted pace and total fluidity of the action. This desire was in part born of necessity, forced upon the playwright by the conditions of his stage. But no one who has actually worked out the sequence of scenes on an Elizabethan stage can believe for a moment that Shakespeare regarded its characteristics as limitations. Like playwrights in any age, he took the stage of his own time for granted. Far more important, the brilliance and ingenuity with which he exploited it prove that he not only accepted it, he gloried in it!

The multitude of short scenes and the intricate way in which different themes and lines of action are intertwined in succeeding scenes are abundant evidence that the internal structure of the plays was conceived in terms of the stage on which they were first performed. It really does not matter, then, whether Shakespeare would have used a modern stage if he had had one. If such a stage had been available, he would have written his plays differently to fit it.

What does matter is that Shakespeare did *not* have a modern stage. He had an Elizabethan stage. And I think it safe to say that no great playwright in history wrote plays so closely and vitally linked to the theatre in which they were first performed.

In my descriptions of my modified Elizabethan staging I have made it clear that this setting is the ideal one for the presentation of Shakespeare's plays. But reconstructed Elizabethan theatres are available only here and there. Many of my own productions were given on modern stages on which certain elements of Elizabethan stages had been temporarily installed. The main thing in adapting a stage to Shakespearean performances is to keep two absolute essentials in mind. First, the stage must have a number of clearly defined zones of interest, areas that give a strong feeling of separation from other zones but which can, with little or no change, be taken to represent different localities. Second, the stage must permit complete freedom of movement from one zone to another so that the zones may be used in a variety of combinations.

As for the direction of the play, every scene with any relation to the action must be retained, though dialogue may be judiciously cut as long as both the sense and the meter are undamaged. In order to respect the "melodic line" of the action, as well as the pace, one scene must follow without interruption upon another.

From this somewhat haphazard memoir the reader must by now have become aware that the accomplishment that gives me the greatest satisfaction is my development of modified Elizabethan staging. In view of this fact it may seem strange that in the final production of my career I turned away from the style with which I had so long been associated. But the play was in some ways one of Shakespeare's least typical, as well as one of his loveliest.

During the week's run of my annual Shakespearean productions at The University of Texas I was repeatedly asked what Shakespeare play I intended to do the following spring. And I had always to reply truthfully that I had given very little thought to the subject. In 1968, however, my answer was different. For some time I had been aware that the time would soon arrive when a Shakespeare production would be too heavy a burden upon my waning physical power. I had decided, therefore, to carry out my long-nurtured resolution to finish my Shakespearean productions with *The Tempest*, since it was also the last play written by Shakespeare.

His last play? It is true that Shakespeare's comrades at the Globe Theatre, John Heminges and Henry Condell, included *King Henry VIII* in their First Folio edition of Shakespeare's plays and that that play is later than *The Tempest*. But there is stylistic proof in the verse that much of *King Henry VIII* was the work of John Fletcher, Shakespeare's successor as the stock provider of plays at the Globe Theatre. There is

190

not the slightest touch of Fletcher in *The Tempest*. No, the play as a whole is infused with a special kind of enchantment not to be found anywhere but in Shakespeare, an enchantment sometimes almost beyond the reaches of the soul.

This is true despite the fact that the version we have—evidently the only one available to Heminges and Condell—has obviously been altered and almost certainly shortened for a performance at court. That it was so performed is proved by the official records. Moreover, there is internal evidence that *The Tempest* was one of several plays presented in celebration of the marriage of Princess Elizabeth, the daughter of Prince Charles, to the elector Palatine. The masque of the goddesses is obviously inserted embroidery. Ceres' two lines "Spring comes to you at the farthest / At the very end of harvest" are directly spoken to the Princess, who was married late in December. "Spring" is thus a shortened form of "offspring" and "harvest" the due nine months for a fulfilled pregnancy. It has also been suggested that the inordinately long act I, scene ii, may originally have been several scenes and that we now have a condensation to make room for the masque.

Whatever alterations and condensations may have been made, the play in performance gives a responsive spectator a spiritual experience of a very unusual character. There must be few who are not moved by Prospero's transcendental realization that appearance is not reality and that, as mere human beings, "We are such stuff as dreams are made on." Or how even Caliban, the acme of earthly foulness, whose life is a miserable catalogue of beatings and enforced labor, hears about him whenever he wakens "sounds and sweet airs that give delight and hurt not." Even the broad comedy, founded on the character of the drunken butler Stephano and the foolish jester Trinculo, has a spiritual undertone as they spontaneously respond to Ariel's invisible piping.

But the spiritual quality of the play is most markedly disclosed when Ariel dissuades Prospero from carrying out his resolution—theretofore the essential burden of the play—from avenging himself against the wrongdoers who are now his powerless victims. He assures Prospero that "If you now beheld them, your affections would become tender." This is a revelation to Prospero. "Dost thou think so, spirit?" he asks Ariel, who tellingly replies, "Mine would, sir, were I human," and Prospero exclaims, "*And mine shall!*" With this the whole play is transformed from a drama of vengeance to a dream of reconciliation.

If I specified that *The Tempest* offers a spititual experience of a very unusual character, it is because I am convinced that *any* theatrical performance partakes of the nature of a ritual. It is well known that

The "Elizabethan stage" constructed at
the Shakespeare Memorial Theatre,
Stratford-upon-Avon, for the 1976 season

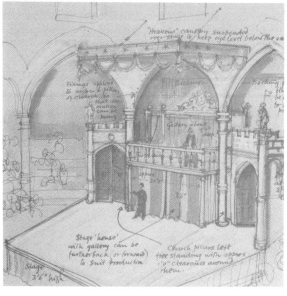

Project for a variable Elizabethan stage
setting in a converted church (St.
Georges, Islington), by C. Walter
Hodges.

the drama had its roots in religious rites. To my mind, it has never wholly lost that character, at least in its unifying effect upon the spectators. That effect can never be achieved by mechanical means. People watching a moving picture do not become a true audience in the theatre sense. They respond—they laugh, they cry, they are convinced by good acting. But these are individual reactions; the spectators do not achieve that collective personality that is the hallmark of the living theatre.

In the theatre, if you respond at all, you cannot be isolated. There something mysterious happens, some magic that is absent in any other form of drama. There is a strange sense of reciprocity between audience and actor and a feeling of community with all the other spectators. Admittedly this does not always happen, but when it does one cannot fail to realize that it is a unique experience that belongs to the living theatre alone. "There is, I swear to you," J. B. Priestley has written, "far more in this queer business than meets the eye. Behind all this tawdry mess of paint and canvas and lights and dog-eared scripts and books of press cuttings and vanity and egoism, there is a mystery. . . . Is there a profound symbolism in this art of the drama that haunts the depths of the mind, rooting its fascination into the unconscious, which is itself a mighty theatre? Does this little dream of the playhouse . . . hint at profound truths for which we have never been able to find the right words?"

Some years ago an experience that I cannot forget reminded me of Priestley's words. I was sitting in the auditorium of a small campus theatre, a converted army recreation hall with no hint of theatrical glamor about it. I had directed the play being performed and for some reason I needed to go backstage. As I stole back to the main doors of the theatre I was impressed by the rapt faces of the audience, concentrating intently on the action of the play. For a few moments I was enfolded by the night, then I went up the wooden steps and quietly opened the stage door. Behind the scenery the light was dim, and I saw no one but the prompter, sitting in his corner. He looked up and instinctively laid his finger to his lips. As I stood there behind the canvas walls listening to the familiar words, I thought of the faces of the entranced audience. Suddenly I was overwhelmed with the realization that, in spite of my intimate association with the play, from the moment when the curtains opened it was no longer in any sense mine. Standing there in the dark, part of neither cast nor audience, I was an outsider intruding upon a mystic communion between the two.

I knew as never before that here was a mystery. Oh, I had known long enough that there were mysterious elements about the theatre, but medieval thinkers distinguished between knowing and knowing *savingly*. For the first time I now knew fully—savingly—the significance of theatre. Truly, drama and the theatre reach down to touch and fructify the deepest elements in our common humanity, lighting up the mind and warming the heart.

In *The Tempest* Shakespeare achieved this ritual quality in a more direct way than in any of his other plays, turning a theatrical theme into a kind of spiritual masque. My desire to capture this quality made me depart for once from my usual method of staging and use a single set, with only occasional changes between scenes in parts of it. The simple but slight alterations could be made by means of a large central revolving rock formation. The drama department's scene designer, Mr. John Rothgeb, carried out the conception skilfully, with the expert aid of the lighting designer, David Nancarrow. I was fortunate also in all my actors.

Shakespearean production had meant so very much to me for so many years that it was not without an undertone of melancholy that I watched the first performance of this my last production. But that feeling gradually evaporated and, after the final curtain, I was suffused by a feeling almost of contentment. When the audience had all left the theatre I remained alone in the body of the house, watching the striking of the scenery. Suddenly and quite unexpectedly I was inundated with the same strange and inexplicable feeling that I had experienced after the dress rehearsal of *Hamlet* at Carnegie Tech. It is difficult to describe, but, though it was vague, it was paradoxically very real. It was almost as if Shakespeare himself were present and expressing a diffused, affectionate approval of what had been accomplished! Again, I do not doubt that this experience could have arisen from the depths of the subconscious. Yet it was so unquestionably there that I feel in duty bound to record its occurrence.

The production of Shakespeare's last play marked the termination of my many years' attempt to present his work in the medium for which he worked, the theatre itself. It was his sole concern, for he never sought publication of his plays. I feel that I can do no better, then, than to conclude this book by addressing the reader with the final couplet of the epilogue to *The Tempest*,

> As you from crimes would pardoned be,
> Let your indulgence set me free.

The B. Iden Payne Theater at The University of Texas, dedicated in 1976.

Payne in 1968

Valedictory: *The Tempest* at The University of Texas at Austin in 1968

BIBLIOGRAPHY

This bibliography was prepared for The University of Texas at Austin by the members of the Memorial Resolution Committee, David Nancarrow (chairman), James Moll, and F. Loren Winship. It is reprinted here with their kind permission.

Acting

Dr. Payne left no complete record of the roles he played. During the years when he was engaged primarily in acting, approximately one-half of his career, he portrayed hundreds of characters. We know that he acted in the works of Barrie, Bennett, Brighouse, Congreve, Galsworthy, Goldsmith, Ibsen, Shaw, Sheridan, Wycherly, and many times in Shakespeare's plays, as well as in those of numerous less well known playwrights. At The University of Texas he performed publicly in only two plays. He celebrated the fiftieth anniversary of his first appearance on the stage by portraying Puff in Richard B. Sheridan's *The Critic*. In 1955 he played a bit role, Matthew Skipps, in Christopher Fry's *The Lady's Not For Burning*.

Articles

"The Undying Theatre," *Bulletin of the National Theatre Conference* (April, 1944)
"Directing the Verse Play," *Educational Theatre Journal* III (1951)
"T. W. Stevens at Carnegie Tech," *Educational Theatre Journal* III (1951)
"Theatre Training in England and America," *Educational Theatre Journal* IV (1952)
"Elizabethan Staging in America," *Theatre* (April 26, 1952)
"Youth and the Fine Arts," *Junior College Journal* XXV (1954)
"The Liberal Arts vs. the Drama Major," *Educational Theatre Journal* VI (1954)
"Shakespeare Was an Actor," *San Diego Magazine* (July, 1956)
"Shakespeare at Work in His Theatre," *Educational Theatre Journal* XIX (1967)

Books

A Life in a Wooden O: A Memoir of the Theatre. Yale University Press, 1977
A Road to William Shakespeare (unpublished manuscript)

Book Reviews

Donald Stauffer, *Shakespeare's World of Images,* in *Educational Theatre Journal* III (1951)
K. J. Holzknecht, *The Backgrounds of Shakespeare's Plays,* in *Educational Theatre Journal* III (1951)
H. C. Goddard, *The Meaning of Shakespeare,* in *Educational Theatre Journal* III (1951)
Allardyce Nicoll, *Shakespeare Survey,* in *Educational Theatre Journal* IV (1951)
Arthur Colby Sprague, *Shakespearean Players and Performances,* in *Educational Theatre Journal* V (1953)
Derek Traversi, *Richard II to Henry V,* in *Educational Theatre Journal* X (1958)
Samuel Selden, *Shakespeare: A Player's Handbook of Short Scenes,* in *Educational Theatre Journal* XIII (1961)
Bertram Joseph, *Acting Shakespeare,* in *Educational Theatre Journal* XIII (1961)
Marvin Rosenberg, *The Masks of Othello,* in *Educational Theatre Journal* XIV (1962)
High Hunt, *An Introduction to the History and Practice of the Stage,* in *The Austin American-Statesman* (October 28, 1962)

Plays

Bird in Hand, 1923–24; *Dolly Jordan,* 1921–22; *The Ghostly Councilor,* 1926–27; *Where Love Is, God Is Also,* 1924–25.
With Rosemary Casey, *Mary Goes to See,* 1938; *The Saint's Husband,* 1934; *Shining Armor,* 1934–35.
With Thomas Wood Stevens, *Pennie Gay,* 1920–21; *Poe,* 1919–20.

Radio Broadcasts

"Variations on a Theatre Theme" and "Shakespeare Sidelights." Twenty-six broadcasts from The University of Texas Radio Station, WFAA, 1956; also from stations associated with the National Association of Educational Broadcasters in the fall of 1957.

Directing

Accurate records of Dr. Payne's career as a director were not kept. He staged hundreds of plays while in England and Ireland, fully two hundred of which were produced while he was with the Manchester Repertory Company. In the United States he directed scores of plays for professional, community, and educational theatres, including almost the entire Shakespeare canon. The following are titles of plays he directed for the Department of Drama at The University of Texas: Shakespeare, William, *The Taming of the Shrew*, 1946–47, 1958–59; Shaw, George B., *Arms and the Man*, 1946–47; Shakespeare, William, *Romeo and Juliet*, 1947–48; author unknown, *Abraham and Isaac*, 1948–49; Goldsmith, Oliver, *She Stoops to Conquer*, 1948–49; Shakespeare, William, *The Tragedy of Richard the Second*, 1948–49; Sheridan, Richard B., *The Critic*, 1949–50; Shakespeare, William, *The Merchant of Venice*, 1949–50; Barrie, James M., *Dear Brutus*, 1950–51; Shakespeare, William, *Much Ado about Nothing*, 1950–51; *The First Part of Henry the Fourth*, 1951–52; *The Second Part of Henry the Fourth*, 1951–52; *Cymbeline*, 1952–53; *A Midsummer Night's Dream*, 1953–54; Brighouse, Harold, *Hobson's Choice*, 1953–54; Shakespeare, William, *Hamlet*, 1954–55; *Love's Labour's Lost*, 1955–56; *The Tragedy of Richard the Third*, 1956–57; Congreve, William *Love for Love*, 1956–57; Shakespeare, William; *The Tragedy of King Lear*, 1957–58; *The Winter's Tale*, 1959–60; *The Tragedy of Macbeth*, 1960–61; *The Merry Wives of Windsor*, 1961–62; *Othello, The Moor of Venice*, 1962–63; *As You Like It*, 1963–64; *Measure for Measure*, 1964–65; *The Tragedy of Julius Caesar*, 1965–66; *Troilus and Cressida*, 1966–67; *Twelfth Night*, 1967–68; *The Tempest*, 1968–69.

Honors

Southwest Theatre Conference Award of Merit, 1954; American Educational Theatre Association Award of Merit for Distinguished Service to Theatre, 1958; American Shakespeare Festival Award for Distinguished Service to Shakespeare, 1958; The University of Texas Student's Association Teaching Excellence Award, 1959; Second Annual Rodgers–Hammerstein Award for Distinguished Theatrical Work in the Southwest, 1962; B. Iden Payne Scholarship Fund founded by former student, Barna Ostertag, 1962; Honorary Life Membership in the American Educational Theatre Association, 1965; Fellow of the American Educational Theatre Association, 1966; Award of Merit for Distinguished Service to the Theatre by the Consular Law Society of New York, 1968; Theta Alpha Phi Medallion of Honor, 1969; First Annual Award of Austin, Texas Circle of Theatres, 1975; Order of the British Empire, 1976; new theatre in the Drama Building of The University of Texas at Austin named for B. Iden Payne by The University of Texas Board of Regents, 1976.

Listed in *Who's Who*, London; *Who's Who in the Theatre*, London; *Who's Who in the American Theatre*, New York.

INDEX